STUDENT LECTURE NOTEBOOK

BIOLOGY
Life on Earth
Seventh Edition

Teresa Audesirk
Gerald Audesirk
University of Colorado at Denver

Bruce E. Byers
University of Massachusetts, Amherst

PEARSON

Prentice
Hall

Upper Saddle River, NJ 07458

Assistant Editor: Colleen Lee
Executive Editor: Teresa Ryu Chung
Editor-in-Chief, Science: John Challice
Vice President of Production & Manufacturing: David W. Riccardi
Executive Managing Editor: Kathleen Schiaparelli
Assistant Managing Editor: Becca Richter
Production Editor: Rhonda Aversa
Supplement Cover Manager: Paul Gourhan
Supplement Cover Designer: Joanne Alexandris
Manufacturing Buyer: Ilene Kahn
Cover Photo Credit: Frantz Lanting/Minden Pictures

© 2005 Pearson Education, Inc.
Pearson Prentice Hall
Pearson Education, Inc.
Upper Saddle River, NJ 07458

The author and publisher of this book have used their best efforts in preparing this book. These efforts include the development, research, and testing of the theories and programs to determine their effectiveness. The author and publisher make no warranty of any kind, expressed or implied, with regard to these programs or the documentation contained in this book. The author and publisher shall not be liable in any event for incidental or consequential damages in connection with, or arising out of, the furnishing, performance, or use of these programs.

Printed in the United States of America

10 9 8 7 6 5 4 3 2

ISBN 0-13-146537-6

Pearson Education Ltd., *London*
Pearson Education Australia Pty. Ltd., *Sydney*
Pearson Education Singapore, Pte. Ltd.
Pearson Education North Asia Ltd., *Hong Kong*
Pearson Education Canada, Inc., *Toronto*
Pearson Educación de Mexico, S.A. de C.V.
Pearson Education—Japan, *Tokyo*
Pearson Education Malaysia, Pte. Ltd.

TABLE OF CONTENTS

TO THE STUDENT

The Student Lecture Notebook is designed to assist you during your biology course. It includes art from the textbook with space available for your note taking needs. Since you will not have to redraw the art in class, you can focus your attention on the lecture while you mark up the pages.

Visit www.prenhall.com/audesirk7 and log in to the Web site selected by your instructor to view additional resources, including self-grading quizzes, animations, and Internet links.

Biosphere	That part of Earth inhabited by living organisms; includes both the living and nonliving components	Earth's surface
Ecosystem	A community together with its nonliving surroundings	snake, antelope, hawk, bushes, grass, rocks, stream
Community	Two or more populations of different species living and interacting in the same area	snake, antelope, hawk, bushes, grass
Species	Very similar, potentially interbreeding organisms	
Population	Members of one species inhabiting the same area	herd of pronghorn antelope
Multicellular Organism	An individual living thing composed of many cells	pronghorn antelope

Figure 1-2   Levels of organization of matter

Multicellular Organism	An individual living thing composed of many cells	pronghorn antelope
Organ System	Two or more organs working together in the execution of a specific bodily function	the nervous system
Organ	A structure usually composed of several tissue types that form a functional unit	the brain
Tissue	A group of similar cells that perform a specific function	nervous tissue
Cell	The smallest unit of life	nerve cell

Figure 1-2   Levels of organization of matter

Cell	The smallest unit of life	
		nerve cell
Organelle	A structure within a cell that performs a specific function	mitochondrion · chloroplast · nucleus
Molecule	A combination of atoms	water · glucose · DNA
Atom	The smallest particle of an element that retains the properties of that element	hydrogen · carbon · nitrogen · oxygen
Subatomic Particle	Particles that make up an atom	proton · neutron · electron

Figure 1-2 Levels of organization of matter

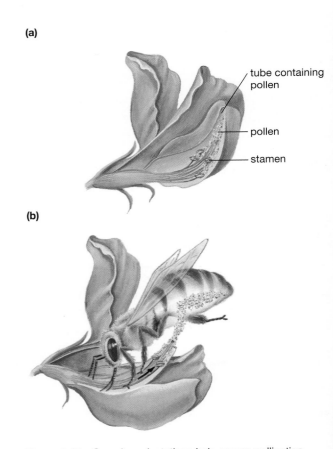

(a)

tube containing pollen

pollen

stamen

(b)

Figure 1-12 Complex adaptations help ensure pollination

Observation:

Flies swarm around meat left in the open;
maggots appear on meat.

Hypothesis:

Flies produce the maggots; keeping flies away
from meat will prevent the appearance of maggots.

Experiment

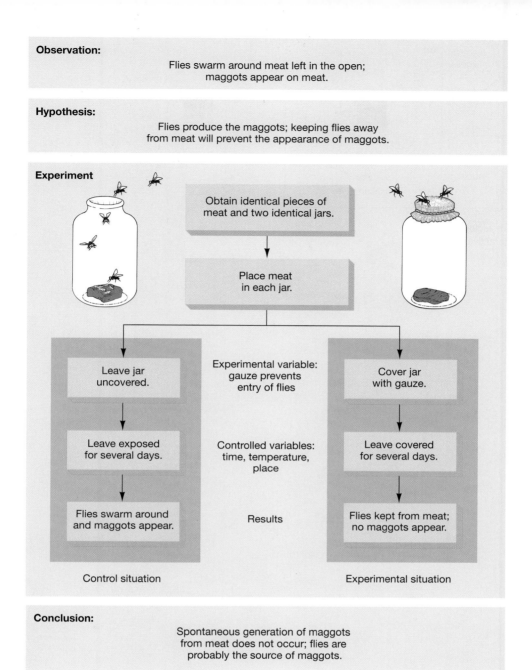

Obtain identical pieces of
meat and two identical jars.

Place meat
in each jar.

| Leave jar uncovered. | Experimental variable: gauze prevents entry of flies | Cover jar with gauze. |

Leave exposed
for several days.

Controlled variables:
time, temperature,
place

Leave covered
for several days.

Flies swarm around
and maggots appear.

Results

Flies kept from meat;
no maggots appear.

Control situation

Experimental situation

Conclusion:

Spontaneous generation of maggots
from meat does not occur; flies are
probably the source of maggots.

Figure E1-1   The experiments of Francesco Redi

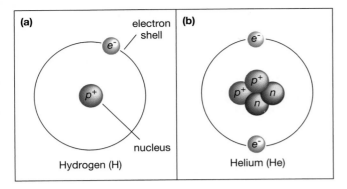

Figure 2-1 Atomic molecules
Media Activity 2.1 Interactive Atoms

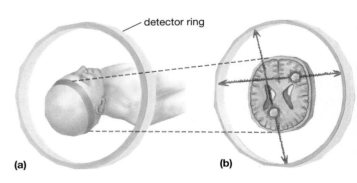

Figure E2-1a,b How positron emission tomography works

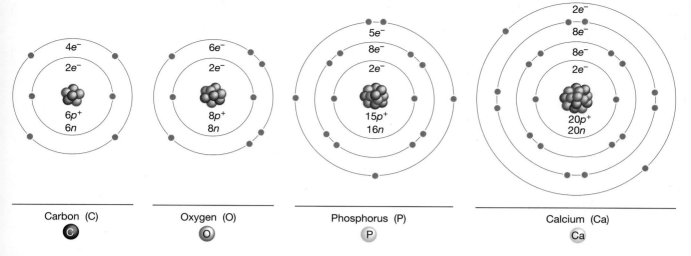

Figure 2-2 Electron shells in atoms
Media Activity 2.1 Interactive Atoms

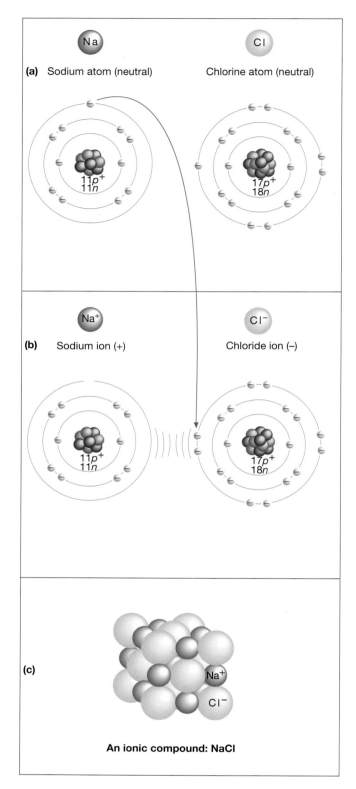

(a) Sodium atom (neutral)   Chlorine atom (neutral)

$11p^+$
$11n$

$17p^+$
$18n$

(b) Sodium ion (+)   Chloride ion (–)

$11p^+$
$11n$

$17p^+$
$18n$

(c)

Na^+

Cl^-

An ionic compound: NaCl

Figure 2-3 The formation of ions and ionic bonds

(a) Nonpolar covalent bonding

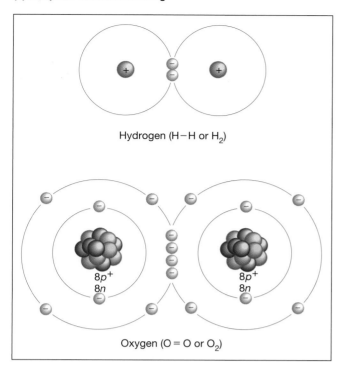

Hydrogen (H−H or H₂)

Oxygen (O = O or O₂)

(b) Polar covalent bonding

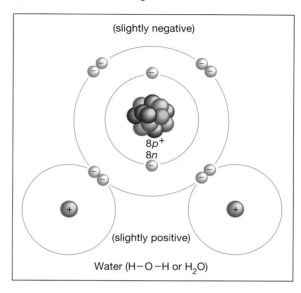

(slightly negative)

$8p^+$
$8n$

(slightly positive)

Water (H−O−H or H₂O)

Figure 2-4   Covalent bonds involve shared electrons

	Table 2-3 Bonding Patterns of Atoms Commonly Found in Biological Molecules			
Atom	Capacity of Outer Electron Shell	Electrons in Outer Shell	Number of Covalent Bonds Usually Formed	Common Bonding Patterns
Hydrogen	2	1	1	—H
Carbon	8	4	4	—C— =C= =C= —C≡
Nitrogen	8	5	3	—N— —N= N≡
Oxygen	8	6	2	—O— O=
Phosphorus	8	5	5	—P=
Sulfur	8	6	2	—S—

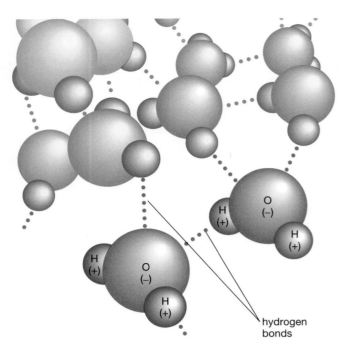

Figure 2-5 Hydrogen bonds
Media Activity 2.2 Water and Life

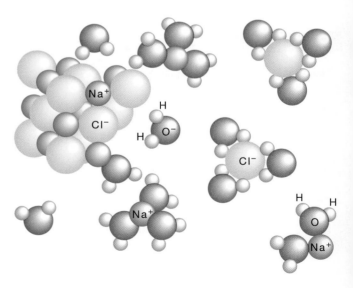

Figure 2-6 Water as a solvent
Media Activity 2.2 Water and Life

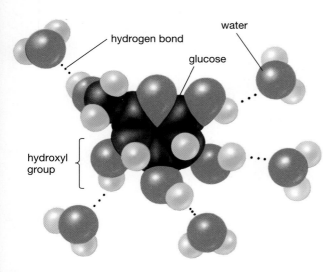

Figure 2-7 Water dissolves many biological molecules
Media Activity 2.2 Water and Life

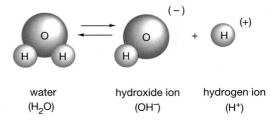

water   hydroxide ion   hydrogen ion
(H₂O)   (OH⁻)   (H⁺)

Figure 2-UN01 Water disassociation
Media Activity 2.2 Water and Life

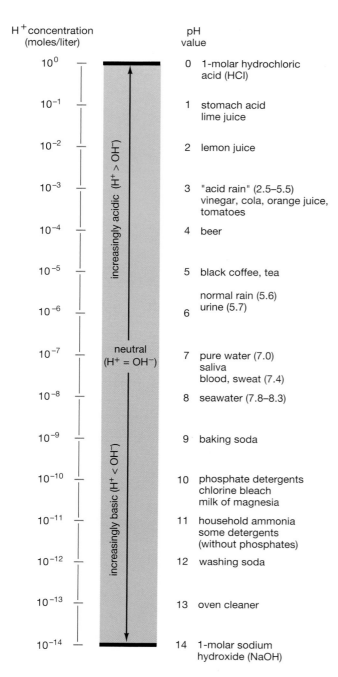

H⁺concentration
(moles/liter)

H$^+$ concentration (moles/liter)	pH value	
10^0	0	1-molar hydrochloric acid (HCl)
10^{-1}	1	stomach acid lime juice
10^{-2}	2	lemon juice
10^{-3}	3	"acid rain" (2.5–5.5) vinegar, cola, orange juice, tomatoes
10^{-4}	4	beer
10^{-5}	5	black coffee, tea
10^{-6}	6	normal rain (5.6) urine (5.7)
10^{-7}	7	pure water (7.0) saliva blood, sweat (7.4)
10^{-8}	8	seawater (7.8–8.3)
10^{-9}	9	baking soda
10^{-10}	10	phosphate detergents chlorine bleach milk of magnesia
10^{-11}	11	household ammonia some detergents (without phosphates)
10^{-12}	12	washing soda
10^{-13}	13	oven cleaner
10^{-14}	14	1-molar sodium hydroxide (NaOH)

increasingly acidic ($H^+ > OH^-$)

neutral ($H^+ = OH^-$)

increasingly basic ($H^+ < OH^-$)

Figure 2-9   The pH scale
Media Activity 2.2 Water and Life

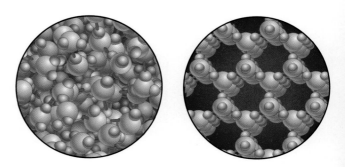

Figures 2-UN02, 2-UN03   Water forms an unusual solid: ice
Media Activity 2.2 Water and Life

Table 3-1 Important Functional Groups in Biological Molecules

Group	Structure	Properties	Types of Molecules
Hydrogen (—H)	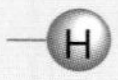	Polar or nonpolar, depending on which atom hydrogen is bonded to; involved in condensation and hydrolysis	Almost all organic molecules
Hydroxyl (—OH)	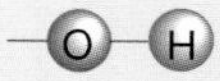	Polar; involved in condensation and hydrolysis	Carbohydrates, nucleic acids, alcohols, some acids, and steroids
Carboxyl (—COOH)	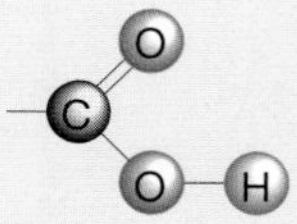	Acidic; negatively charged when H^+ dissociates; involved in peptide bonds	Amino acids, fatty acids
Amino (—NH$_2$)	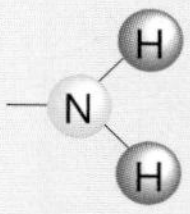	Basic; may bond an additional H^+, becoming positively charged; involved in peptide bonds	Amino acids, nucleic acids
Phosphate (—H$_2$PO$_4$)	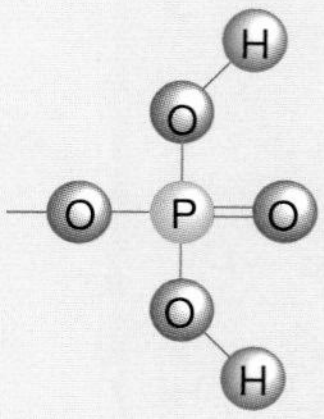	Acidic; up to two negative charges when H^+ dissociates; links nucleotides in nucleic acids; energy-carrier group in ATP	Nucleic acids, phospholipids
Methyl (—CH$_3$)	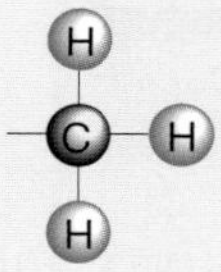	Nonpolar; tends to make molecules hydrophobic	Many organic molecules; especially common in lipids

Media Activity 3.1 Structure of Biological Molecules

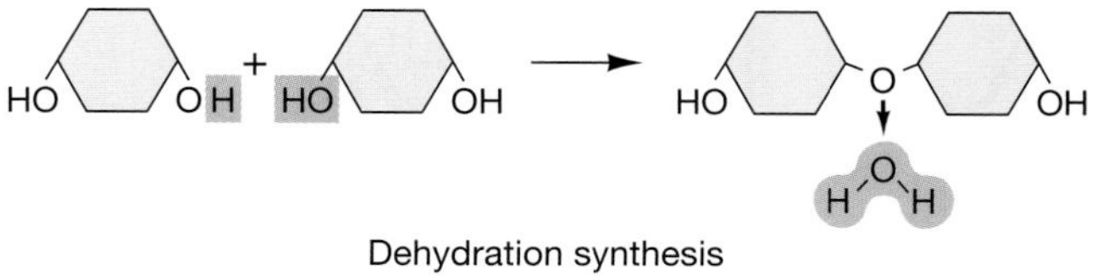

Dehydration synthesis

Figure 3-UN01 Dehydration synthesis

11

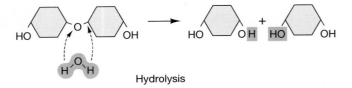

Figure 3-UN02 Hydrolysis

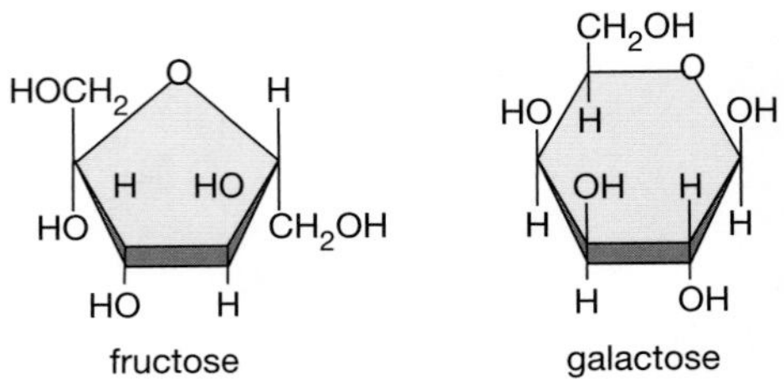

Figure 3-UN03 Fructose and galactose

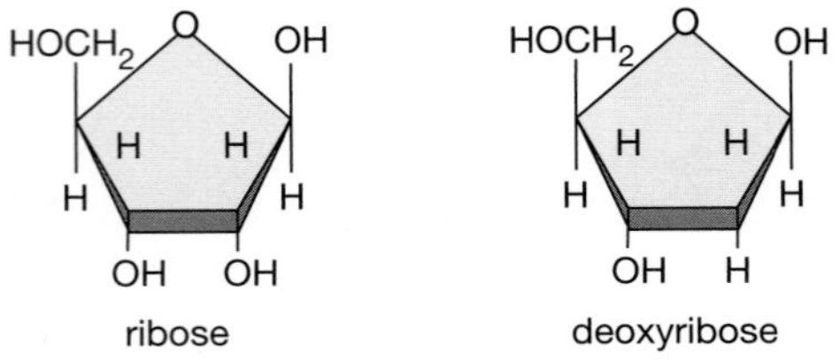

fructose

galactose

ribose

deoxyribose

Figure 3-UN04 Ribose and deoxyribose

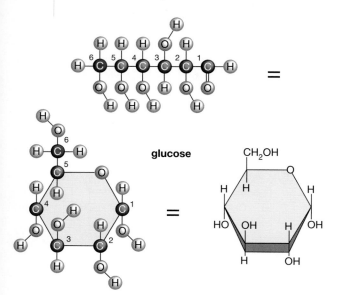

Figure 3-1 Glucose structure

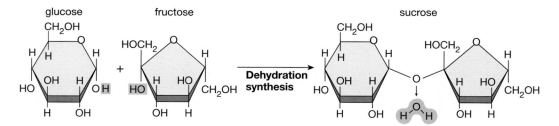

Figure 3-2 Synthesis of a disaccharide

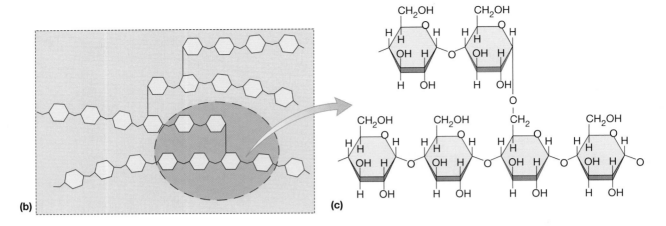

Figure 3-3b,c Starch is an energy-storage polysaccharide made of glucose subunits

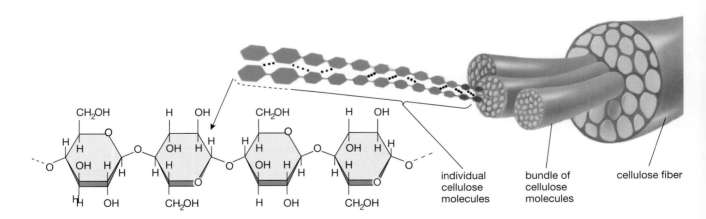

Figure 3-4 Cellulose structure and function

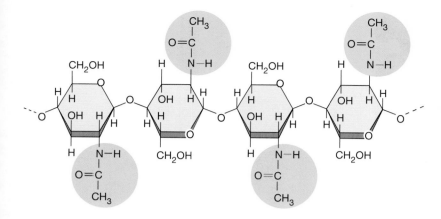

Figure 3-5 Chitin: a unique polysaccharide

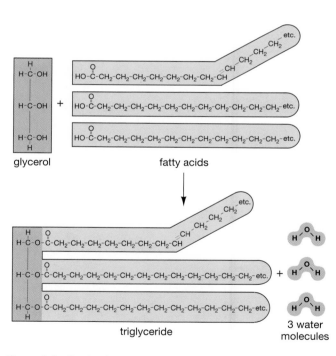

glycerol

fatty acids

triglyceride

3 water molecules

Figure 3-6 Synthesis of a triglyceride

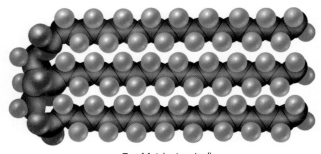

Beef fat (saturated)

Figure 3-UN05   Beef fat (saturated)

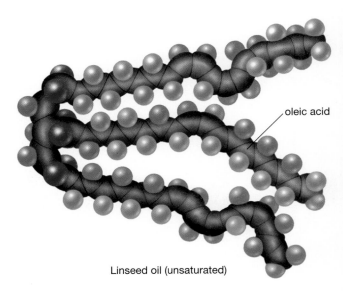

oleic acid

Linseed oil (unsaturated)

Figure 3-UN06   Linseed oil (unsaturated)

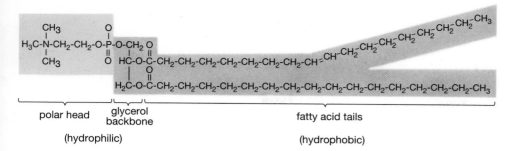

polar head   glycerol backbone   fatty acid tails

(hydrophilic)   (hydrophobic)

Figure 3-8 Phospholipids

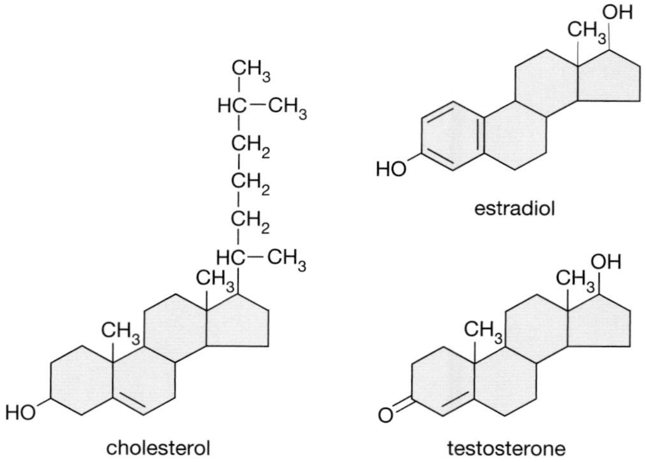

cholesterol

estradiol

testosterone

Figure 3-9 Steroids

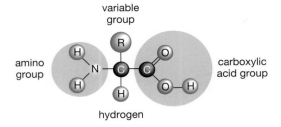

Figure 3-UN07 Amino acid functional group

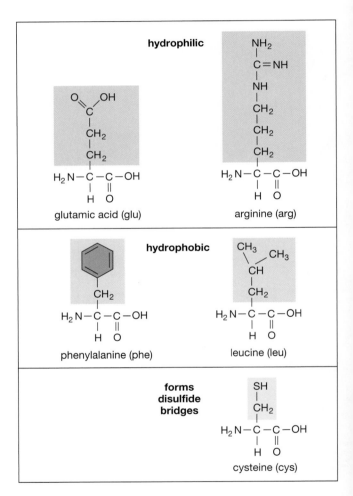

Figure 3-11 Amino acid diversity

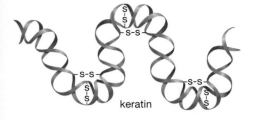

Figure 3-UN08 Keratin

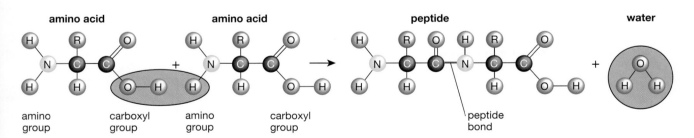

Figure 3-12 Protein synthesis

Figure 3-13   The four levels of protein structure

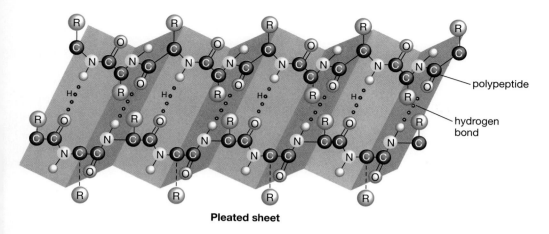

Pleated sheet

Figure 3-14 The pleated sheet is an example of protein secondary structure

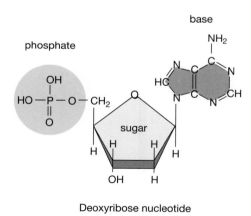

Deoxyribose nucleotide

Figure 3-UN09 Deoxyribose nucleotide

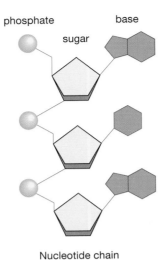

phosphate   base

sugar

Nucleotide chain

Figure 3-UN10   Nucleotide chain

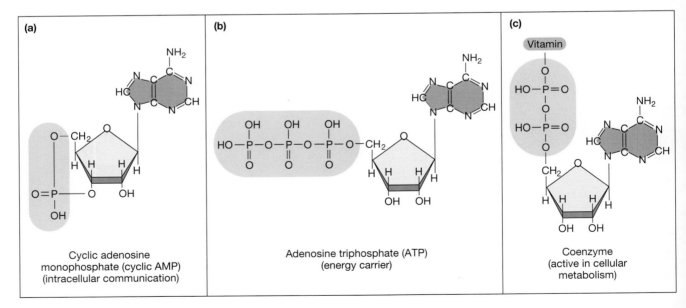

Cyclic adenosine
monophosphate (cyclic AMP)
(intracellular communication)

Adenosine triphosphate (ATP)
(energy carrier)

Coenzyme
(active in cellular
metabolism)

Figure 3-15   A sampling of the diversity of nucleotides

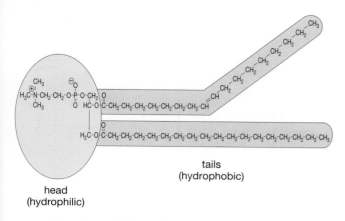

Figure 4-UN01   A phospholipid

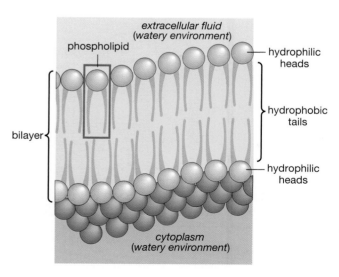

Figure 4-UN02   Phospholipid bilayer

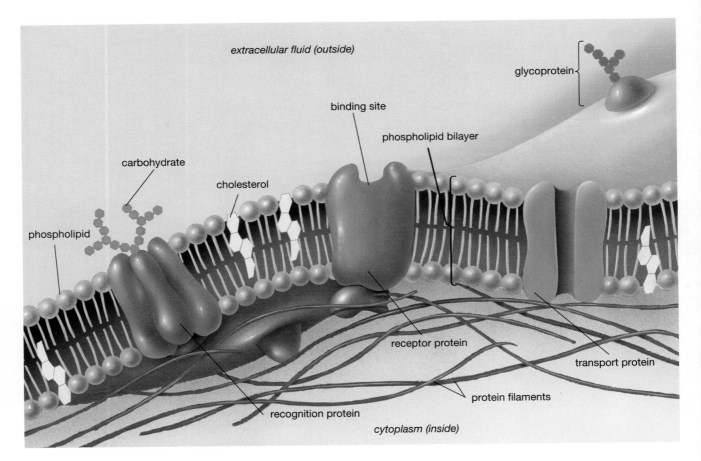

Figure 4-1   The plasma membrane is a fluid mosaic
Media Activity 4.1 Membrane Structure and Transport

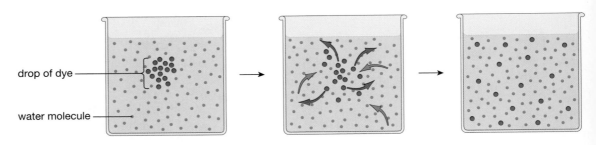

Figure 4-2   Diffusion of a dye in water

Table 4-1 Transport Across Membranes

Passive transport	Movement of substances across a membrane, going down a gradient of concentration, pressure, or electrical charge. Does not require the cell to expend energy.
Simple diffusion	Diffusion of water, dissolved gases, or lipid-soluble molecules through the phospholipid bilayer of a membrane.
Facilitated diffusion	Diffusion of (usually water-soluble) molecules through a channel or carrier protein.
Osmosis	Diffusion of water across a selectively permeable membrane—that is, a membrane that is more permeable to water than to dissolved molecules.
Energy-requiring transport	Movement of substances into or out of a cell using cellular energy.
Active transport	Movement of individual small molecules or ions through membrane-spanning proteins, using cellular energy, usually ATP.
Endocytosis	Movement of large particles, including large molecules or entire microorganisms, into a cell by engulfing extracellular material, as the plasma membrane forms membrane-bound sacs that enter the cytoplasm.
Exocytosis	Movement of materials out of a cell by enclosing the material in a membranous sac that moves to the cell surface, fuses with the plasma membrane, and opens to the outside, allowing its contents to diffuse away.

(a) Simple diffusion

(extracellular fluid)

lipid-soluble molecules
(O_2, CO_2, H_2O)

(cytoplasm)

(b) Facilitated diffusion through a channel

ions

channel
protein

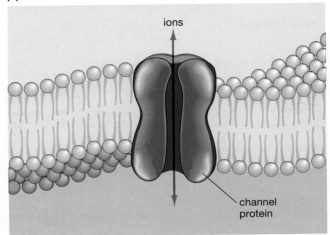

(c) Facilitated diffusion through a carrier

amino acids,
sugars,
small proteins

carrier
protein

(extracellular fluid)

(cytoplasm)

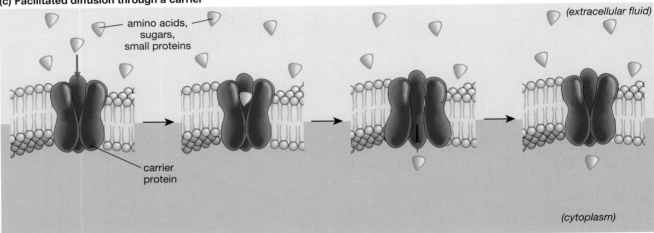

Figure 4-3 Diffusion through the plasma membrane

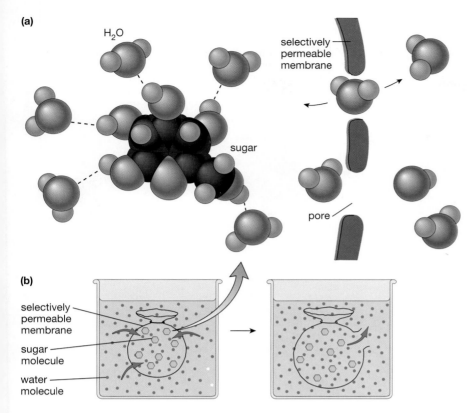

(a)

H₂O

selectively
permeable
membrane

sugar

pore

(b)

selectively
permeable
membrane

sugar
molecule

water
molecule

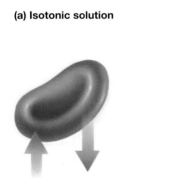

Figure 4-4   Osmosis
Media Activity 4.2 Osmosis

(a) Isotonic solution

(b) Hypertonic solution

(c) Hypotonic solution

Figure 4-5   The effects of osmosis
Media Activity 4.2 Osmosis

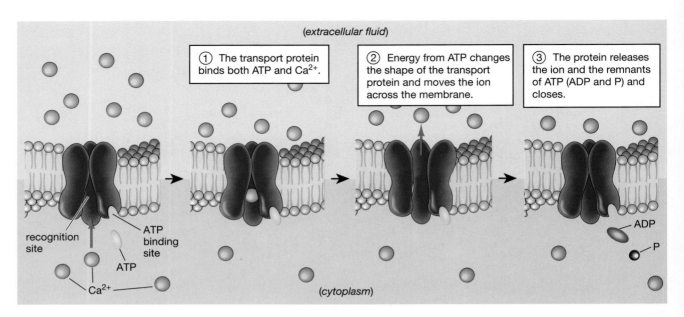

Figure 4-6 Active transport

(a) Pinocytosis

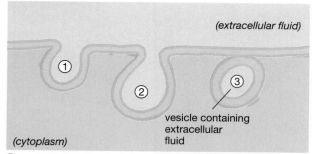

(1) A dimple forms in the plasma membrane, which (2) deepens and surrounds the extracellular fluid. (3) The membrane encloses the extracellular fluid, forming a vesicle.

(b) Receptor-mediated endocytosis

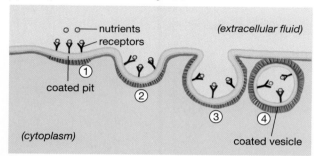

(1) Receptor proteins for specific molecules or complexes of molecules are localized at coated pit sites. (2) The receptors bind the molecules and the membrane dimples inward. (3) The coated pit region of the membrane encloses the receptor-bound molecules. (4) A vesicle ("coated vesicle") containing the bound molecules is released into the cytoplasm.

Figure 4-7 Three types of endocytosis

(c) Phagocytosis

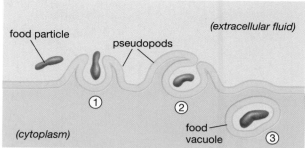

(1) The plasma membrane extends pseudopods toward an extracellular particle (for example, food). (2) The ends of the pseudopods fuse, encircling the particle. (3) A vesicle called a food vacuole is formed containing the engulfed particle.

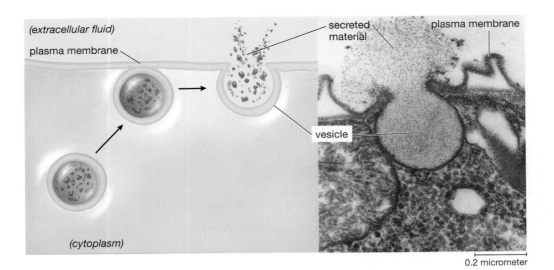

Figure 4-9 Exocytosis

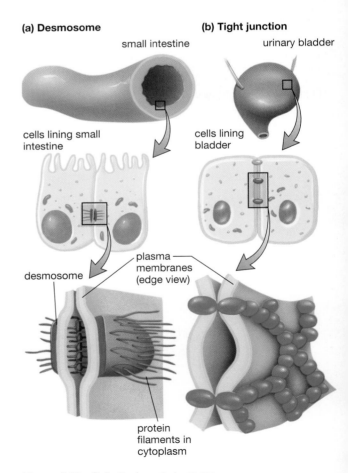

(a) Desmosome

small intestine

cells lining small intestine

desmosome

plasma membranes (edge view)

protein filaments in cytoplasm

(b) Tight junction

urinary bladder

cells lining bladder

Figure 4-10 Cell attachment structures

(a) Gap junctions

(b) Plasmodesmata

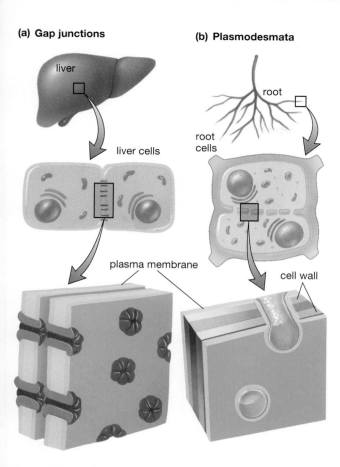

liver

liver cells

root

root cells

plasma membrane

cell wall

Figure 4-11   Cell communication structures

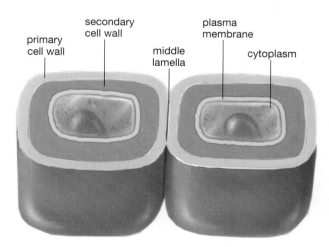

primary cell wall

secondary cell wall

middle lamella

plasma membrane

cytoplasm

Figure 4-12   Plant cell walls

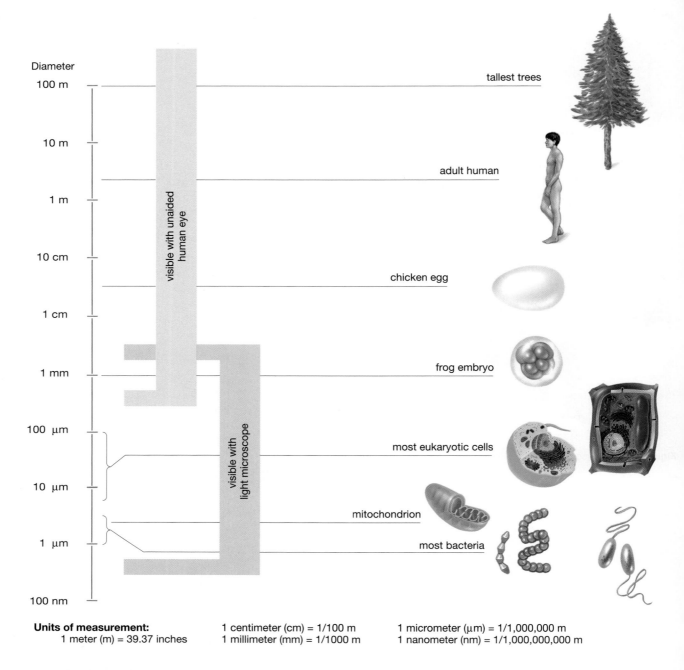

Diameter

100 m — tallest trees

10 m —

1 m — adult human

visible with unaided human eye

10 cm —

1 cm — chicken egg

1 mm — frog embryo

100 μm —

visible with light microscope

most eukaryotic cells

10 μm —

mitochondrion

1 μm — most bacteria

100 nm —

Units of measurement:
1 meter (m) = 39.37 inches

1 centimeter (cm) = 1/100 m
1 millimeter (mm) = 1/1000 m

1 micrometer (μm) = 1/1,000,000 m
1 nanometer (nm) = 1/1,000,000,000 m

Figure 5-1 Relative sizes

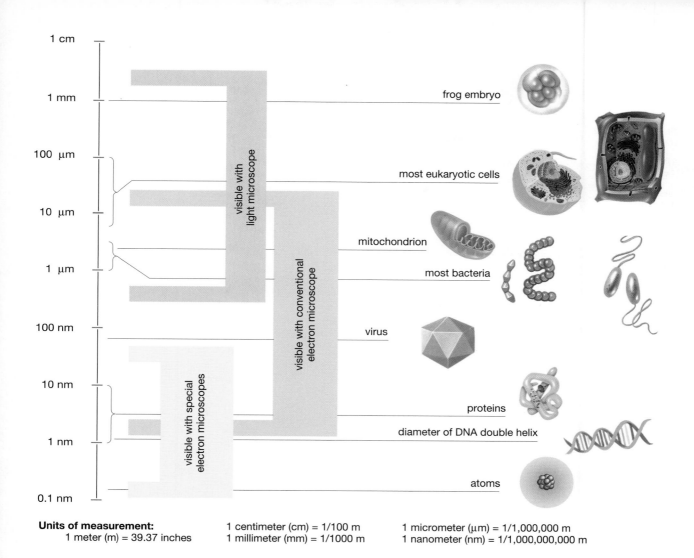

1 cm	
1 mm	frog embryo
100 µm	most eukaryotic cells
10 µm	
	mitochondrion
1 µm	most bacteria
100 nm	virus
10 nm	
	proteins
1 nm	diameter of DNA double helix
	atoms
0.1 nm	

visible with light microscope

visible with conventional electron microscope

visible with special electron microscopes

Units of measurement:
1 meter (m) = 39.37 inches

1 centimeter (cm) = 1/100 m
1 millimeter (mm) = 1/1000 m

1 micrometer (µm) = 1/1,000,000 m
1 nanometer (nm) = 1/1,000,000,000 m

Figure 5-1   Relative sizes

distance to center (r)	1.0	3.0	1.0
surface area ($4\pi r^2$)	12.6	113.1	339.4
volume ($4/3\ \pi r^3$)	4.2	113.1	113.1
area/volume	3.0	1.0	3.0

Figure 5-UN01   Geometrical considerations limit the size of relatively spherical cells

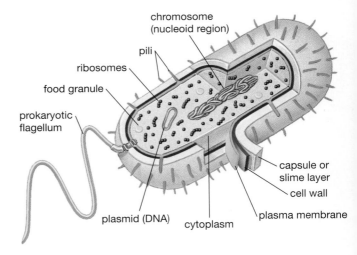

Figure 5-2   A generalized prokaryotic cell

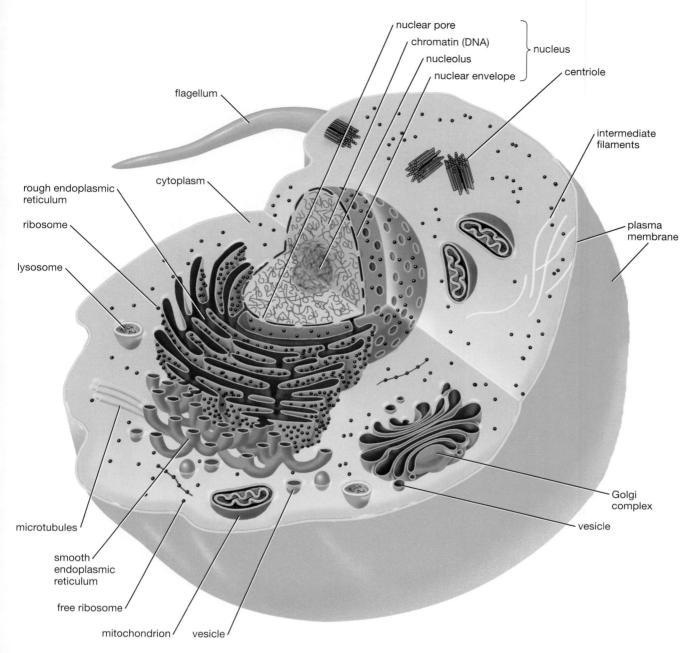

nuclear pore
chromatin (DNA)
nucleolus
nuclear envelope
nucleus
centriole
flagellum
intermediate filaments
cytoplasm
plasma membrane
rough endoplasmic reticulum
ribosome
lysosome
Golgi complex
vesicle
microtubules
smooth endoplasmic reticulum
free ribosome
mitochondrion
vesicle

Figure 5-3 A generalized animal cell
Media Activity 5.1 Cell Structure

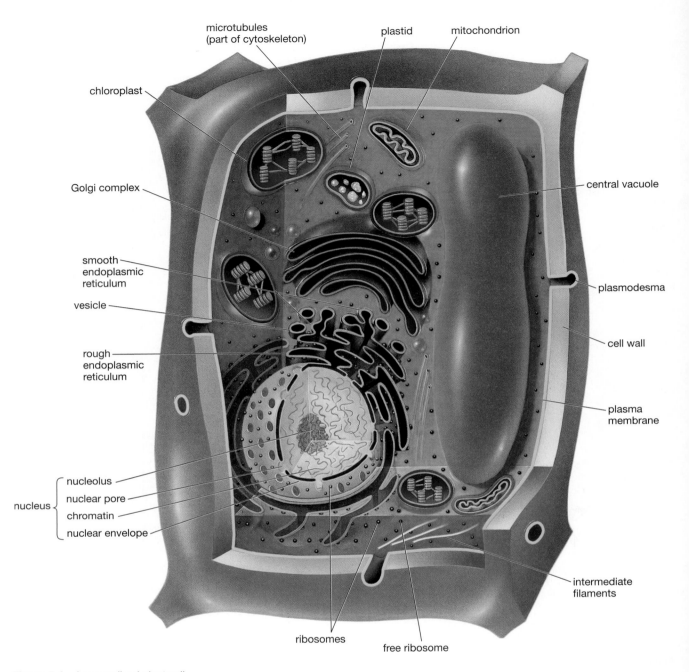

Figure 5-4 A generalized plant cell

microtubules
(part of cytoskeleton)

plastid

mitochondrion

chloroplast

Golgi complex

central vacuole

smooth
endoplasmic
reticulum

plasmodesma

vesicle

cell wall

rough
endoplasmic
reticulum

plasma
membrane

nucleus
{
  nucleolus
  nuclear pore
  chromatin
  nuclear envelope
}

intermediate
filaments

ribosomes

free ribosome

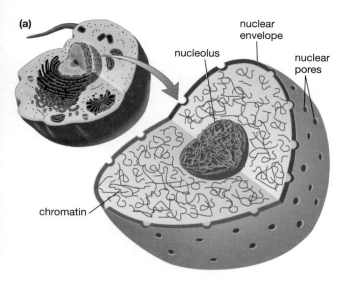

Figure 5-5a The nucleus

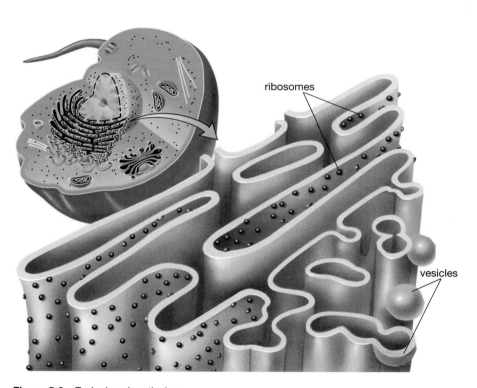

Figure 5-8 Endoplasmic reticulum

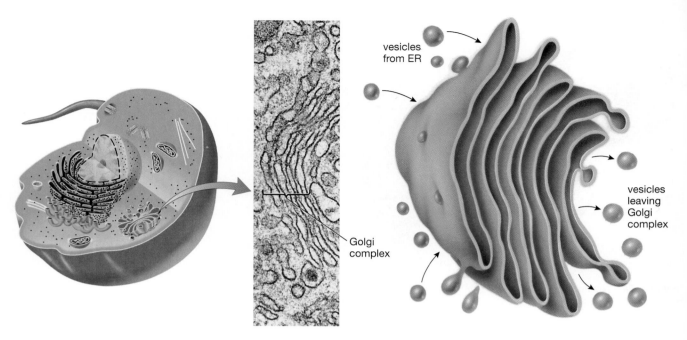

vesicles from ER

vesicles leaving Golgi complex

Golgi complex

Figure 5-9   The Golgi complex

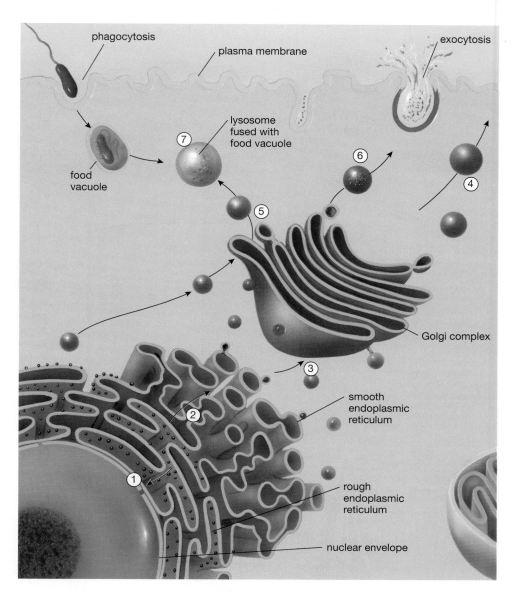

phagocytosis

plasma membrane

exocytosis

lysosome
fused with
food vacuole

⑦

⑥

④

food
vacuole

⑤

③

②

①

Golgi complex

smooth
endoplasmic
reticulum

rough
endoplasmic
reticulum

nuclear envelope

Figure 5-10   The flow of membrane within the cell
Media Activity 5.2 Membrane Traffic

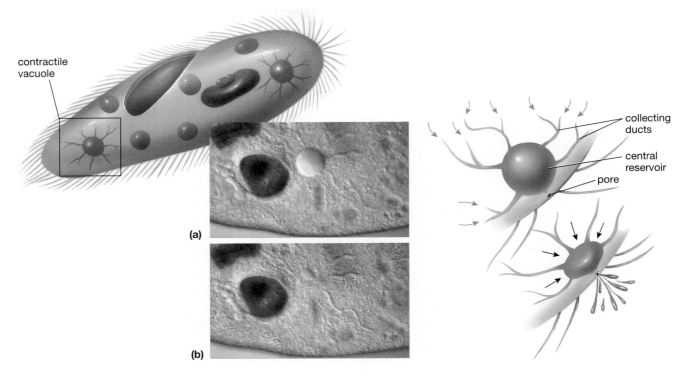

contractile
vacuole

collecting
ducts

central
reservoir

pore

(a)

(b)

Figure 5-11   Contractile vacuoles

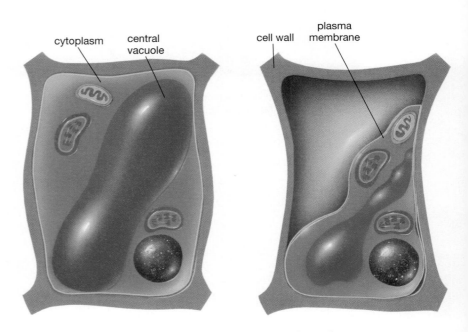

cytoplasm

central
vacuole

cell wall

plasma
membrane

Figure 5-12   The central vacuole and turgor pressure in plant cells

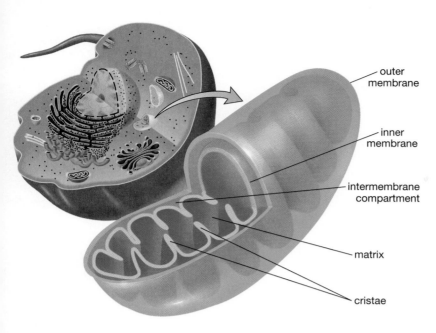

Figure 5-13   A mitochondrion

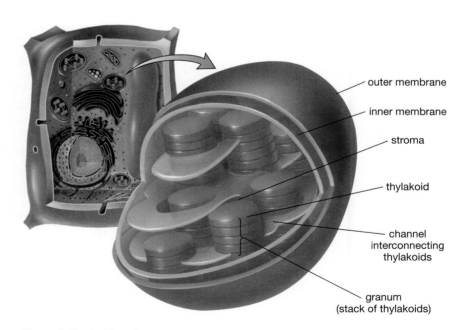

Figure 5-14   A chloroplast

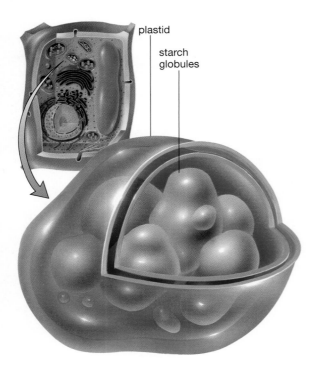

Figure 5-15 A plastid

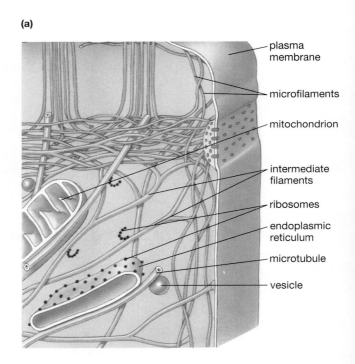

Figure 5-16a The cytoskeleton

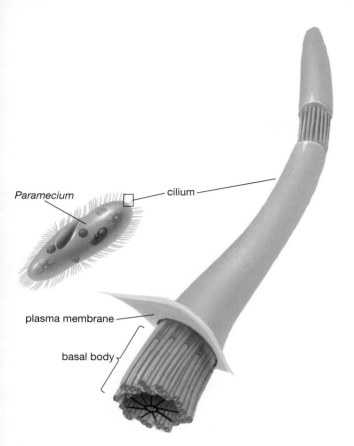

Figure 5-17 Cilia and flagella

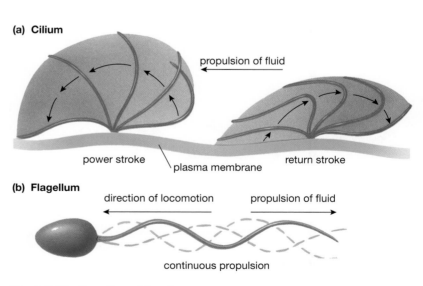

(a) Cilium

propulsion of fluid

power stroke   plasma membrane   return stroke

(b) Flagellum

direction of locomotion   propulsion of fluid

continuous propulsion

Figure 5-18 How cilia and flagella move

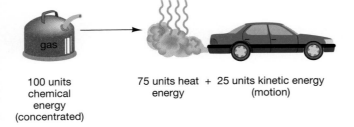

100 units
chemical
energy
(concentrated)

75 units heat + 25 units kinetic energy
energy   (motion)

Figure 6-UN01   Chemical energy changes to kinetic energy

Exergonic reaction

energy
released

reactants

products

Figure 6-UN02   Exergonic reaction

Endergonic reaction

energy
used

products

reactants

Figure 6-UN03   Endergonic reaction

Burning glucose

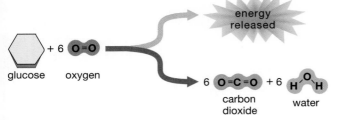

Figure 6-UN04 Exergonic reactions release energy

Photosynthesis

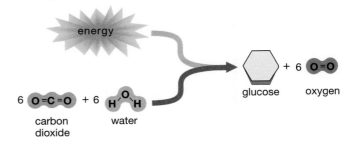

Figure 6-UN05 Endergonic reactions require an input of energy

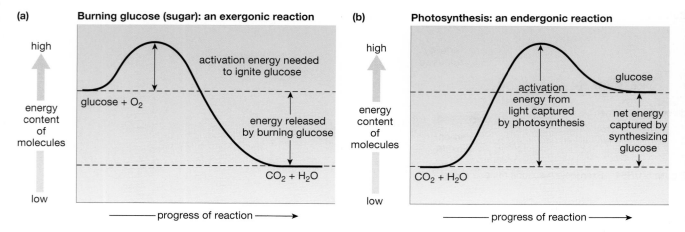

Figure 6-2 Energy relations in exergonic and endergonic reactions

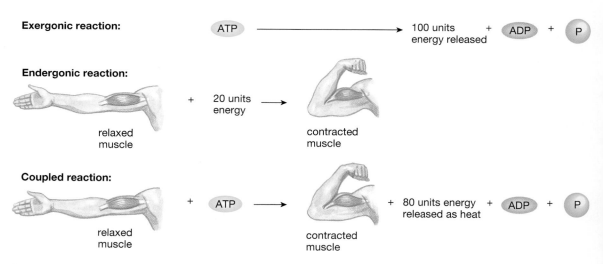

Figure 6-3 Coupled reactions

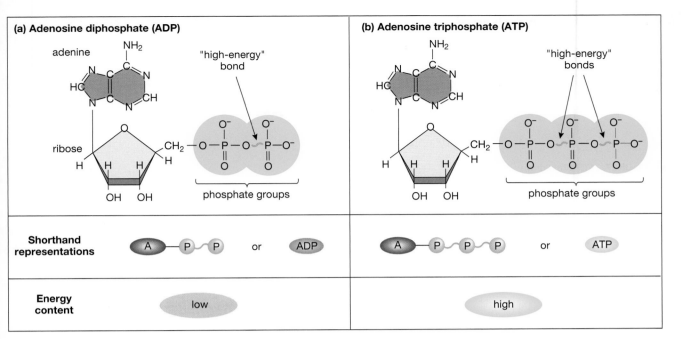

	(a) Adenosine diphosphate (ADP)	(b) Adenosine triphosphate (ATP)
Shorthand representations	A—P~P or ADP	A—P~P~P or ATP
Energy content	low	high

Figure 6-4 ADP and ATP
Media Activity 6.2 Energy and Life

ATP synthesis: Energy is stored in ATP

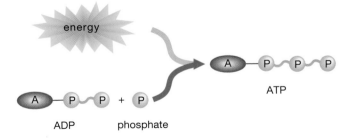

Figure 6-UN06 ATP synthesis

ATP breakdown: Energy of ATP is released

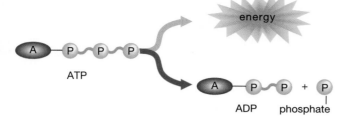

Figure 6-UN07 ATP breakdown

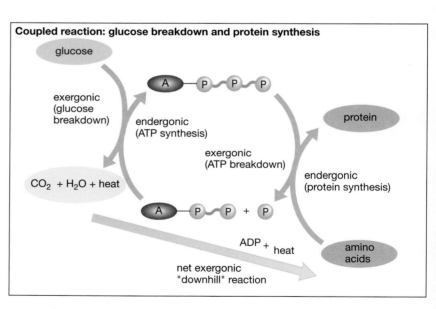

Figure 6-5 Coupled reactions within living cells

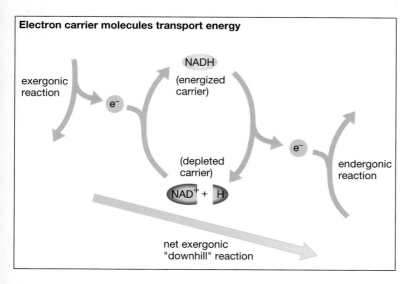

Figure 6-6 Electron carriers

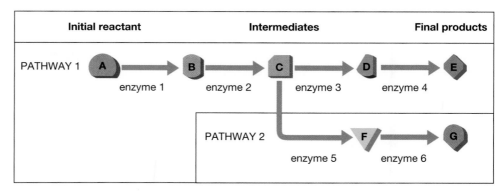

Figure 6-7 Simplified view of metabolic pathways
Media Activity 6.3 Enzymes

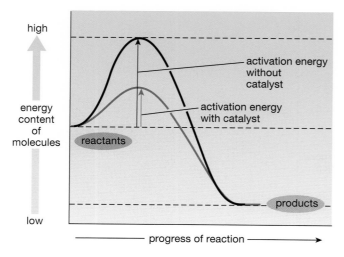

Figure 6-8 Catalysts lower activation energy, increasing the rate of reactions

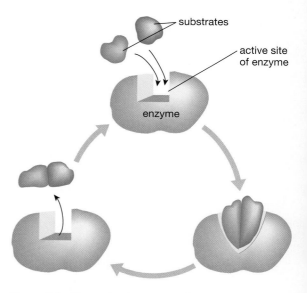

Figure 6-9 The cycle of enzyme–substrate interactions

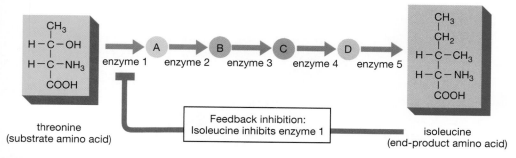

Figure 6-10 Enzyme regulation by feedback inhibition

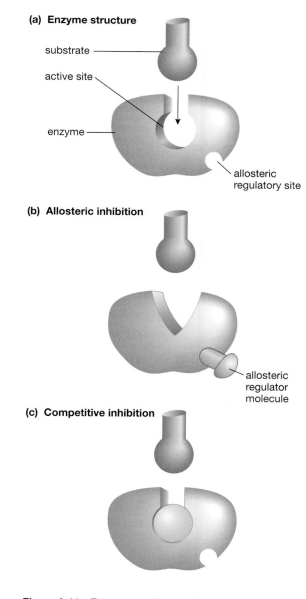

Figure 6-11 Enzyme regulation by allosteric regulation and competitive inhibition

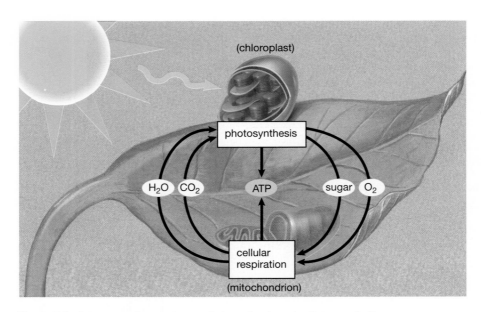

Figure 7-1   Interconnections between photosynthesis and cellular respiration

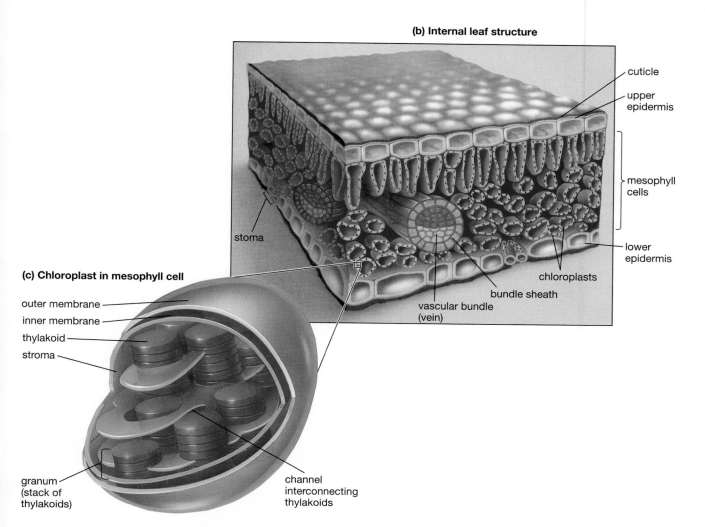

(b) Internal leaf structure

cuticle

upper epidermis

mesophyll cells

lower epidermis

chloroplasts

bundle sheath

vascular bundle (vein)

stoma

(c) Chloroplast in mesophyll cell

outer membrane

inner membrane

thylakoid

stroma

granum (stack of thylakoids)

channel interconnecting thylakoids

Figure 7-2b,c   An overview of photosynthetic structures

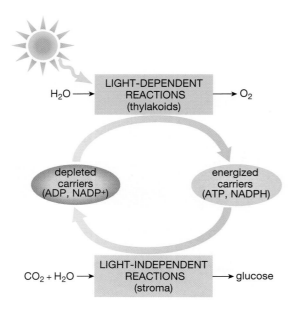

Figure 7-UN01 Light-dependent and light-independent reactions

(a) Visible light ("rainbow colors")

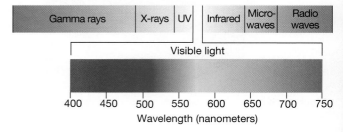

(b) Absorbance of photosynthetic pigments

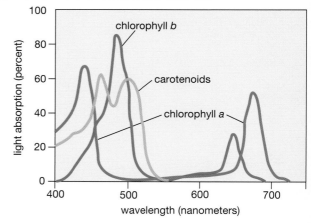

Figure 7-3 Light, chloroplast pigments, and photosynthesis
Media Activity 7.1 Properties of Light

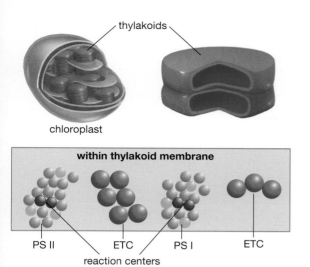

thylakoids

chloroplast

within thylakoid membrane

PS II   ETC   PS I   ETC

reaction centers

Figure 7-UN02 Light-dependent reactions of photosynthesis
Media Activity 7.2 Photosynthesis

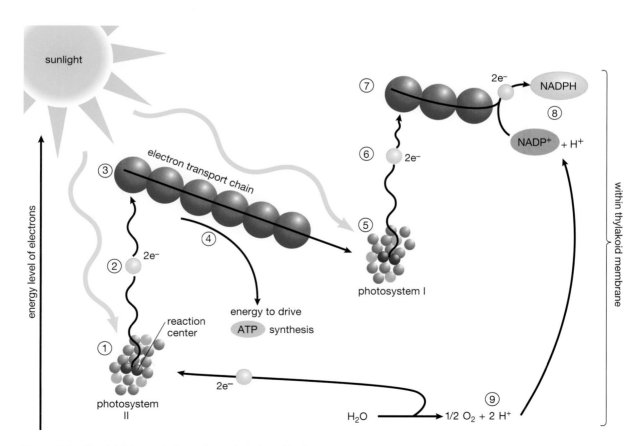

sunlight

energy level of electrons

electron transport chain

③

② 2e⁻

④

⑦ 2e⁻ → NADPH

⑧

NADP⁺ + H⁺

⑥ 2e⁻

⑤

photosystem I

energy to drive
ATP synthesis

reaction
center

①

photosystem
II

2e⁻

H₂O → 1/2 O₂ + 2 H⁺

⑨

within thylakoid membrane

Figure 7-4 The light-dependent reactions of photosynthesis
Media Activity 7.2 Photosynthesis

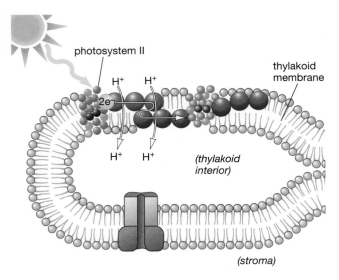

Figure E7-UN01 Chemiosmosis
Media Activity 7.3 Chemiosmosis

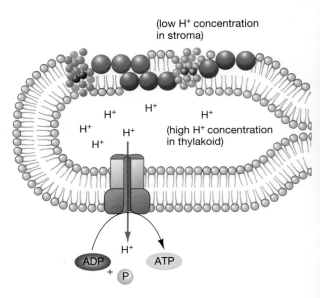

Figure E7-UN02 Chemiosmosis
Media Activity 7.3 Chemiosmosis

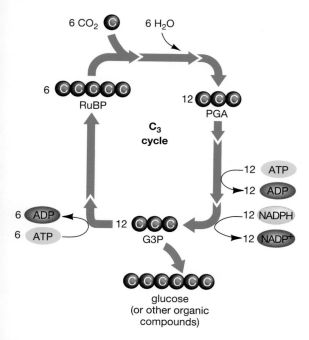

Figure 7-6 The C$_3$ cycle of carbon fixation

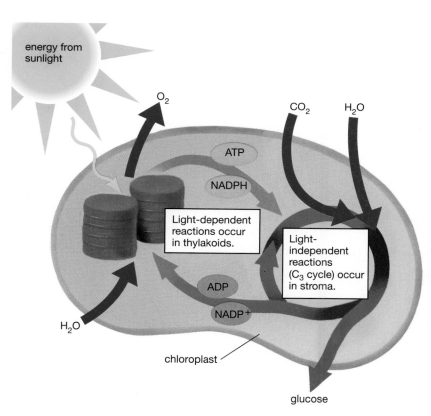

Figure 7-7 A summary diagram of photosynthesis

(a) C₃ plants use the C₃ pathway

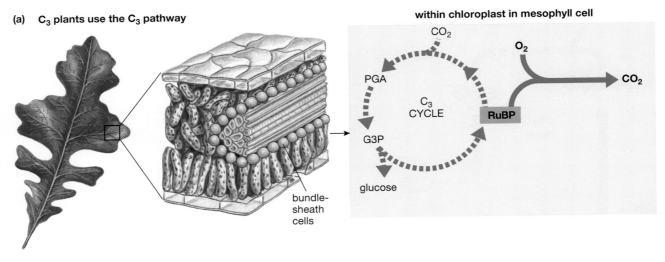

within chloroplast in mesophyll cell

CO₂

PGA

C₃ CYCLE

O₂

CO₂

G3P

RuBP

glucose

bundle-sheath cells

(b) C₄ plants use the C₄ pathway

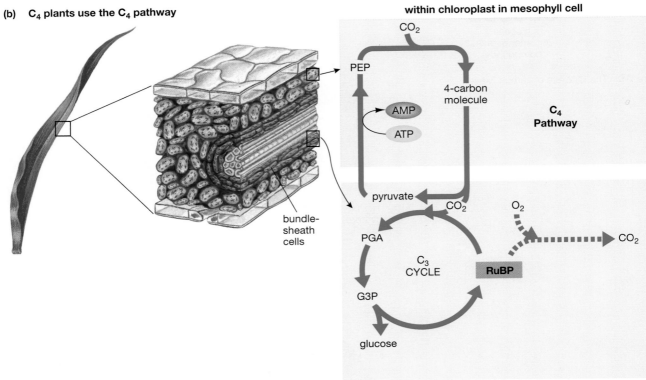

within chloroplast in mesophyll cell

CO₂

PEP

AMP

ATP

4-carbon molecule

C₄ Pathway

pyruvate

CO₂

O₂

CO₂

PGA

C₃ CYCLE

RuBP

G3P

glucose

bundle-sheath cells

within chloroplast in bundle-sheath cell

Figure 7-8 Comparison of C₃ and C₄ plants

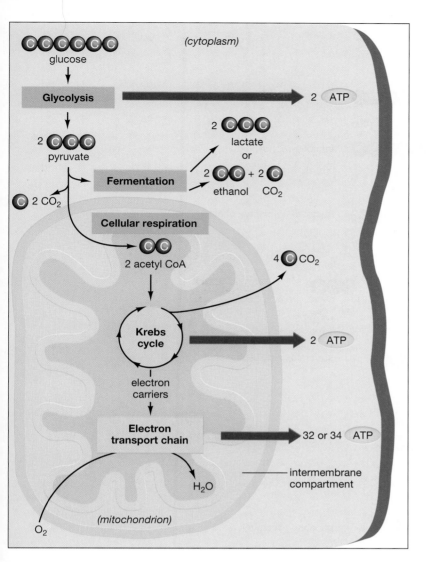

Figure 8-1 A summary of glucose metabolism
Media Activity 8.1 Glucose Metabolism

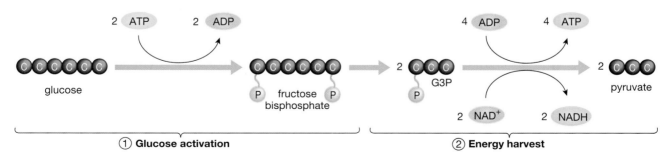

Figure 8-2 The essentials of glycolysis

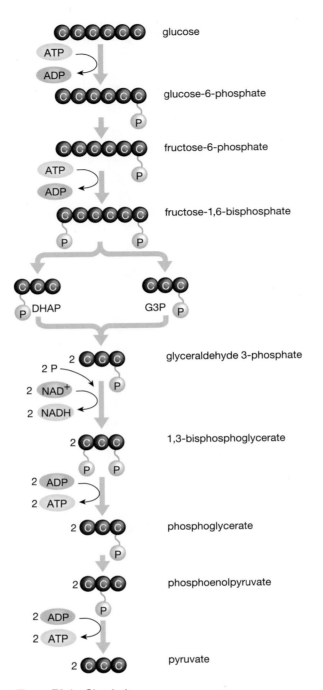

Figure E8-1 Glycolysis

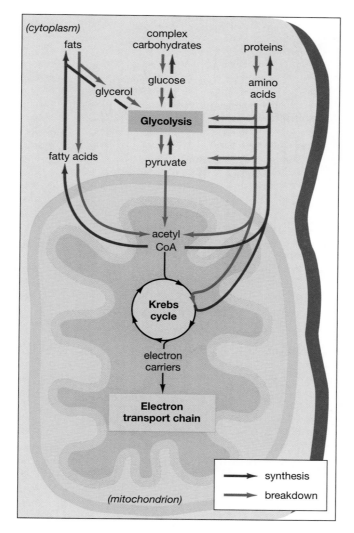

Figure E8-2 How various nutrients yield energy and can be inter-converted

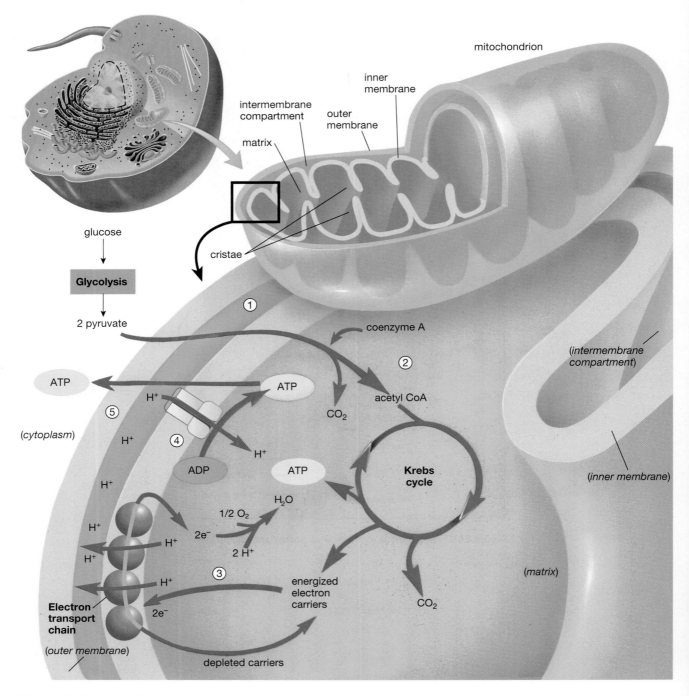

Labels in figure:

mitochondrion

inner membrane

intermembrane compartment

outer membrane

matrix

cristae

glucose

Glycolysis

2 pyruvate

coenzyme A

① ②

(intermembrane compartment)

ATP

H⁺ ATP

⑤

(cytoplasm)

④

H⁺

ADP

H⁺ ATP

CO_2

acetyl CoA

Krebs cycle

(inner membrane)

H⁺

H_2O

$1/2 O_2$

$2e^-$

2 H⁺

③

energized electron carriers

(matrix)

H⁺

CO_2

Electron transport chain

$2e^-$

(outer membrane)

depleted carriers

Figure 8-4   Cellular respiration

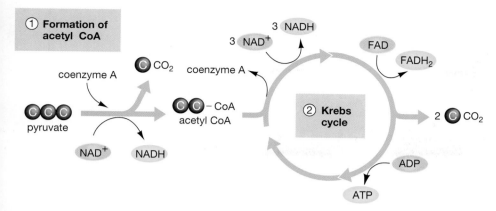

Figure 8-5 The reactions in the mitochondrial matrix

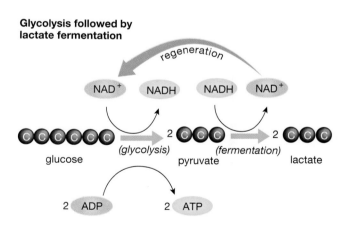

Glycolysis followed by lactate fermentation

Figure 8-UN01 Lactate fermentation

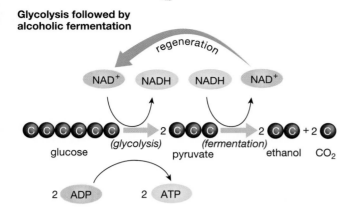

Glycolysis followed by alcoholic fermentation

glucose (glycolysis) 2 pyruvate (fermentation) 2 ethanol + 2 CO_2

2 ADP → 2 ATP

Figure 8-UN02 Alcoholic fermentation

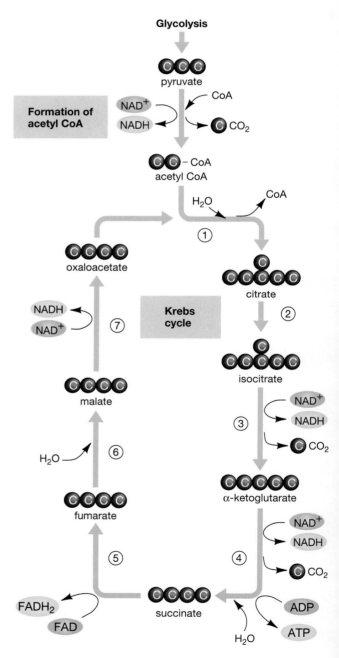

Figure E8-3 The mitochondrial matrix reactions

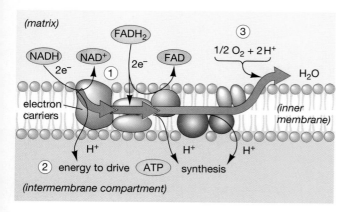

Figure 8-6 The electron transport chain of mitochondria

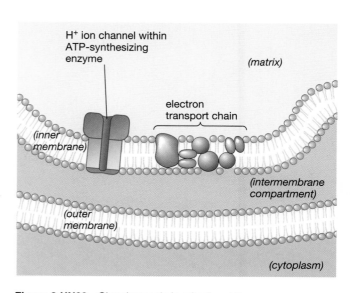

Figure 8-UN03 Chemiosmosis in mitochondria

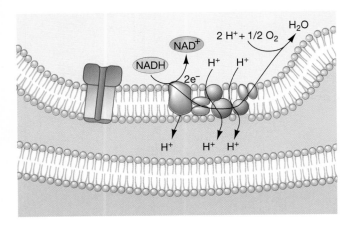

Figure 8-UN04   Chemiosmosis in mitochondria

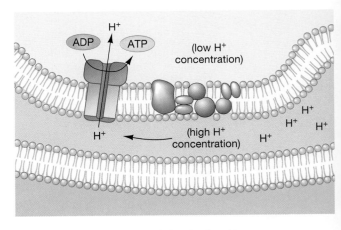

Figure 8-UN05   Chemiosmosis in mitochondria

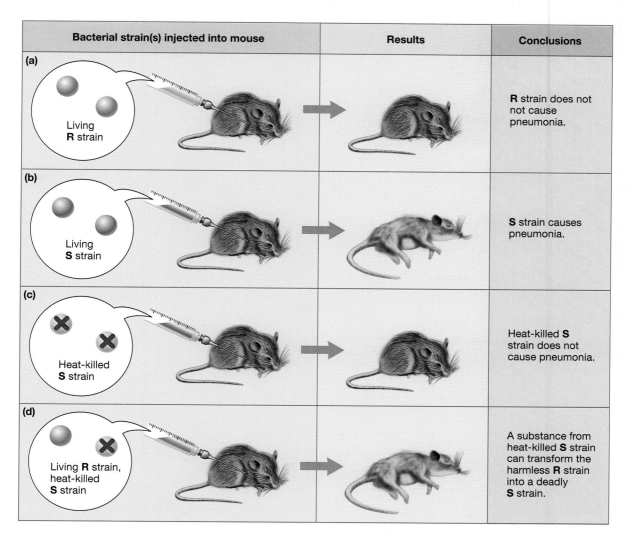

Figure 9-1 Transformed bacteria

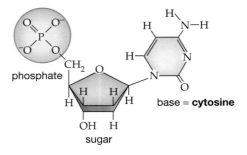

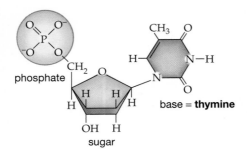

Figure 9-UN01 Two DNA nucleotides: thymine and cytosine

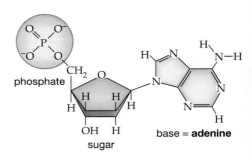

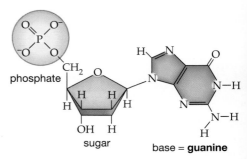

Figure 9-UN02 Two DNA nucleotides: adenine and guanine

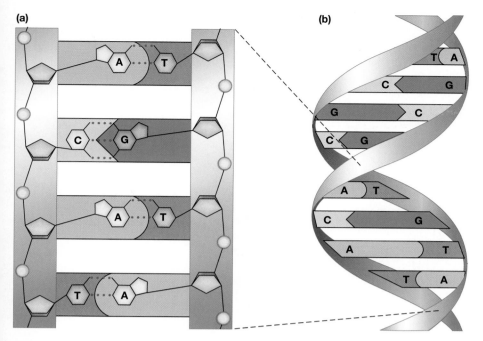

Figure 9-3a,b The Watson-Crick model of DNA structure
Media Activity 9.1 DNA Structure

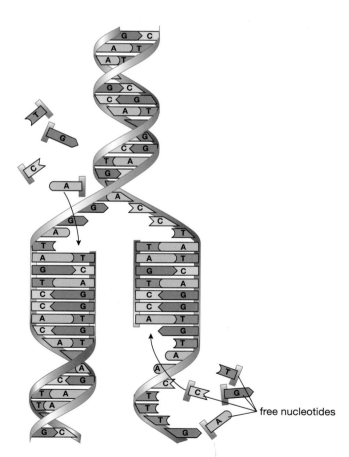

free nucleotides

Figure 9-4 Basic features of DNA replication
Media Activity 9.2 DNA Replication

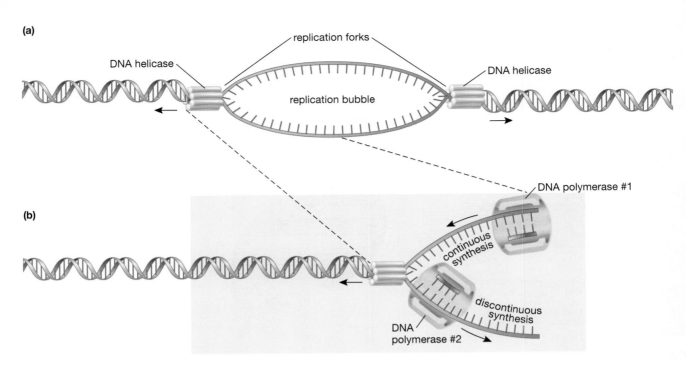

Figure E9-2a,b Details of DNA replication
Media Activity 9.2 DNA Replication

(c)

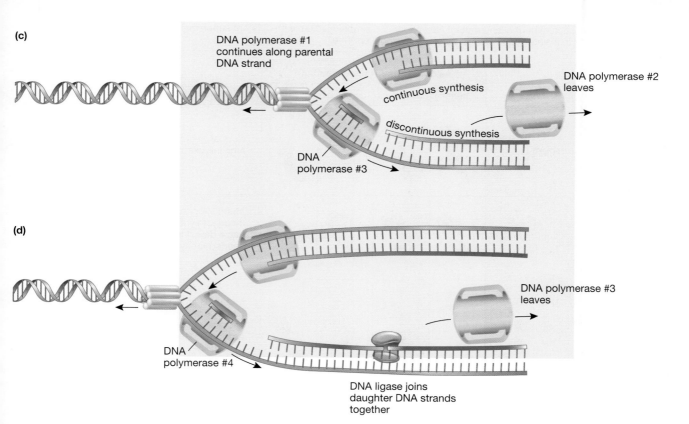

DNA polymerase #1
continues along parental
DNA strand

continuous synthesis

DNA polymerase #2
leaves

discontinuous synthesis

DNA
polymerase #3

(d)

DNA polymerase #3
leaves

DNA
polymerase #4

DNA ligase joins
daughter DNA strands
together

Figure E9-2c,d Details of DNA replication
Media Activity 9.2 DNA Replication

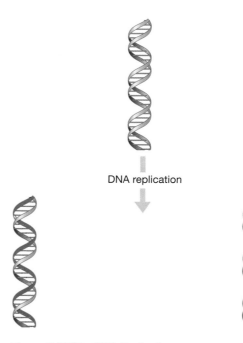

DNA replication

Figure 9-UN03 DNA Replication
Media Activity 9.2 DNA Replication

(a) Growth characteristics of normal and mutant *Neurospora* on simple medium with different supplements show that defects in a single gene lead to defects in a single enzyme.

		Supplements Added to Medium				Conclusions
		none	ornithine	citrulline	arginine	
Normal *Neurospora*						Normal *Neurospora* can synthesize arginine, citrulline, and ornithine.
Mutants with single gene defect	A					Mutant A grows only if arginine is added. It cannot synthesize arginine because it has a defect in enzyme 2; gene A is needed for synthesis of arginine.
	B					Mutant B grows if either arginine or citrulline are added. It cannot synthesize arginine because it has a defect in enzyme 1. Gene B is needed for synthesis of citrulline.

(b) The biochemical pathway for synthesis of the amino acid arginine involves two steps, each catalyzed by a different enzyme.

ornithine → (enzyme 1 / gene B) → citrulline → (enzyme 2 / gene A) → arginine — amino acid needed in protein synthesis

Figure 10-1 Beadle and Tatum's experiments with *Neurospora* mutants

Table 10-1 A Comparison of DNA and RNA

	DNA	RNA	
Strands	2	1	
Sugar	deoxyribose	ribose	
Types of Bases	adenine (A), thymine (T) cytosine (C), guanine (G)	adenine (A), uracil (U) cytosine (C), guanine (G)	
Base Pairs	DNA:DNA	RNA:DNA	RNA:RNA
	A–T	A–T	A–U
	T–A	U–A	U–A
	C–G	C–G	C–G
	G–C	G–C	G–C
Function	Contains genes; sequence of bases in most genes determines the amino acid sequence of a protein	**Messenger RNA (mRNA):** carries the code for a protein-coding gene from DNA to ribosomes **Ribosomal RNA (rRNA):** combines with proteins to form ribosomes, the structures that link amino acids to form a protein **Transfer RNA (tRNA):** carries amino acids to the ribosomes	

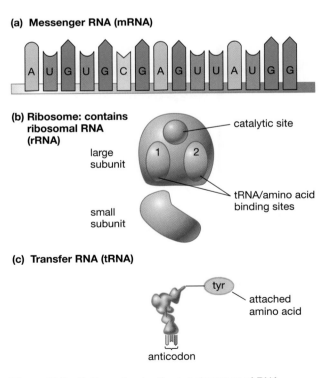

(a) Messenger RNA (mRNA)

A U G U G C G A G U U A U G G

(b) Ribosome: contains ribosomal RNA (rRNA)

catalytic site

large subunit

small subunit

tRNA/amino acid binding sites

(c) Transfer RNA (tRNA)

tyr

attached amino acid

anticodon

Figure 10-2   Cells synthesize three major types of RNA

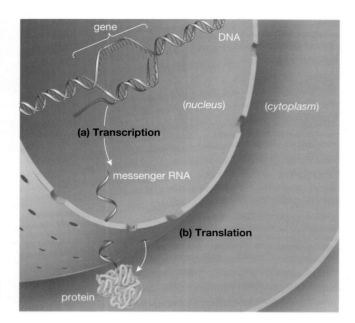

Figure 10-3 Genetic information flows from DNA to RNA to protein

Table 10-3 The Genetic Code (Codons of mRNA)

		Second Base				
		U	**C**	**A**	**G**	
First Base	**U**	UUU Phenylalanine (Phe) UUC Phenylalanine UUA Leucine (Leu) UUG Leucine	UCU Serine (Ser) UCC Serine UCA Serine UCG Serine	UAU Tyrosine (Tyr) UAC Tyrosine UAA Stop UAG Stop	UGU Cysteine (Cys) UGC Cysteine UGA Stop UGG Tryptophan (Trp)	U C A G
	C	CUU Leucine CUC Leucine CUA Leucine CUG Leucine	CCU Proline (Pro) CCC Proline CCA Proline CCG Proline	CAU Histidine (His) CAC Histidine CAA Glutamine (Gln) CAG Glutamine	CGU Arginine (Arg) CGC Arginine CGA Arginine CGG Arginine	U C A G
	A	AUU Isoleucine (Ile) AUC Isoleucine AUA Isoleucine AUG Methionine (Met)	ACU Threonine (Thr) ACC Threonine ACA Threonine ACG Threonine	AAU Asparagine (Asp) AAC Asparagine AAA Lysine (Lys) AAG Lysine	AGU Serine (Ser) AGC Serine AGA Arginine (Arg) AGG Arginine	U C A G
	G	GUU Valine (Val) GUC Valine GUA Valine GUG Valine	GCU Alanine (Ala) GCC Alanine GCA Alanine GCG Alanine	GAU Aspartic acid (Asp) GAC Aspartic acid GAA Glutamic acid (Glu) GAG Glutamic acid	GGU Glycine (Gly) GGC Glycine GGA Glycine GGG Glycine	U C A G

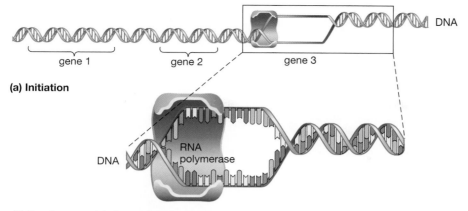

gene 1   gene 2   gene 3   DNA

(a) Initiation

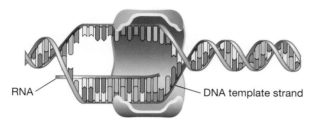

DNA   RNA polymerase

RNA polymerase binds to the promoter region of DNA near the beginning of a gene, separating the double helix near the promoter.

(b) Elongation

RNA   DNA template strand

RNA polymerase travels along the DNA template strand, catalyzing the addition of ribose nucleotides into an RNA molecule. The nucleotides in the RNA are complementary to the template strand of the DNA.

Figure 10-4a,b   Transcription: initiation and elongation
Media Activity 10.1 Transcription

(c) Termination

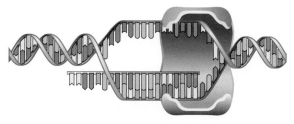

At the end of a gene, RNA polymerase encounters a sequence of DNA called a termination signal. RNA polymerase detaches from the DNA and releases the RNA molecule.

(d) Conclusion of transcription

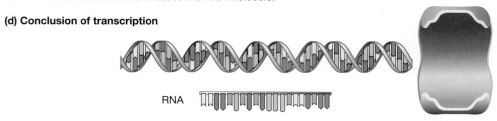

RNA

After termination, the DNA completely rewinds into a double helix. The RNA molecule is free to move from the nucleus to the cytoplasm for translation, and RNA polymerase may move to another gene and begin transcription once again.

Figure 10-4c,d   Transcription: termination and conclusion
Media Activity 10.1 Transcription

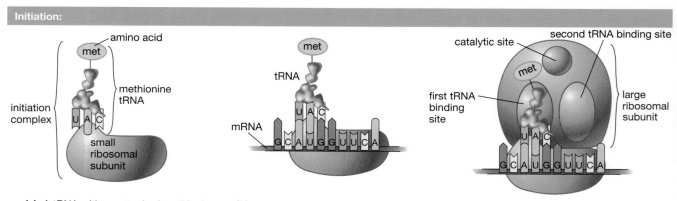

Initiation:

(a) A tRNA with an attached methionine amino acid binds to a small ribosomal subunit, forming an initiation complex.

(b) The initiation complex binds to an mRNA molecule. The methionine (met) tRNA anticodon (UAC) base-pairs with the start codon (AUG) of the mRNA.

(c) The large ribosomal subunit binds to the small subunit. The methionine tRNA binds to the first tRNA site on the large subunit.

Figure 10-6a,b,c   Translation is the process of protein synthesis
Media Activity 10.2 Translation

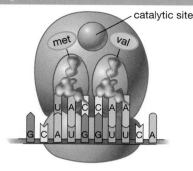

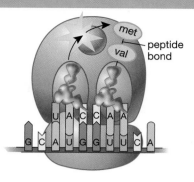

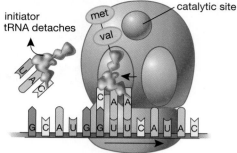

ribosome moves one codon to right

(d) The second codon of mRNA (GUU) base-pairs with the anticodon (CAA) of a second tRNA carrying the amino acid valine (val). This tRNA binds to the second tRNA site on the large subunit.

(e) The catalytic site on the large subunit catalyzes the formation of a peptide bond linking the amino acids methionine and valine. The two amino acids are now attached to the tRNA in the second binding position.

(f) The "empty" tRNA is released and the ribosome moves down the mRNA, one codon to the right. The tRNA that is attached to the two amino acids is now in the first tRNA binding site and the second tRNA binding site is empty.

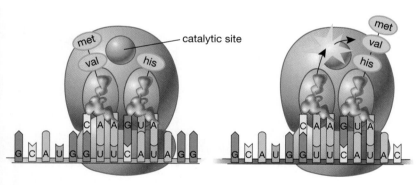

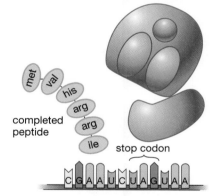

(g) The third codon of mRNA (CAU) base-pairs with the anticodon (GUA) of a tRNA carrying the amino acid histidine (his). This tRNA enters the second tRNA binding site on the large subunit.

(h) The catalytic site forms a new peptide bond between valine and histidine. A three-amino-acid chain is now attached to the tRNA in the second binding site. The tRNA in the first site leaves, and the ribosome moves one codon over on the mRNA.

(i) This process repeats until a stop codon is reached; the mRNA and the completed peptide are released from the ribosome, and the subunits separate.

Figure 10-6d-i Translation is the process of protein synthesis
Media Activity 10.2 Translation

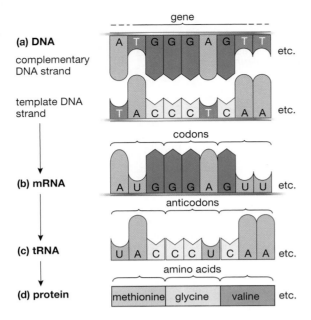

Figure 10-7 Complementary base pairing is critical to decode genetic information

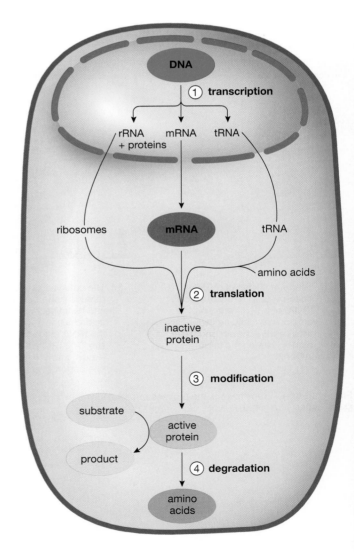

Figure 10-8 An overview of information flow in a cell, from gene transcription to chemical reactions catalyzed by enzymes

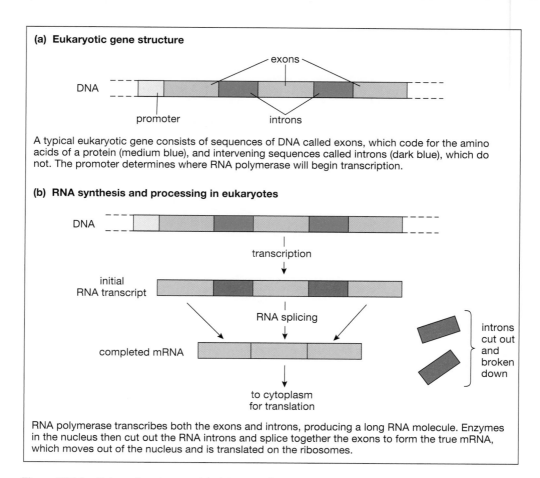

(a) Eukaryotic gene structure

exons

DNA

promoter

introns

A typical eukaryotic gene consists of sequences of DNA called exons, which code for the amino acids of a protein (medium blue), and intervening sequences called introns (dark blue), which do not. The promoter determines where RNA polymerase will begin transcription.

(b) RNA synthesis and processing in eukaryotes

DNA

transcription

initial RNA transcript

RNA splicing

completed mRNA

introns cut out and broken down

to cytoplasm for translation

RNA polymerase transcribes both the exons and introns, producing a long RNA molecule. Enzymes in the nucleus then cut out the RNA introns and splice together the exons to form the true mRNA, which moves out of the nucleus and is translated on the ribosomes.

Figure E10-1   Eukaryotic genes contain introns and exons

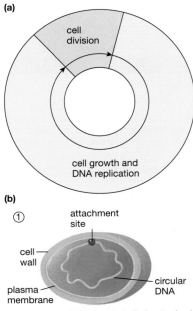

(a)

cell
division

cell growth and
DNA replication

(b)

① attachment
site

cell
wall

plasma
membrane

circular
DNA

The circular DNA double helix is attached
to the plasma membrane at one point.

②

The DNA replicates and the two
DNA double helices attach to the
plasma membrane at nearby points.

③

New plasma membrane is added
between the attachment points,
pushing them further apart.

④

The plasma membrane grows inward
at the middle of the cell.

⑤

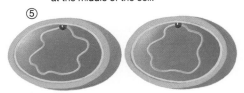

The parent cell divides into two
daughter cells.

Figure 11-2   The prokaryotic cell cycle

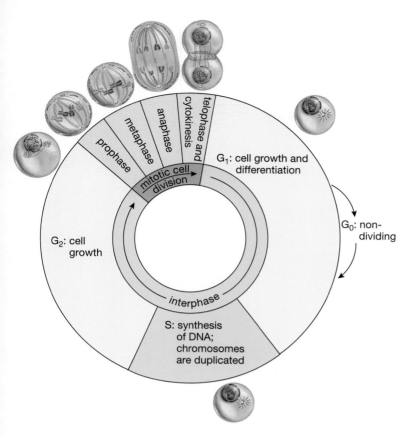

Figure 11-3   The eukaryotic cell cycle

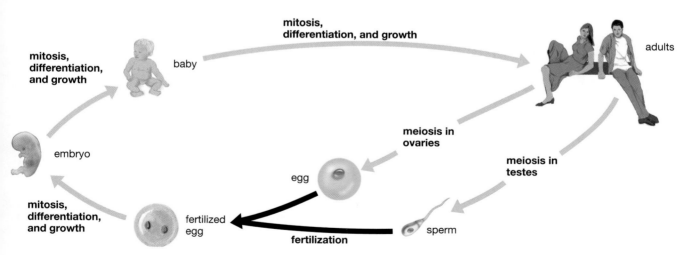

Figure 11-4   Mitotic and meiotic cell division in the human life cycle
Media Activity 11.1 Cell Division in Humans

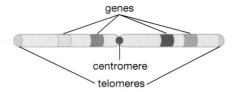

Figure 11-UN01 Chromosomes

Figure 11-UN02 Chromosomes

Figure 11-UN03 Chromosomes

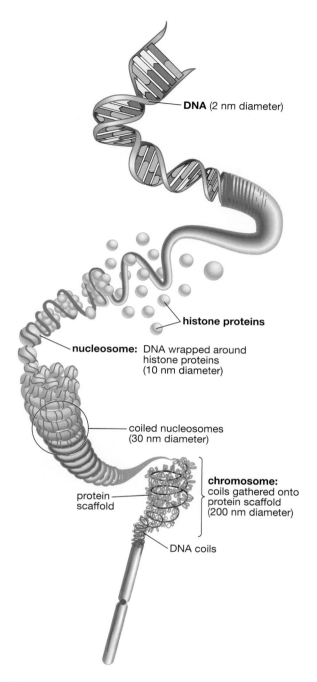

Figure 11-5   Chromosome structure

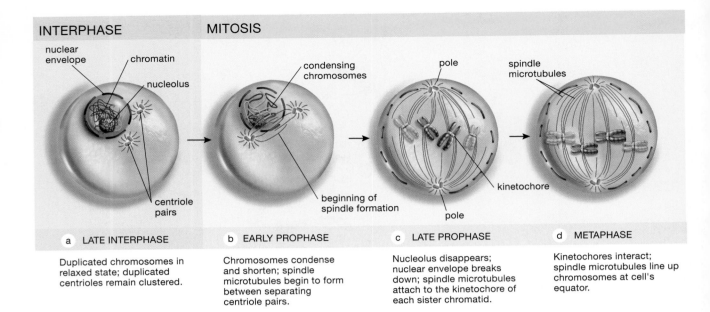

INTERPHASE | MITOSIS

a LATE INTERPHASE

Duplicated chromosomes in relaxed state; duplicated centrioles remain clustered.

b EARLY PROPHASE

Chromosomes condense and shorten; spindle microtubules begin to form between separating centriole pairs.

c LATE PROPHASE

Nucleolus disappears; nuclear envelope breaks down; spindle microtubules attach to the kinetochore of each sister chromatid.

d METAPHASE

Kinetochores interact; spindle microtubules line up chromosomes at cell's equator.

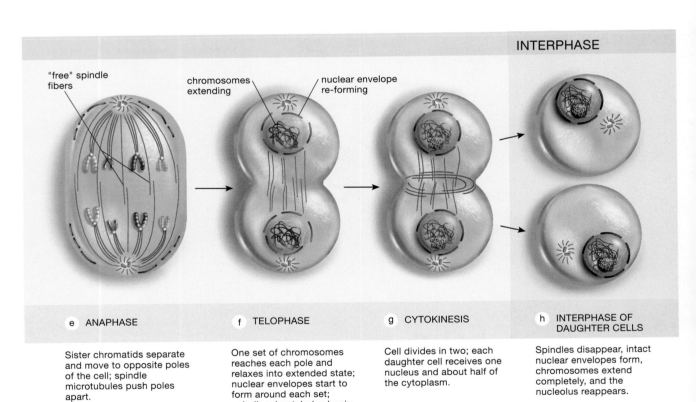

INTERPHASE

e ANAPHASE

Sister chromatids separate and move to opposite poles of the cell; spindle microtubules push poles apart.

f TELOPHASE

One set of chromosomes reaches each pole and relaxes into extended state; nuclear envelopes start to form around each set; spindle microtubules begin to disappear.

g CYTOKINESIS

Cell divides in two; each daughter cell receives one nucleus and about half of the cytoplasm.

h INTERPHASE OF DAUGHTER CELLS

Spindles disappear, intact nuclear envelopes form, chromosomes extend completely, and the nucleolus reappears.

Figure 11-8 Mitotic cell division in an animal cell
Media Activity 11.2 Cell Cycle and Mitosis

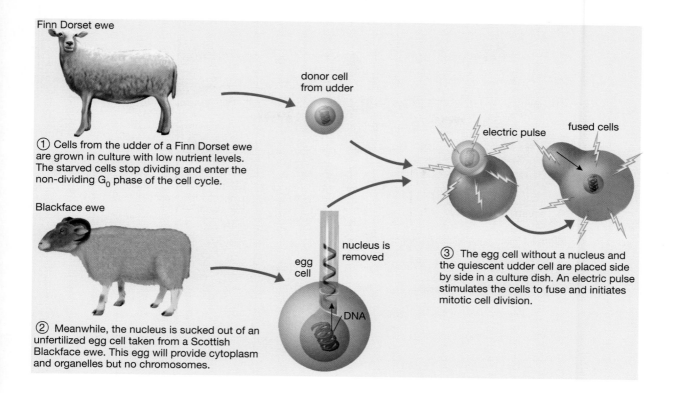

Finn Dorset ewe

① Cells from the udder of a Finn Dorset ewe are grown in culture with low nutrient levels. The starved cells stop dividing and enter the non-dividing G_0 phase of the cell cycle.

donor cell from udder

Blackface ewe

egg cell

nucleus is removed

DNA

② Meanwhile, the nucleus is sucked out of an unfertilized egg cell taken from a Scottish Blackface ewe. This egg will provide cytoplasm and organelles but no chromosomes.

electric pulse   fused cells

③ The egg cell without a nucleus and the quiescent udder cell are placed side by side in a culture dish. An electric pulse stimulates the cells to fuse and initiates mitotic cell division.

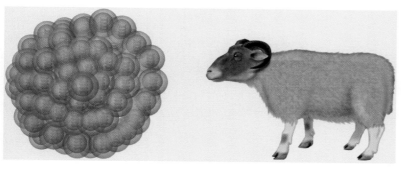

④ The cell divides, forming an embryo that consists of a hollow ball of cells.

⑤ The ball of cells is implanted into the uterus of another Blackface ewe.

⑥ The Blackface ewe gives birth to Dolly, a female Finn Dorset lamb, a genetic twin of the Finn Dorset ewe.

Figure E11-1   The making of Dolly

(a)

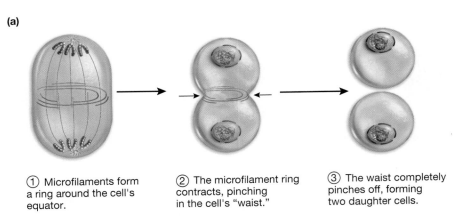

① Microfilaments form a ring around the cell's equator.

② The microfilament ring contracts, pinching in the cell's "waist."

③ The waist completely pinches off, forming two daughter cells.

Figure 11-9a Cytokinesis in an animal cell

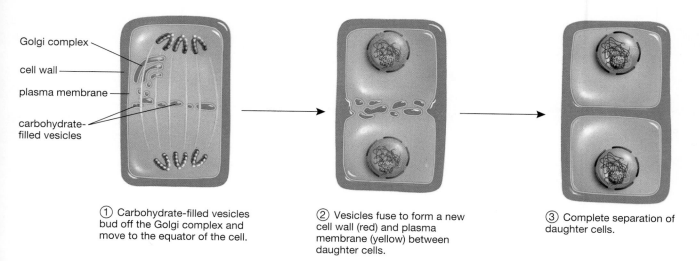

Golgi complex
cell wall
plasma membrane
carbohydrate-
filled vesicles

① Carbohydrate-filled vesicles bud off the Golgi complex and move to the equator of the cell.

② Vesicles fuse to form a new cell wall (red) and plasma membrane (yellow) between daughter cells.

③ Complete separation of daughter cells.

Figure 11-10   Cytokinesis in a plant cell

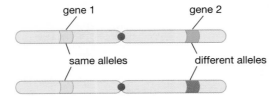

Figure 11-UN04   Mutations

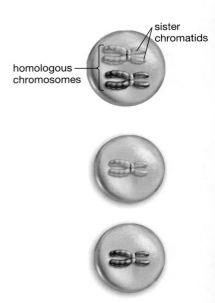

Figures 11-UN05, 11-UN06   Meiosis I

Figure 11-UN07 Meiosis II

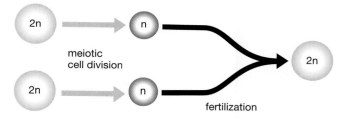

Figure 11-UN08 Meiotic cell division

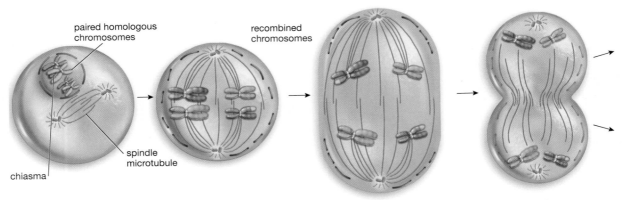

paired homologous chromosomes

recombined chromosomes

spindle microtubule

chiasma

(a) Prophase I. Duplicated chromosomes condense. Homologous chromosomes pair up and chiasmata occur as chromatids of homologues exchange parts. The nuclear envelope disintegrates, and spindle microtubules form.

(b) Metaphase I. Paired homologous chromosomes line up along the equator of the cell. One homologue of each pair faces each pole of the cell and attaches to spindle microtubules via its kinetochore (blue).

(c) Anaphase I. Homologues separate, one member of each pair going to each pole of the cell. Sister chromatids do not separate.

(d) Telophase I. Spindle microtubules disappear. Two clusters of chromosomes have formed, each containing one member of each pair of homologues. The daughter nuclei are therefore haploid. Cytokinesis commonly occurs at this stage. There is little or no interphase between meiosis I and meiosis II.

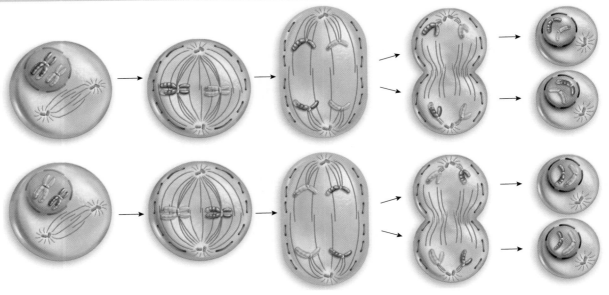

(e) Prophase II. If chromosomes have relaxed after telophase I, they recondense. Spindle microtubules re-form and attach to the sister chromatids.

(f) Metaphase II. Chromosomes line up along the equator, with sister chromatids of each chromosome attached to spindle microtubules that lead to opposite poles.

(g) Anaphase II. Chromatids separate into independent daughter chromosomes, one former chromatid moving toward each pole.

(h) Telophase II. Chromosomes finish moving to opposite poles. Nuclear envelopes re-form, and the chromosomes become extended again (not shown here).

(i) Four haploid cells. Cytokinesis results in four haploid cells, each containing one member of each pair of homologous chromosomes (shown here in condensed state).

Figure 11-11 Meiotic cell division in an animal cell
Media Activity 11.3 Meiosis

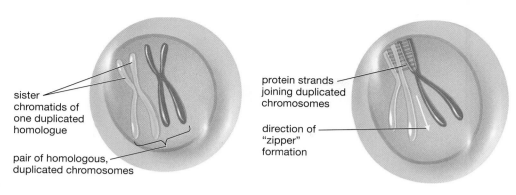

(a) Duplicated homologous chromosomes pair up side by side.

sister chromatids of one duplicated homologue

pair of homologous, duplicated chromosomes

protein strands joining duplicated chromosomes

direction of "zipper" formation

(b) Protein strands "zip" the homologous chromosomes together.

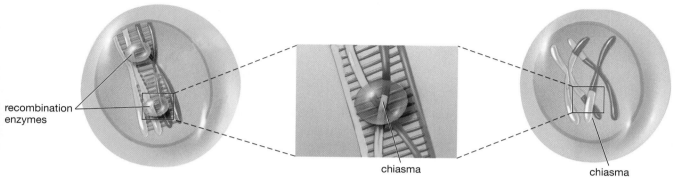

recombination enzymes

chiasma

chiasma

(c) Recombination enzymes bind to the joined chromosomes.

(d) Recombination enzymes snip chromatids apart and reattach the free ends. Chiasmata (the sites of crossing over) form when one end of the paternal chromatid (yellow) attaches to the other end of a maternal chromatid (purple).

(e) Recombination enzymes and protein zippers leave. Chiasmata remain, helping to hold homologous chromosomes together.

Figure 11-12   The mechanism of crossing over

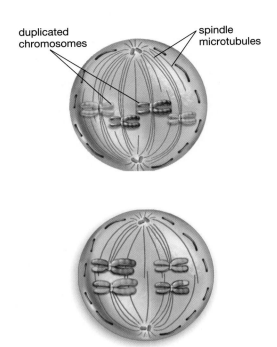

duplicated
chromosomes

spindle
microtubules

Figures 11-UN09, 11-UN10 Mitosis and meiosis I

Table 11-1 A Comparison of Mitotic and Meiotic Cell Divisions in Animal Cells

Feature	Mitotic Cell Division	Meiotic Cell Division
Cells in which it occurs	Body cells	Gamete-producing cells
Final chromosome number	Diploid—2n; two copies of each type of chromosome (homologous pairs)	Haploid—1n; one member of each homologous pair
Number of daughter cells	Two, identical to the parent cell and to each other	Four, containing recombined chromosomes due to crossing over
Number of cell divisions per DNA replication	One	Two
Function in animals	Development, growth, repair and maintenance of tissues, asexual reproduction	Gamete production for sexual reproduction

MITOSIS

no stages comparable to meiosis I

interphase   prophase   metaphase   anaphase   telophase   2 diploid cells

MEIOSIS

Recombination occurs.

Homologues pair.

Sister chromatids remain attached.

interphase   prophase   metaphase   anaphase   telophase   prophase   metaphase   anaphase   telophase   4 haploid cells

MEIOSIS I   MEIOSIS II

In these diagrams, comparable phases are aligned. In both mitosis and meiosis, chromosomes are replicated during interphase. Meiosis I, with the pairing of homologous chromosomes, formation of chiasmata, exchange of chromosome parts, and separation of homologues to form haploid daughter nuclei, has no counterpart in mitosis. Meiosis II, however, is similar to mitosis.

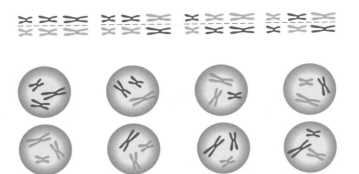

Figures 11-UN11, 11-UN12   Shuffling homologues and genetic variability

Media Activity 11.4 How Meiosis Produces Genetic Variability

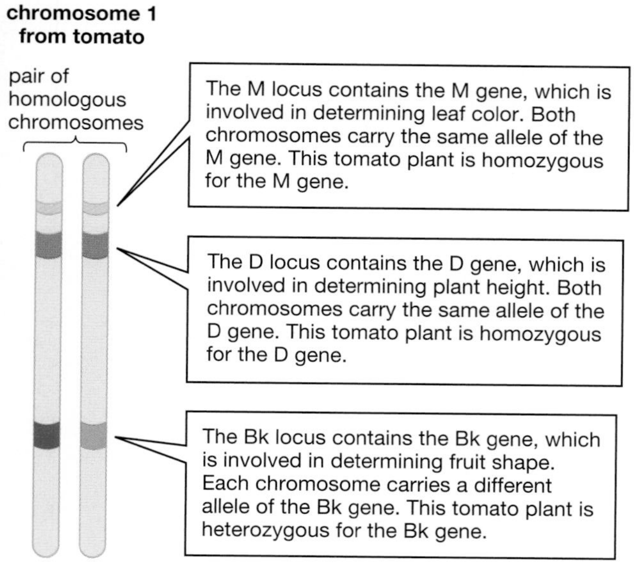

**chromosome 1
from tomato**

pair of
homologous
chromosomes

The M locus contains the M gene, which is involved in determining leaf color. Both chromosomes carry the same allele of the M gene. This tomato plant is homozygous for the M gene.

The D locus contains the D gene, which is involved in determining plant height. Both chromosomes carry the same allele of the D gene. This tomato plant is homozygous for the D gene.

The Bk locus contains the Bk gene, which is involved in determining fruit shape. Each chromosome carries a different allele of the Bk gene. This tomato plant is heterozygous for the Bk gene.

Figure 12-2   The relationships among genes, alleles, and chromosomes

intact pea flower

flower dissected to show
reproductive structures

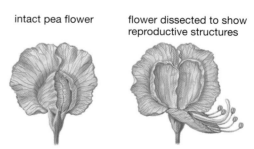

Figure 12-3   The flowers of the edible pea

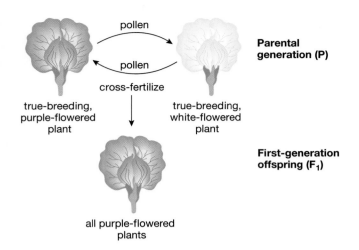

pollen

Parental generation (P)

cross-fertilize

true-breeding, purple-flowered plant

true-breeding, white-flowered plant

First-generation offspring (F₁)

all purple-flowered plants

Figure 12-UN01 Mendel pea experiments, flower color: cross fertilization
Media Activity 12.1 Monohybrid Crosses

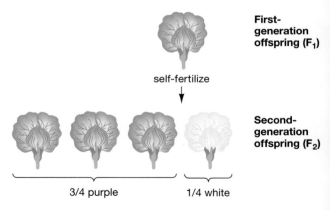

First-generation offspring (F₁)

self-fertilize

Second-generation offspring (F₂)

3/4 purple

1/4 white

Figure 12-UN02 Mendel pea experiments, flower color: self fertilization
Media Activity 12.1 Monohybrid Crosses

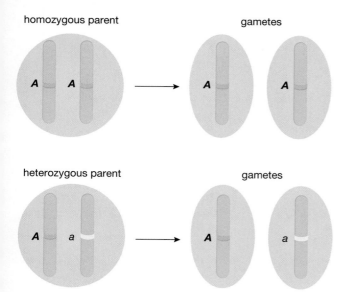

Figures 12-UN03, 12-UN04 Mendel pea experiments, flower color: gametes of a homozygous parent and heterozygous parent
Media Activity 12.1 Monohybrid Crosses

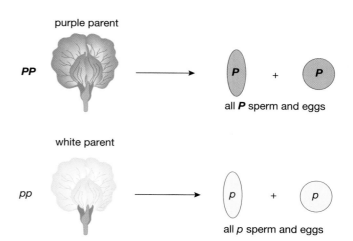

Figure 12-UN05 Mendel pea experiments, flower color: gametes of a homozygous parent
Media Activity 12.1 Monohybrid Crosses

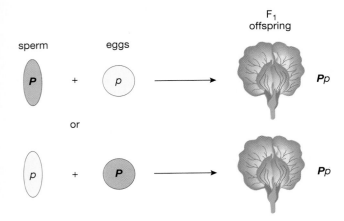

Figure 12-UN06 Mendel pea experiments, flower color: F1
generation of a homozygous parent
Media Activity 12.1 Monohybrid Crosses

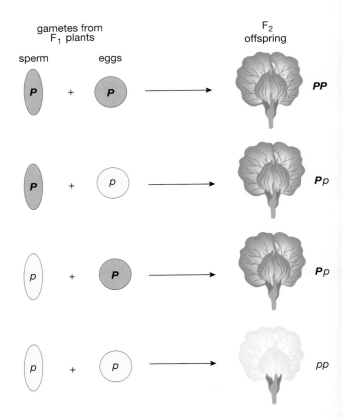

Figure 12-UN07 Mendel pea experiments, flower color: F2 from
heterozygous F1
Media Activity 12.1 Monohybrid Crosses

(a)

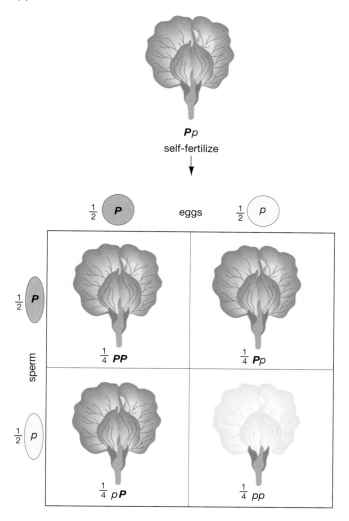

(b)

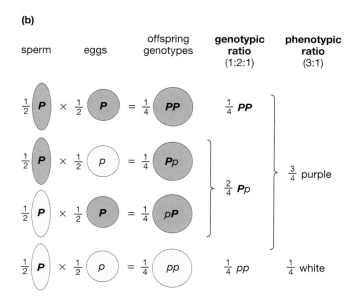

Figure 12-4 Determining the outcome of a single-trait cross

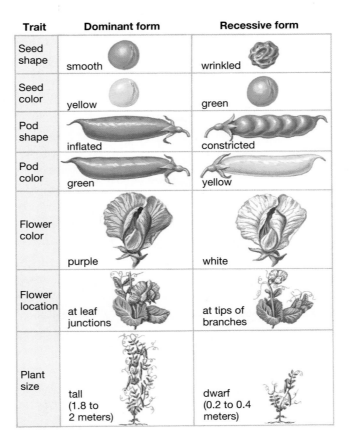

Trait	Dominant form		Recessive form	
Seed shape	smooth		wrinkled	
Seed color	yellow		green	
Pod shape	inflated		constricted	
Pod color	green		yellow	
Flower color	purple		white	
Flower location	at leaf junctions		at tips of branches	
Plant size	tall (1.8 to 2 meters)		dwarf (0.2 to 0.4 meters)	

Figure 12-5 Trait of pea plants that Mendel studied
Media Activity 12.2 Dihybrid Crosses

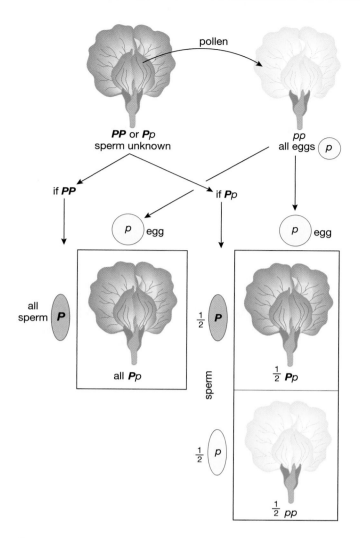

Figure 12-UN08 Test cross
Media Activity 12.2 Dihybrid Crosses

(a)

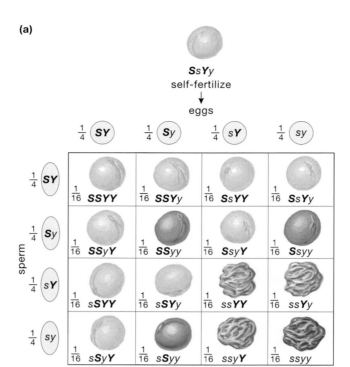

(b)

seed shape		seed color		phenotypic ratio (9:3:3:1)
$\frac{3}{4}$ smooth	×	$\frac{3}{4}$ yellow	=	$\frac{9}{16}$ smooth yellow
$\frac{3}{4}$ smooth	×	$\frac{1}{4}$ green	=	$\frac{3}{16}$ smooth green
$\frac{1}{4}$ wrinkled	×	$\frac{3}{4}$ yellow	=	$\frac{3}{16}$ wrinkled yellow
$\frac{1}{4}$ wrinkled	×	$\frac{1}{4}$ green	=	$\frac{1}{16}$ wrinkled green

Figure 12-6 Predicting genotypes and phenotypes for a cross between gametes that are heterozygous for two traits

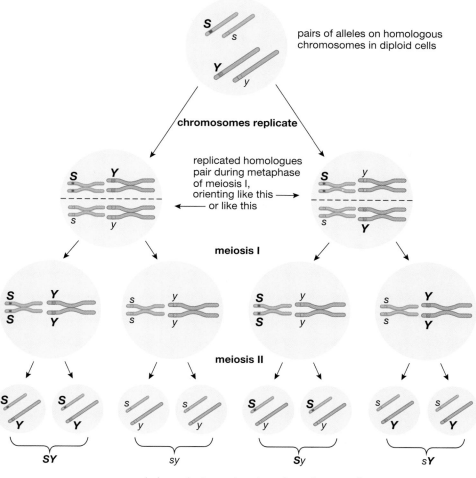

pairs of alleles on homologous chromosomes in diploid cells

chromosomes replicate

replicated homologues pair during metaphase of meiosis I, orienting like this ⟶ ⟵ or like this

meiosis I

meiosis II

SY sy Sy sY

independent assortment produces four equally likely allele combinations during meiosis

Figure 12-7 Independent assortment of alleles

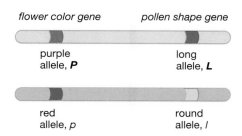

flower color gene   *pollen shape gene*

purple   long
allele, **P**   allele, **L**

red   round
allele, *p*   allele, *l*

Figure 12-UN09 Linkage

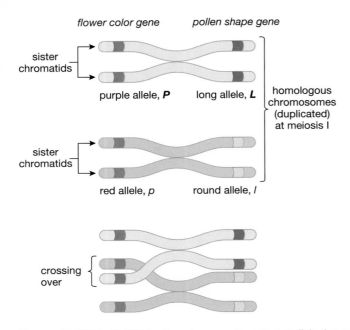

Figures 12-UN10, 12-UN11 Crossing over may separate linked genes

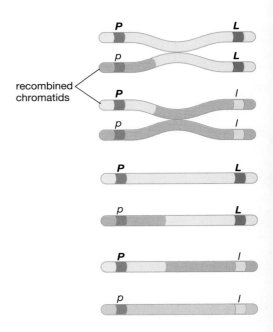

Figures 12-UN12, 12-UN13 Crossing over may separate linked genes

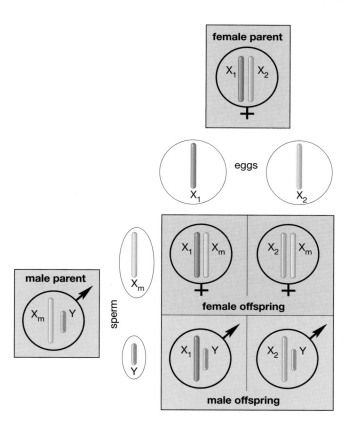

Figure 12-9 Sex determination in mammals

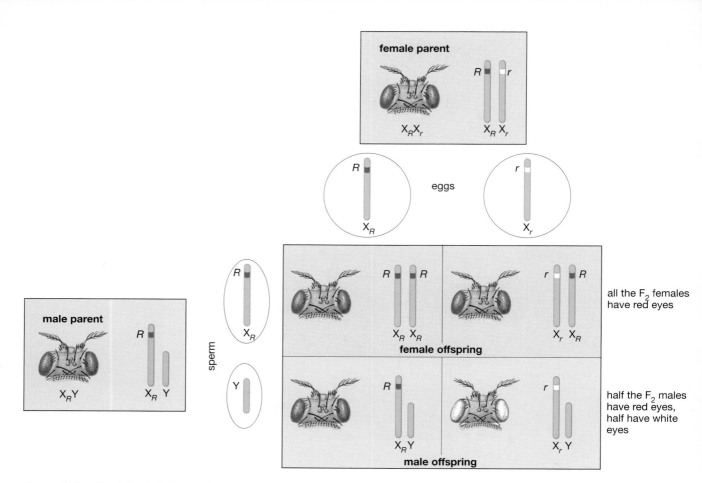

Figure 12-10   Sex-linked inheritance of eye color in fruit flies

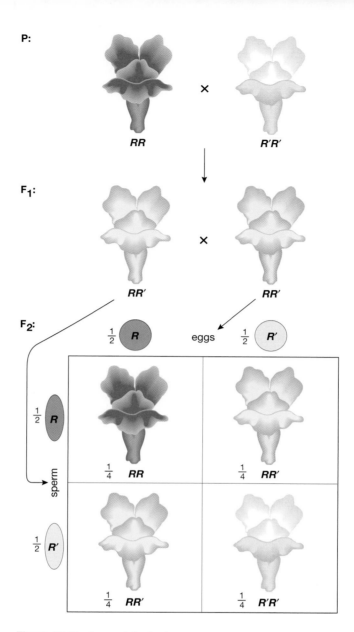

Figure 12-11 Incomplete dominance

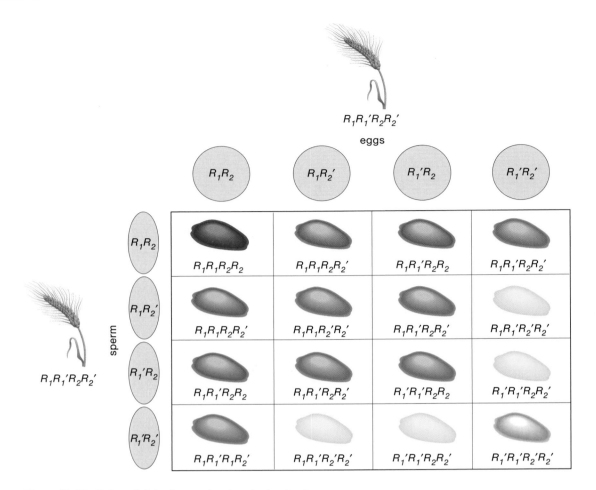

Figure 12-12 Polygenic inheritance of grain color in wheat

(a) A pedigree for a dominant trait

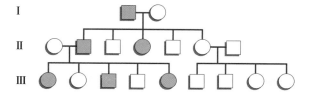

(b) A pedigree for a recessive trait

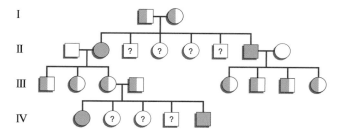

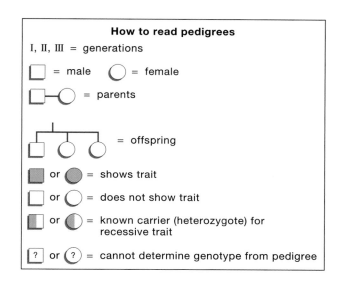

How to read pedigrees

I, II, III = generations

☐ = male   ○ = female

☐—○ = parents

offspring

■ or ● = shows trait

☐ or ○ = does not show trait

◨ or ◐ = known carrier (heterozygote) for recessive trait

? or ? = cannot determine genotype from pedigree

Figure 12-14 Family pedigrees

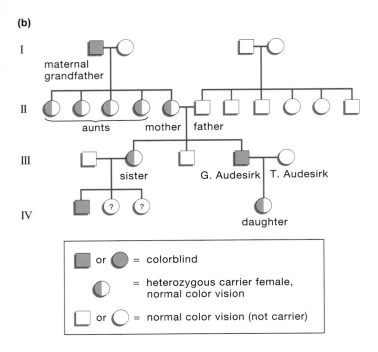

(b)

maternal
grandfather

aunts   mother   father

sister   G. Audesirk T. Audesirk

daughter

■ or ● = colorblind

◐ = heterozygous carrier female,
     normal color vision

□ or ○ = normal color vision (not carrier)

Figure 12-17b   Color blindness, a sex-linked recessive trait

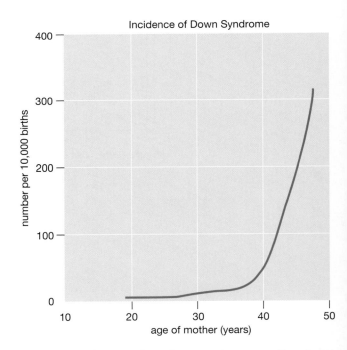

Figure 12-20   Down syndrome frequency increases with maternal age

Table 12-1 Human Blood Group Characteristics

Blood Type	Genotype	Red Blood Cells	Has Plasma Antibodies to:	Can Receive Blood from:	Can Donate Blood to:	Frequency in U.S.
A	AA or Ao	A glycoprotein	B glycoprotein	A or O (no blood with B glycoprotein)	A or AB	40%
B	BB or Bo	B glycoprotein	A glycoprotein	B or O (no blood with A glycoprotein)	B or AB	10%
AB	AB	Both A and B glycoproteins	Neither A nor B glycoprotein	AB, A, B, O (universal recipient)	AB	4%
O	oo	Neither A nor B glycoprotein	Both A and B glycoproteins	O (no blood with A or B glycoprotein)	O, AB, A, B (universal donor)	46%

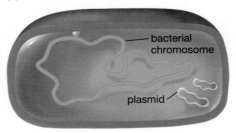

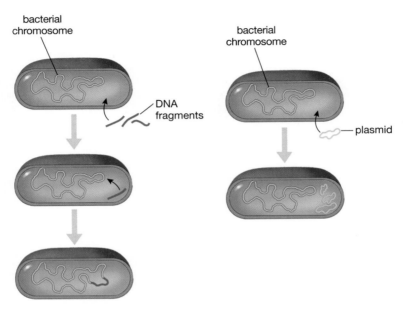

(b) Transformation with DNA fragment

(c) Transformation with plasmid

Figure 13-1   Recombination in bacteria
Media Activity 13.1 Genetic Recombination in Bacteria

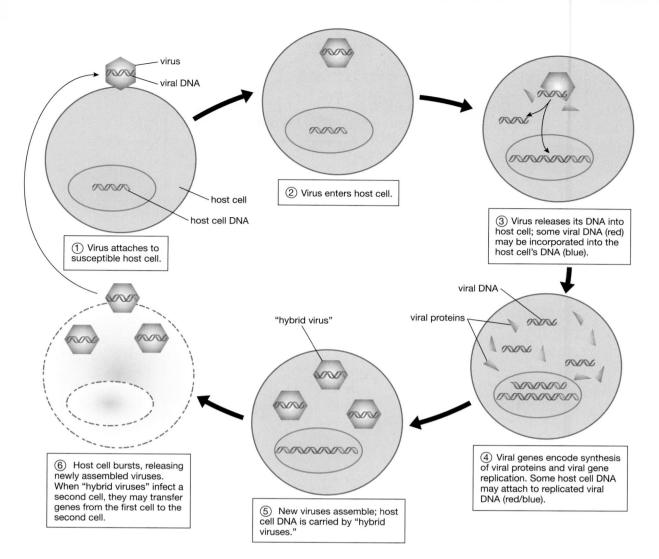

virus
viral DNA

host cell
host cell DNA

① Virus attaches to susceptible host cell.

② Virus enters host cell.

③ Virus releases its DNA into host cell; some viral DNA (red) may be incorporated into the host cell's DNA (blue).

viral DNA
viral proteins

④ Viral genes encode synthesis of viral proteins and viral gene replication. Some host cell DNA may attach to replicated viral DNA (red/blue).

"hybrid virus"

⑤ New viruses assemble; host cell DNA is carried by "hybrid viruses."

⑥ Host cell bursts, releasing newly assembled viruses. When "hybrid viruses" infect a second cell, they may transfer genes from the first cell to the second cell.

Figure 13-2 Viruses may transfer genes between cells

(a) One PCR cycle

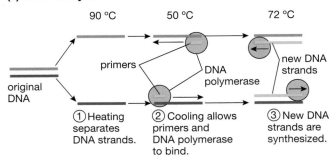

90 °C 50 °C 72 °C

primers

DNA
polymerase

new DNA
strands

original
DNA

① Heating
separates
DNA strands.

② Cooling allows
primers and
DNA polymerase
to bind.

③ New DNA
strands are
synthesized.

(b) Each PCR cycle doubles the number of copies of the DNA

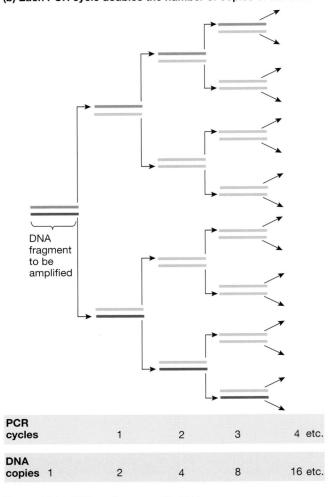

DNA
fragment
to be
amplified

PCR cycles		1	2	3	4 etc.
DNA copies	1	2	4	8	16 etc.

Figure 13-3   PCR copies a specific DNA sequence
Media Activity 13.2 Polymerase Chain Reaction (PCR)

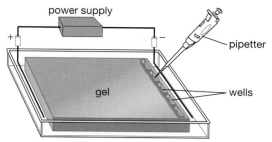

(a) DNA samples are pipetted into wells (shallow slots) in the gel. Electrical current is sent through the gel (negative at end with wells, positive at opposite end.)

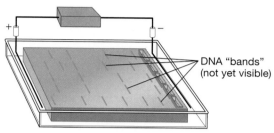

(b) Electrical current moves DNA segments through the gel. Smaller pieces of DNA move farther toward the positive electrode.

(c) Gel is placed on special nylon "paper." Electrical current drives DNA out of gel onto nylon.

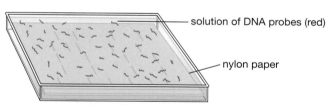

(d) Nylon paper with DNA is bathed in a solution of labeled DNA probes (red) that are complementary to specific DNA segments in the original DNA sample.

(e) Complementary DNA segments are labeled by probes (red bands).

Figure 13-5   Gel electrophoresis is used to separate and identify segments of DNA

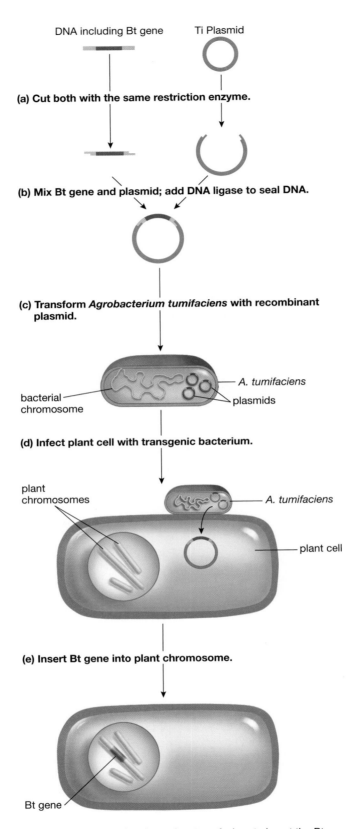

DNA including Bt gene   **Ti Plasmid**

(a) Cut both with the same restriction enzyme.

(b) Mix Bt gene and plasmid; add DNA ligase to seal DNA.

(c) Transform *Agrobacterium tumifaciens* with recombinant plasmid.

A. tumifaciens

bacterial chromosome

plasmids

(d) Infect plant cell with transgenic bacterium.

plant chromosomes

A. tumifaciens

plant cell

(e) Insert Bt gene into plant chromosome.

Bt gene

Figure 13-7   Using *Agrobacterium tumefaciens* to insert the Bt gene into plants

(a) Mst II cuts a normal globin allele in 2 places, but cuts the sickle-cell allele in 1 place.

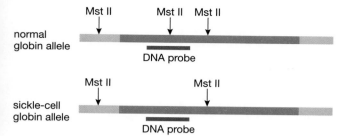

(b) Gel electrophoresis of globin alleles

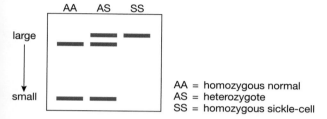

AA = homozygous normal
AS = heterozygote
SS = homozygous sickle-cell

Figure 13-9 Diagnosing sickle-cell anemia with restriction enzymes
Media Activity 13.3 Human Genome Sequencing

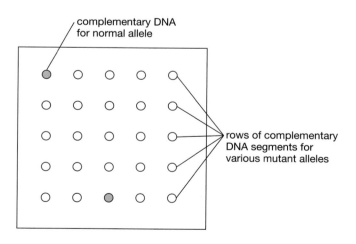

Figure 13-10 Diagnosing cystic fibrosis with a DNA array

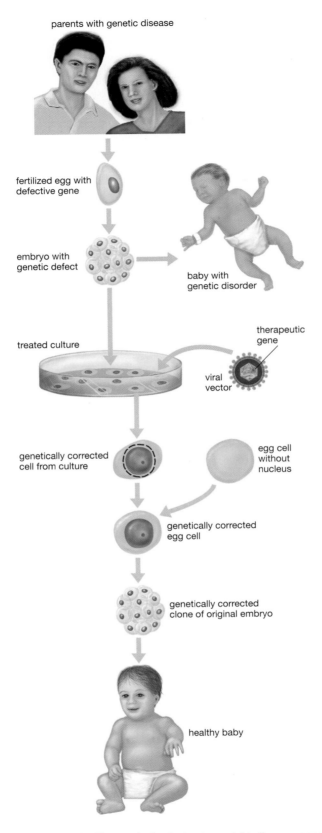

parents with genetic disease

fertilized egg with defective gene

embryo with genetic defect

baby with genetic disorder

treated culture

therapeutic gene

viral vector

genetically corrected cell from culture

egg cell without nucleus

genetically corrected egg cell

genetically corrected clone of original embryo

healthy baby

Figure 13-11 Human cloning technology might allow permanent correction of genetic defects

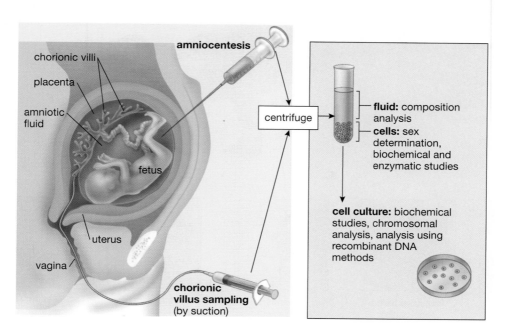

Figure E13-3 Prenatal cell sampling techniques

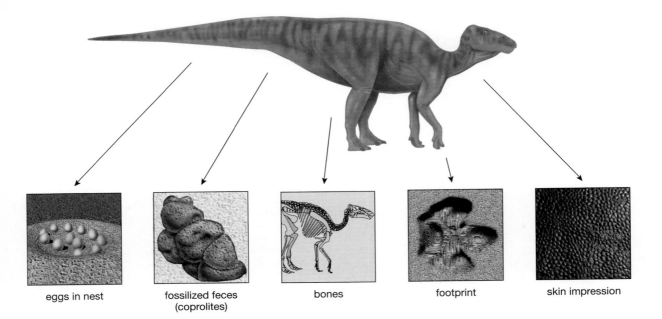

eggs in nest | fossilized feces (coprolites) | bones | footprint | skin impression

Figure 14-2 Types of fossils

(a) Large ground finch, beak suited to large seeds

(b) Small ground finch, beak suited to small seeds

(c) Warbler finch, beak suited to insects

(d) Vegetarian tree finch, beak suited to leaves

Figure 14-4 Darwin's finches, residents of the Galapagos Islands

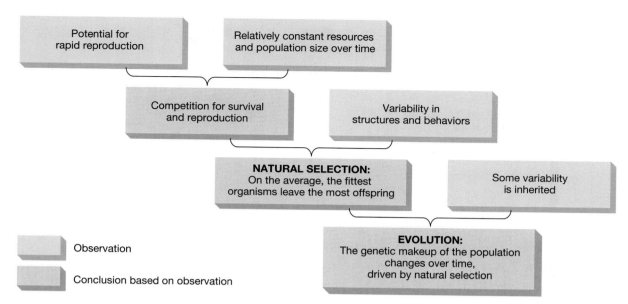

Observation

Conclusion based on observation

Figure 14-5   A Flow Chart of Evolutionary Reasoning

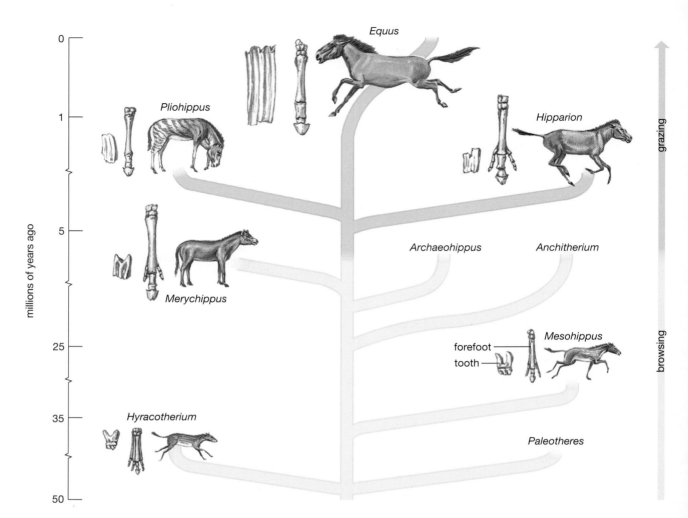

Figure 14-6   The evolution of the horse

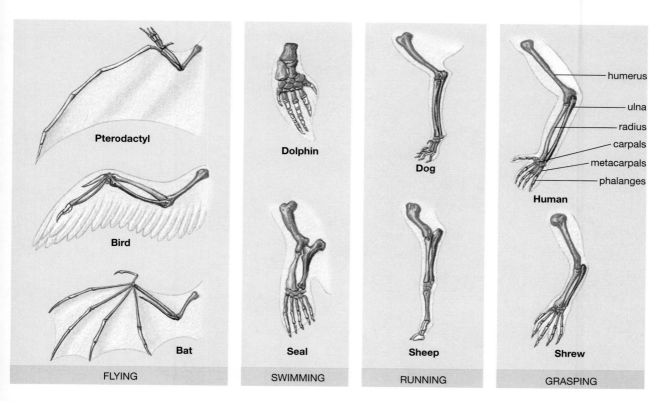

Figure 14-7 Homologous structures
Media Activity 14.1 Analagous and Homologous Structures

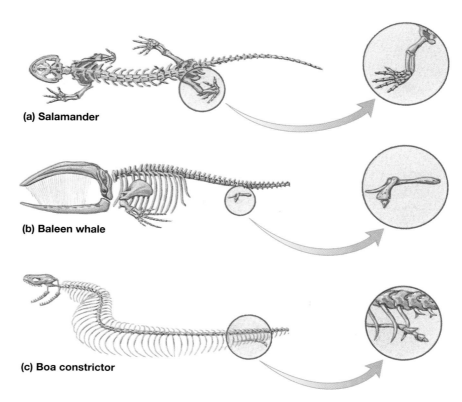

(a) Salamander

(b) Baleen whale

(c) Boa constrictor

Figure 14-8 Vestigial structures

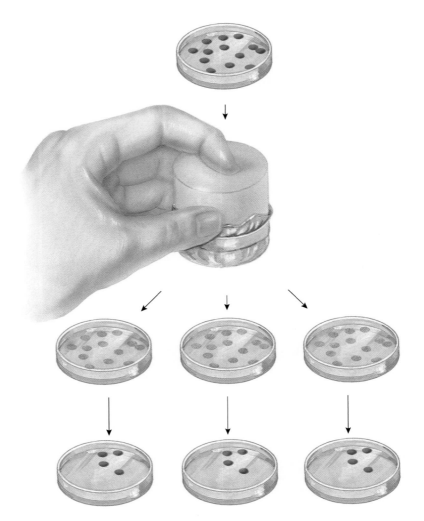

Figure 15-1 Mutations occur spontaneously
Media Activity 15.1 Agents of Change

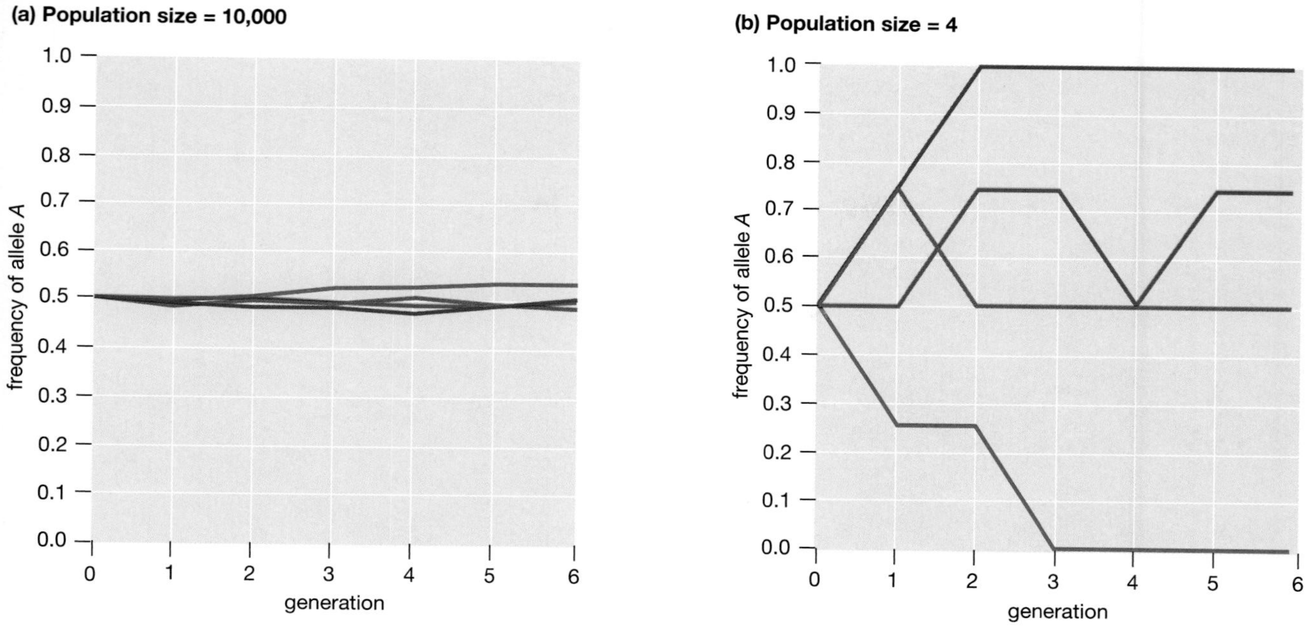

(a) Population size = 10,000

frequency of allele A — generation

(b) Population size = 4

frequency of allele A — generation

Figure 15-2   The effect of population size on genetic drift

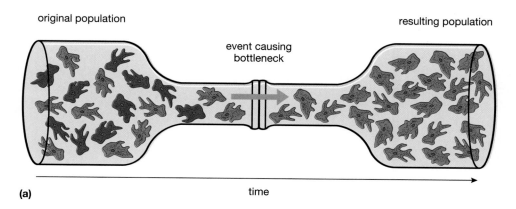

original population

event causing
bottleneck

resulting population

(a)   time

Figure 15-3a   Population bottlenecks reduce variation
Media Activity 15.2 The Bottleneck Effect

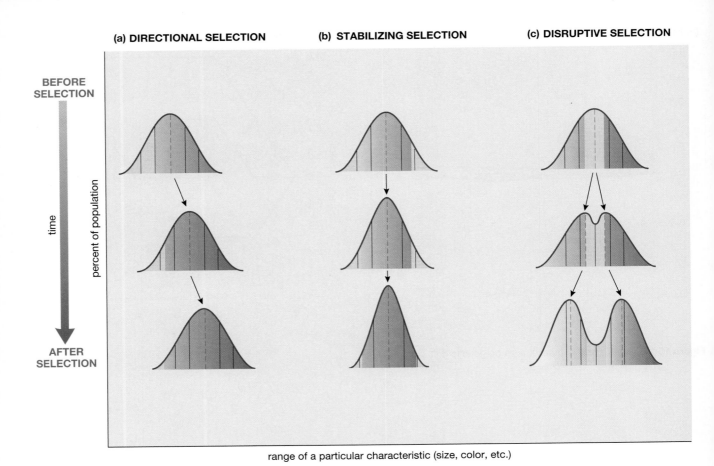

(a) DIRECTIONAL SELECTION   (b) STABILIZING SELECTION   (c) DISRUPTIVE SELECTION

BEFORE SELECTION

time

percent of population

AFTER SELECTION

range of a particular characteristic (size, color, etc.)

Figure 15-9 Three ways that selection affects a population over time
Media Activity 15.3 Three Modes of Natural Selection

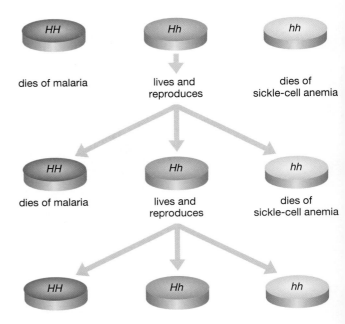

HH   Hh   hh

dies of malaria   lives and reproduces   dies of sickle-cell anemia

HH   Hh   hh

dies of malaria   lives and reproduces   dies of sickle-cell anemia

HH   Hh   hh

Figure 15-10 A balanced polymorphism

Allopatric speciation

time

Sympatric speciation

① original population

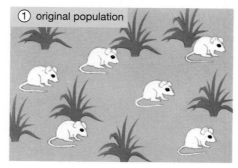

② geographical isolation

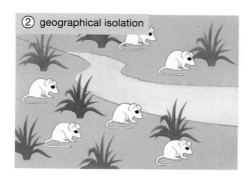

② ecological isolation

③ genetic divergence

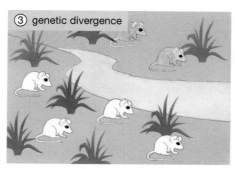

③ genetic divergence

④ reproductive isolation

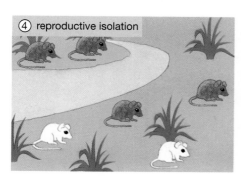

④ reproductive isolation

Figure 16-2 Models of allopatric and sympatric speciation
Media Activity 16.2 Allopatric Speciation
Media Activity 16.3 Sympatric Speciation

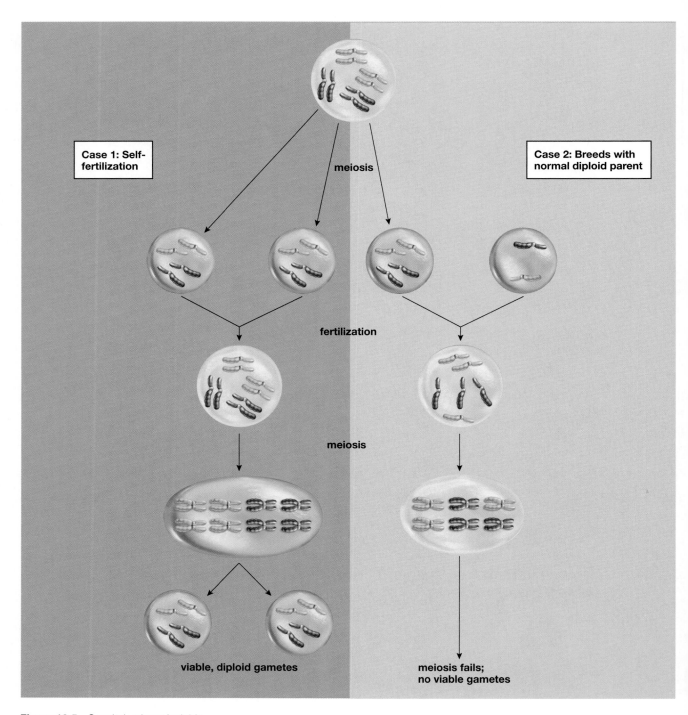

Case 1: Self-fertilization

meiosis

Case 2: Breeds with normal diploid parent

fertilization

meiosis

viable, diploid gametes

meiosis fails;
no viable gametes

Figure 16-5 Speciation by polyploidy
Media Activity 16.4 Speciation by Polyploidy

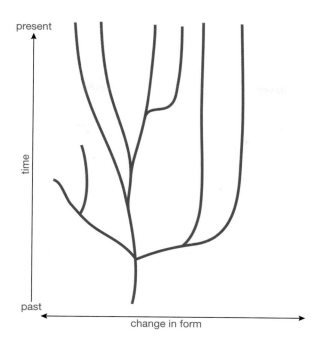

Figure 16-6 Interpreting an evolutionary tree

Figure 17-1 Spontaneous generation refuted

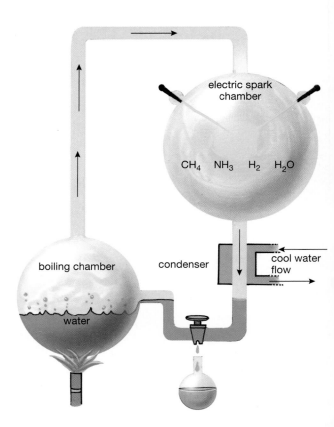

Figure 17-2 The experimental apparatus of Stanley Miller and Harold Urey

Table 17-1 The History of Life on Earth

Era	Period	Epoch	Millions of Years Ago*	Major Events
Precambrian			4600	Origin of solar system and Earth.
			4000–3900	Appearance of first rocks on Earth.
			3900–3500	First living cells (prokaryotes).
			3500	Origin of photosynthesis (in cyanobacteria).
			2200	Accumulation of free oxygen in atmosphere.
			2000–1700	First eukaryotes.
			By 1000	First multicellular organisms.
			About 1000	First animals (soft-bodied marine invertebrates).
Paleozoic	Cambrian		544–505	Primitive marine algae flourish; origin of most marine invertebrate types; first fishes.
	Ordovician		505–440	Invertebrates, especially arthropods and mollusks, dominant in sea; first fungi.
	Silurian		440–410	Many fishes, trilobites, mollusks in sea; first vascular plants; invasion of land by plants; invasion of land by arthropods.
	Devonian		410–360	Fishes and trilobites flourish in sea; first amphibians and insects; first seeds and pollen.
	Carboniferous		360–286	Swamp forests of tree ferns and club mosses; first conifers; dominance of amphibians; numerous insects; first reptiles.
	Permian		286–245	Massive marine extinctions, including last of trilobites; flourishing of reptiles and decline of amphibians; aggregation of continents into one land mass, Pangaea.
Mesozoic	Triassic		245–208	First mammals and dinosaurs; forests of gymnosperms and tree ferns; beginning of breakup of Pangaea.
	Jurassic		208–146	Dominance of dinosaurs and conifers; first birds; continents partially separated.
	Cretaceous		146–65	Flowering plants appear and become dominant; mass extinctions of marine life and some terrestrial life, including last dinosaurs; modern continents well separated.
Cenozoic	Tertiary	Paleocene	65–54	Widespread flourishing of birds, mammals, insects, and flowering plants; shifting of continents into modern positions; mild climate at beginning of period, with extensive mountain building and cooling toward end.
		Eocene	54–38	
		Oligocene	38–23	
		Miocene	23–5	
		Pliocene	5–1.8	
	Quaternary	Pleistocene	1.8–0.01	Evolution of genus *Homo*; repeated glaciations in Northern Hemisphere; extinction of many giant mammals.
		Recent	0.01–present	

*From University of California Museum of Paleontology, April 2000.

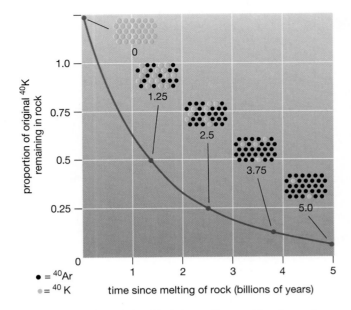

Figure E17-1 The relationship between time and the decay of radioactive ⁴⁰K to ⁴⁰Ar

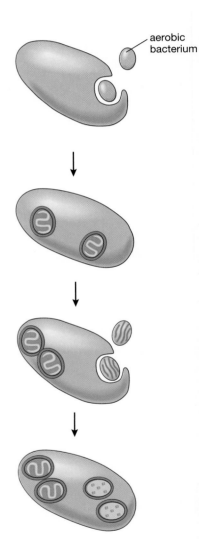

Figure 17-4 The probable origin of mitochondria and chloroplasts in eukaryotic cells
Media Activity 17.1 Endosymbiosis

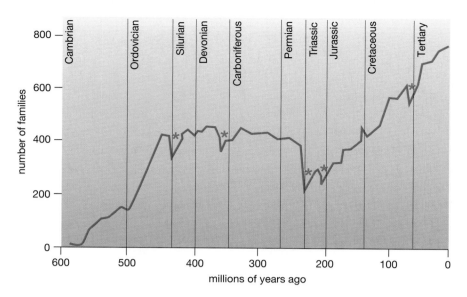

Figure 17-10 Mass extinctions

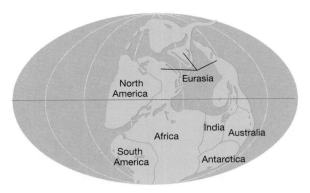

(a) 340 million years ago

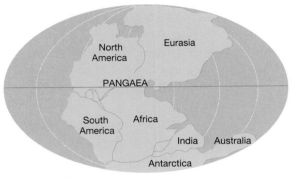

(b) 225 million years ago

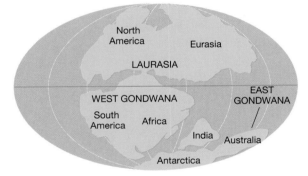

(c) 135 million years ago

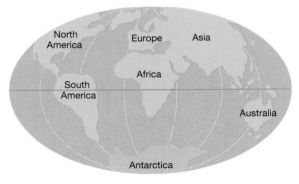

(d) Present

Figure 17-11 Continental drift from plate tectonics
Media Activity 17.3 Plate Tectonics

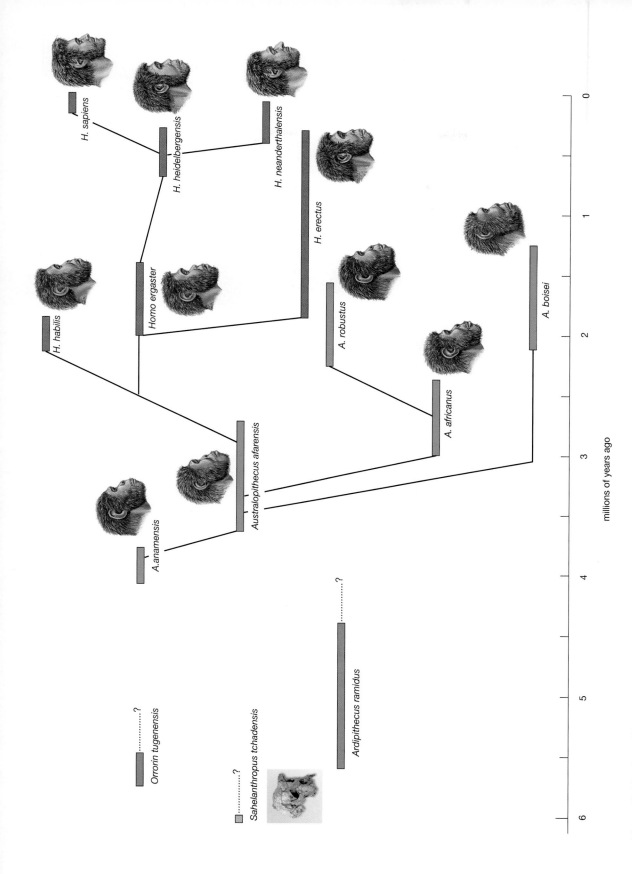

Figure 17-14 A possible evolutionary tree for humans

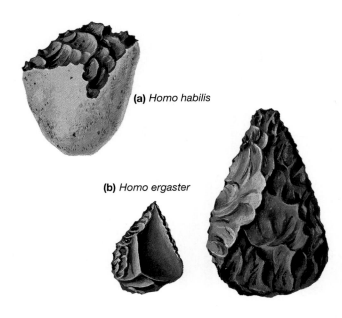

(a) *Homo habilis*

(b) *Homo ergaster*

(c) *Homo neanderthalensis*

Figure 17-15   Representative hominid tools

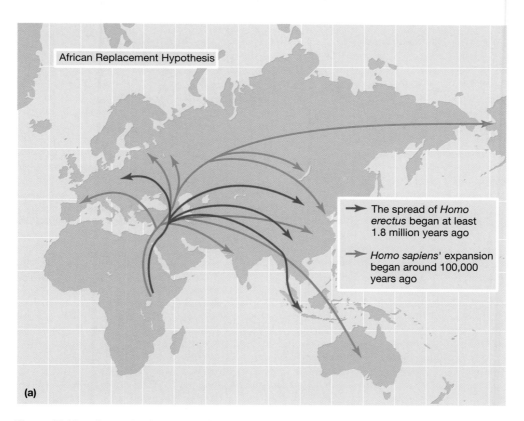

Figure 17-18a Competing hypotheses for the evolution of Homo sapiens

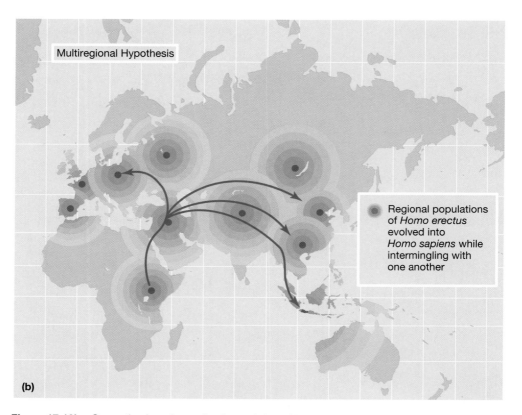

Figure 17-18b Competing hypotheses for the evolution of Homo sapiens

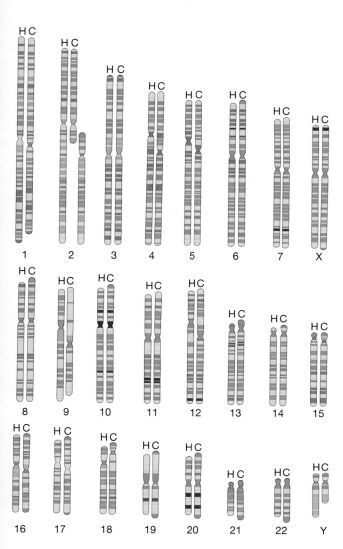

Figure 18-3   Human and chimp chromosomes are similar

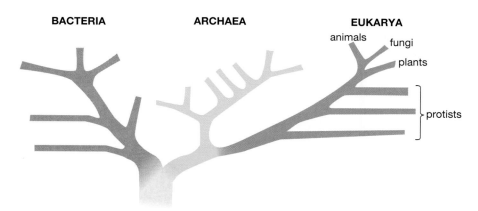

Figure 18-5   The tree of life
Media Activity 18.2 Tree of Life

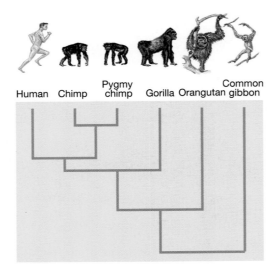

Figure E18-1 Relatedness can be determined by comparing DNA sequences

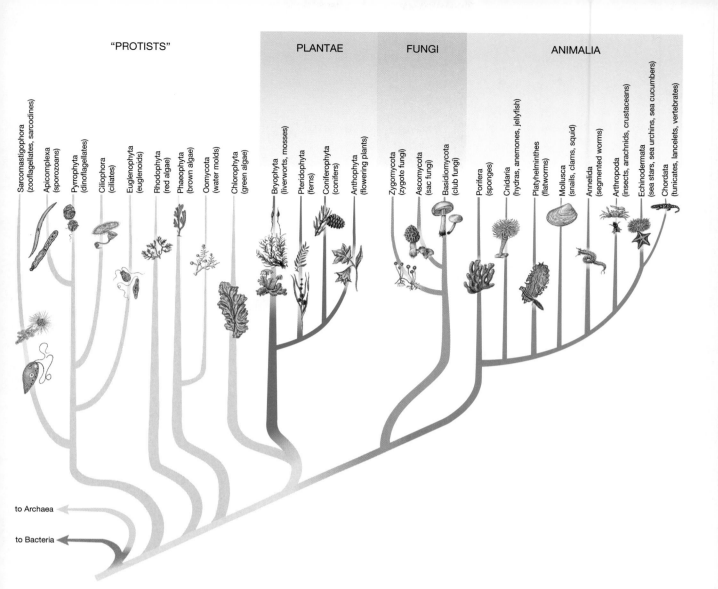

Figure 18-6 A closer look at the eukaryotic tree of life

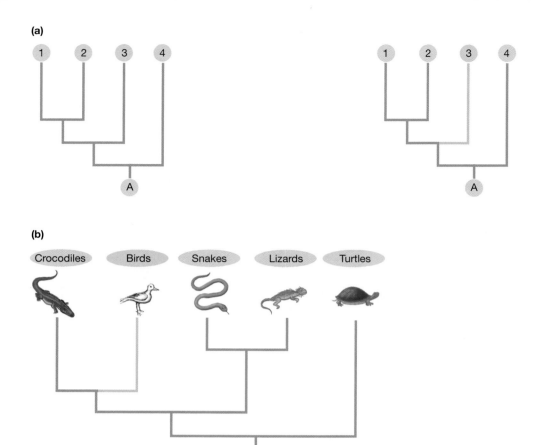

Figure 18-8 Reptiles are not a monophyletic group

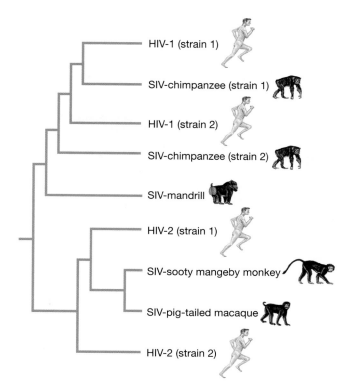

Figure 18-9 Evolutionary analysis helps reveal the origin of HIV

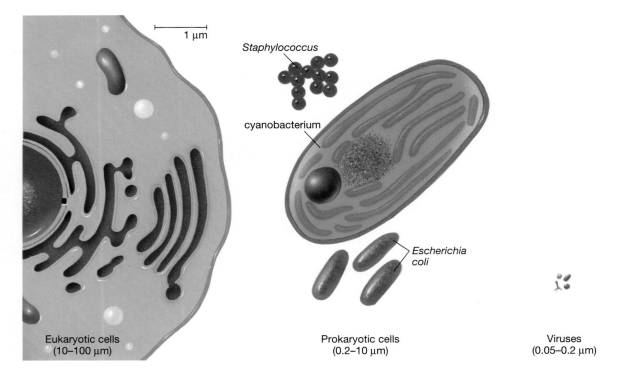

Figure 19-1   The sizes of microorganisms

Eukaryotic cells
(10–100 μm)

Prokaryotic cells
(0.2–10 μm)

Viruses
(0.05–0.2 μm)

Staphylococcus

cyanobacterium

Escherichia coli

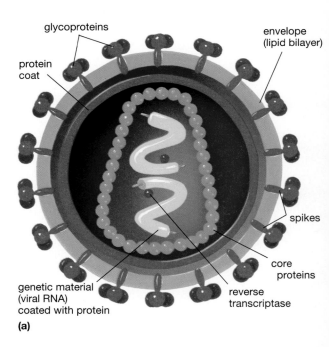

glycoproteins

envelope
(lipid bilayer)

protein
coat

spikes

core
proteins

genetic material
(viral RNA)
coated with protein

reverse
transcriptase

(a)

Figure 19-2a   Viral structure and replication

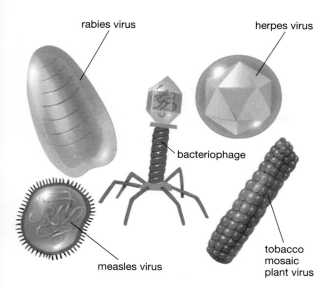

Figure 19-3 Viruses come in a variety of shapes

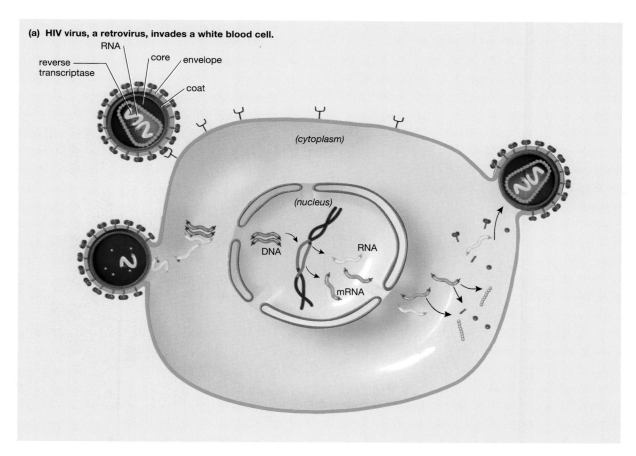

(a) HIV virus, a retrovirus, invades a white blood cell.

Figure E19-1a How viruses replicate
Media Activity 19.1 Retrovirus Replication

(b) Herpes virus, a double-stranded DNA virus, invades a skin cell.

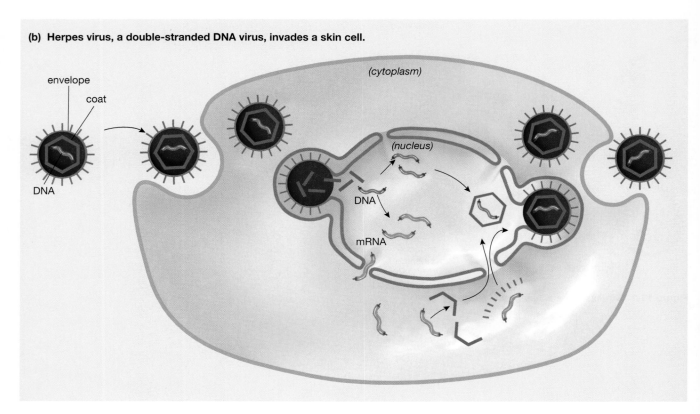

Figure E19-1b How viruses replicate
Media Activity 19.2 Herpes Virus Replication

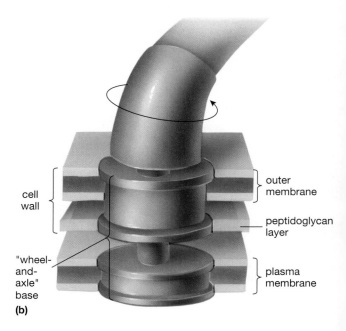

Figure 19-7b The prokaryote flagellum

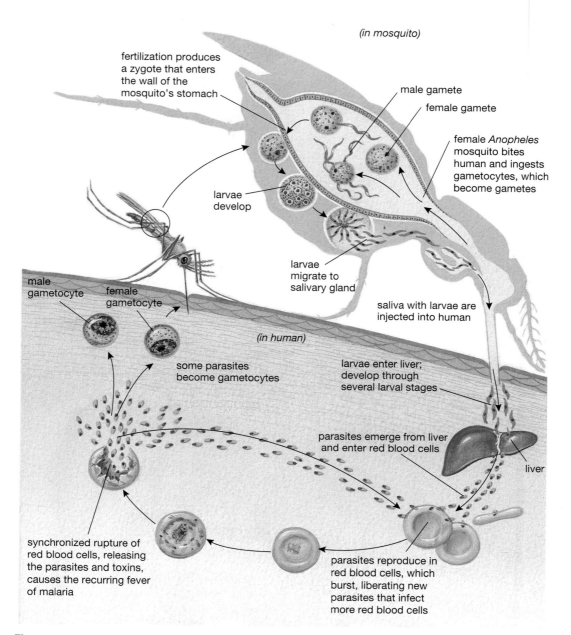

(in mosquito)

fertilization produces a zygote that enters the wall of the mosquito's stomach

male gamete

female gamete

female *Anopheles* mosquito bites human and ingests gametocytes, which become gametes

larvae develop

larvae migrate to salivary gland

saliva with larvae are injected into human

male gametocyte

female gametocyte

(in human)

some parasites become gametocytes

larvae enter liver; develop through several larval stages

parasites emerge from liver and enter red blood cells

liver

synchronized rupture of red blood cells, releasing the parasites and toxins, causes the recurring fever of malaria

parasites reproduce in red blood cells, which burst, liberating new parasites that infect more red blood cells

Figure 19-21   The life cycle of the malaria parasite

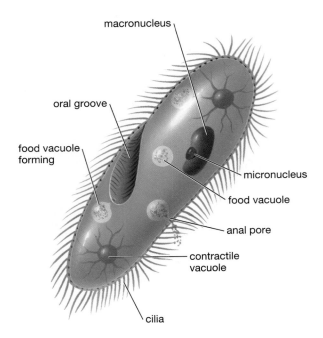

macronucleus

oral groove

food vacuole
forming

micronucleus

food vacuole

anal pore

contractile
vacuole

cilia

Figure 19-22   The complexity of ciliates

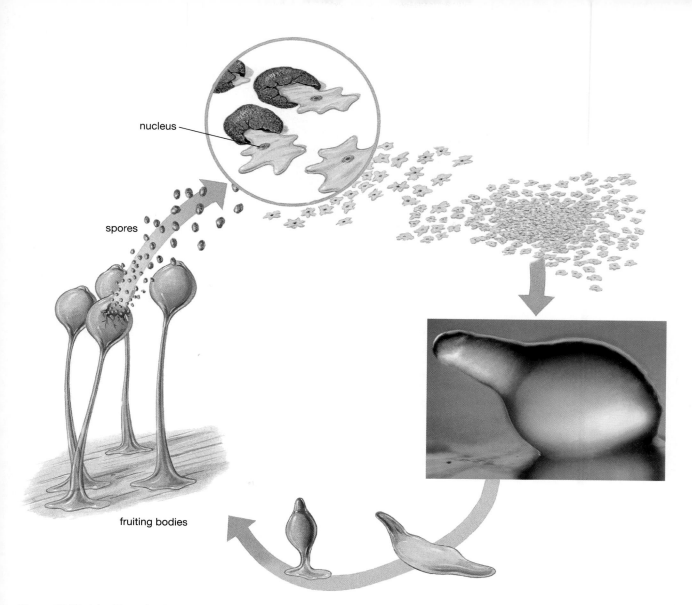

nucleus

spores

fruiting bodies

Figure 19-25 The life cycle of a cellular slime mold

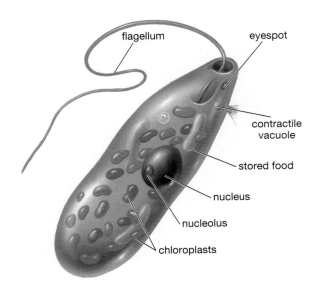

flagellum

eyespot

contractile
vacuole

stored food

nucleus

nucleolus

chloroplasts

Figure 19-26 *Euglena*, a representative euglenoid

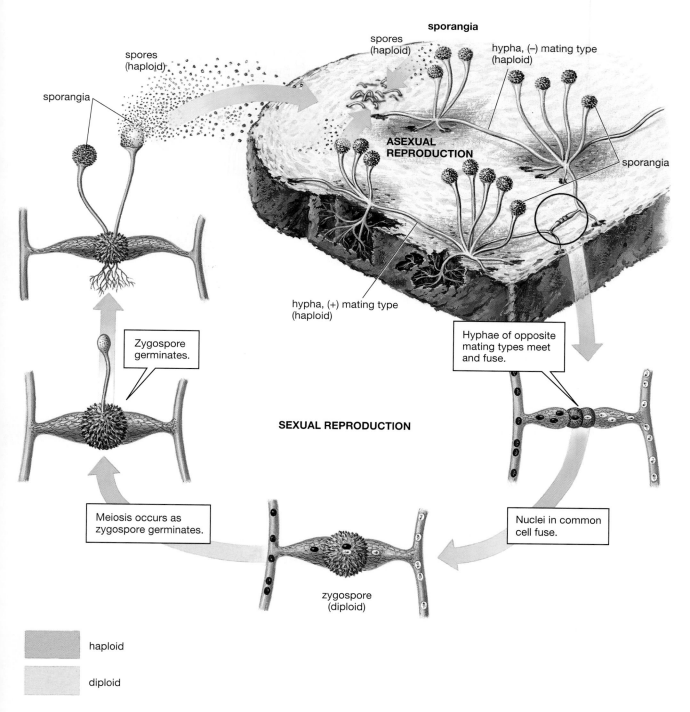

spores (haploid)

sporangia

sporangia

spores (haploid)

hypha, (−) mating type (haploid)

sporangia

ASEXUAL REPRODUCTION

hypha, (+) mating type (haploid)

Zygospore germinates.

Hyphae of opposite mating types meet and fuse.

SEXUAL REPRODUCTION

Nuclei in common cell fuse.

Meiosis occurs as zygospore germinates.

zygospore (diploid)

haploid

diploid

Figure 20-4   The life cycle of a zygomycete

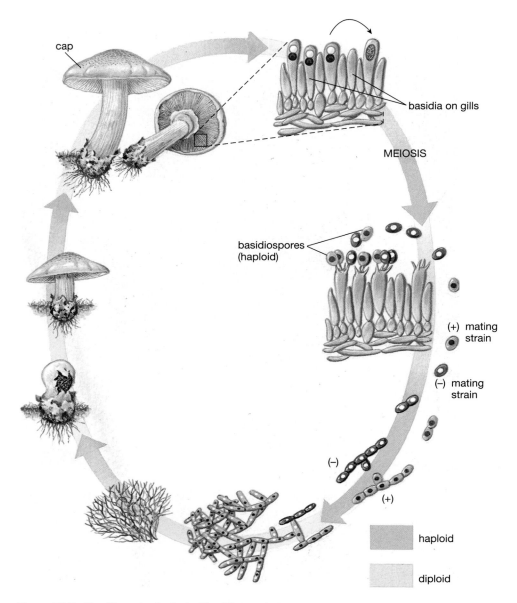

cap

basidia on gills

MEIOSIS

basidiospores (haploid)

(+) mating strain

(−) mating strain

(−)

(+)

haploid

diploid

Figure 20-6   The life cycle of a typical basidiomycete

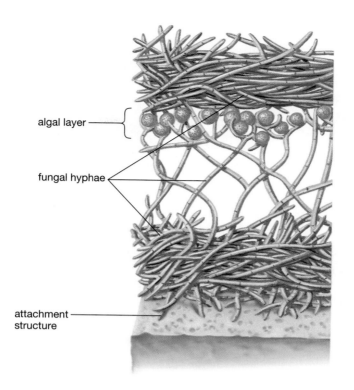

algal layer

fungal hyphae

attachment structure

Figure 20-9   The lichen: a symbiotic partnership

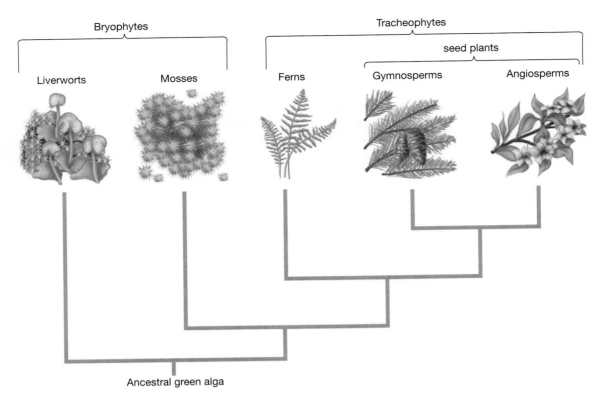

Bryophytes

Tracheophytes

seed plants

Liverworts   Mosses   Ferns   Gymnosperms   Angiosperms

Ancestral green alga

Figure 21-1 Evolutionary tree of some major plant groups
Media Activity 21.1 Evolution of Plant Structure

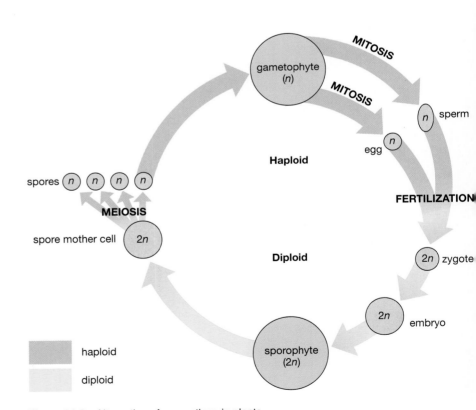

MITOSIS

gametophyte
(*n*)

MITOSIS

n sperm

egg *n*

Haploid

FERTILIZATION

spores *n* *n* *n* *n*

MEIOSIS

spore mother cell   2*n*

2*n* zygote

Diploid

2*n* embryo

sporophyte
(2*n*)

haploid

diploid

Figure 21-2 Alternation of generations in plants

154

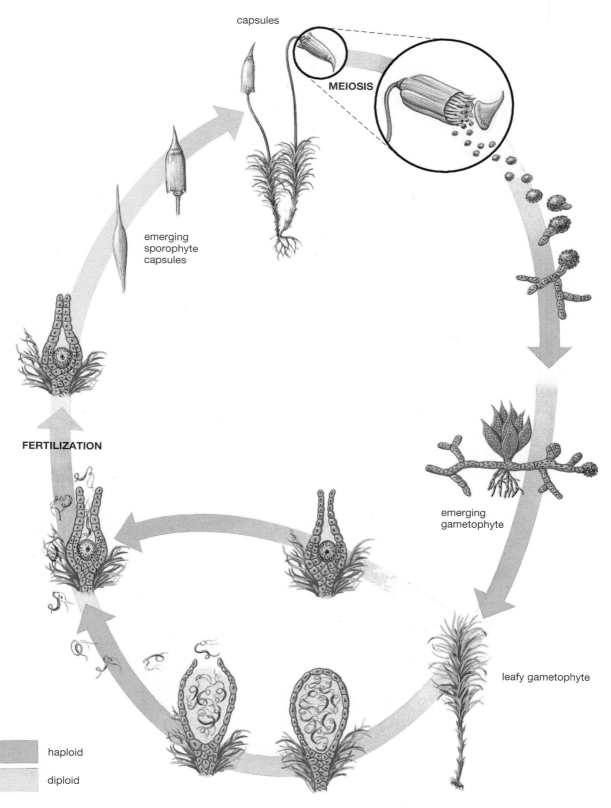

capsules

MEIOSIS

emerging
sporophyte
capsules

FERTILIZATION

emerging
gametophyte

leafy gametophyte

haploid

diploid

Figure 21-4 Life cycle of a moss

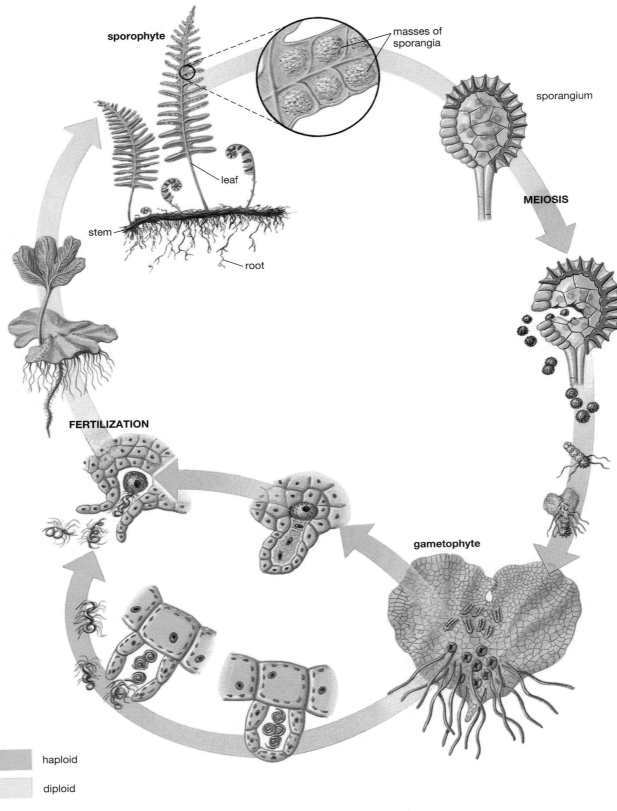

sporophyte

masses of
sporangia

sporangium

MEIOSIS

leaf

stem

root

FERTILIZATION

gametophyte

haploid

diploid

Figure 21-6 Life cycle of a fern
Media Activity 21.2 Fern Life Cycle

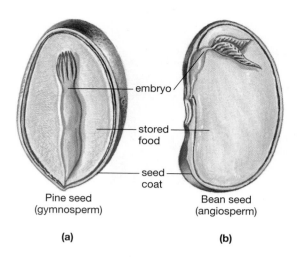

embryo

stored food

seed coat

Pine seed (gymnosperm)

Bean seed (angiosperm)

(a)

(b)

Figure 21-7a,b   Seeds

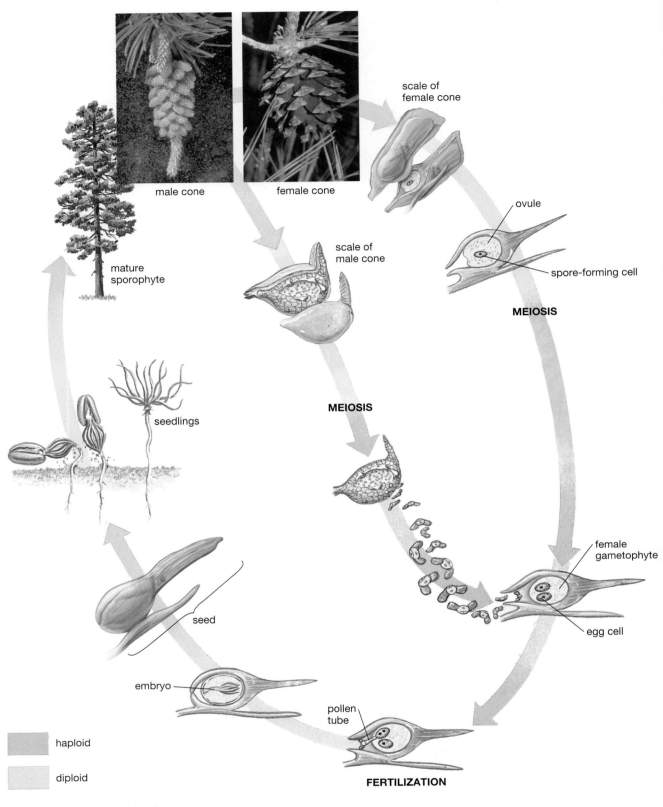

scale of
female cone

ovule

spore-forming cell

MEIOSIS

male cone

female cone

mature
sporophyte

scale of
male cone

MEIOSIS

seedlings

female
gametophyte

egg cell

seed

embryo

pollen
tube

haploid

diploid

FERTILIZATION

Figure 21-8   Life cycle of the pine

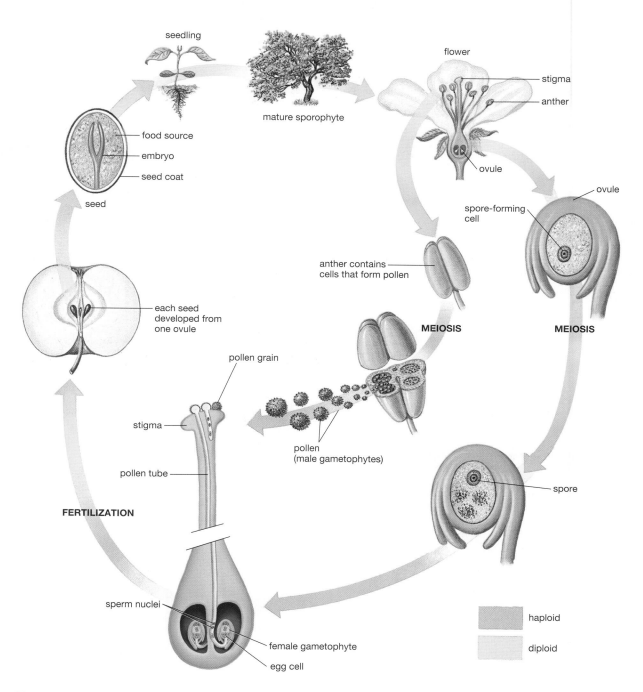

Figure 21-11 Life cycle of a flowering plant

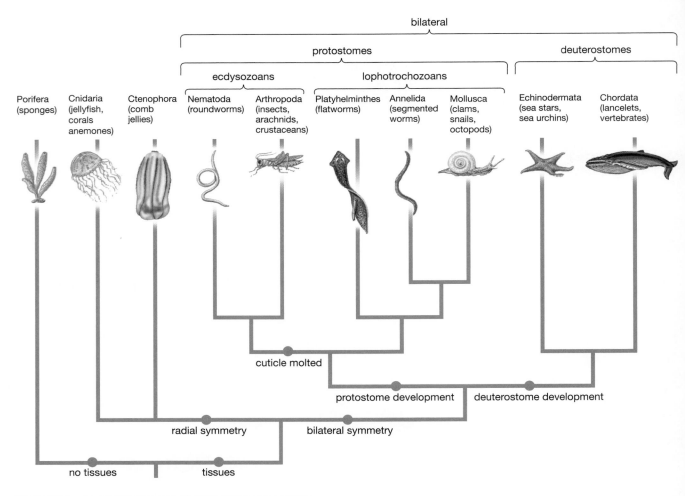

Figure 22-1 An evolutionary tree of some major animal phyla
Media Activity 22.1 Architecture of Animals

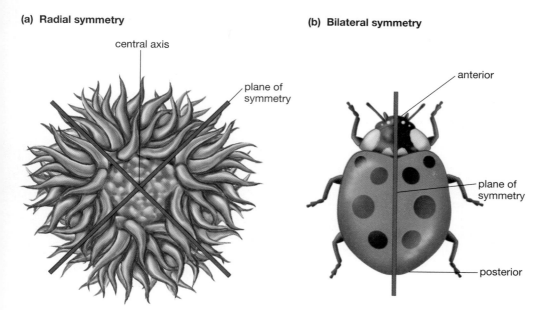

(a) Radial symmetry

central axis

plane of
symmetry

(b) Bilateral symmetry

anterior

plane of
symmetry

posterior

Figure 22-2 Body symmetry and cephalization

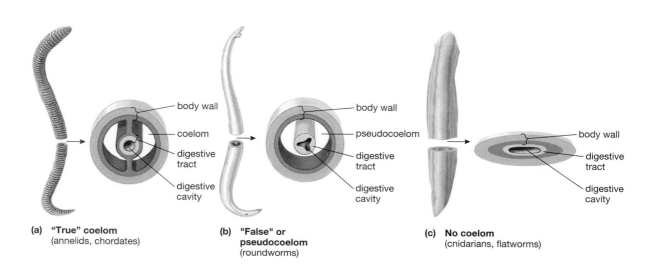

body wall

coelom

digestive
tract

digestive
cavity

(a) "True" coelom
(annelids, chordates)

body wall

pseudocoelom

digestive
tract

digestive
cavity

**(b) "False" or
pseudocoelom**
(roundworms)

body wall

digestive
tract

digestive
cavity

(c) No coelom
(cnidarians, flatworms)

Figure 22-3 Body cavities

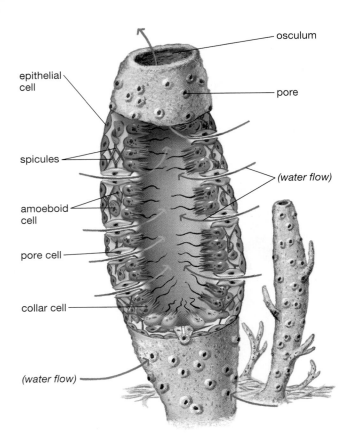

Figure 22-4   The body plan of sponges

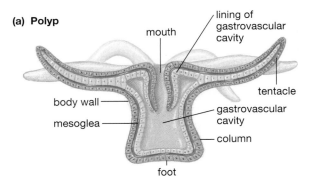

Figure 22-7   Polyp and medusa

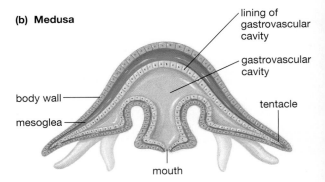

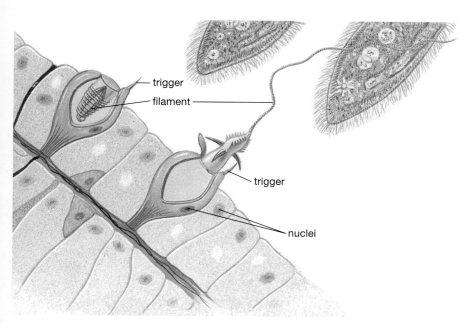

Figure 22-8 Cnidarian weaponry: the cnidocyte

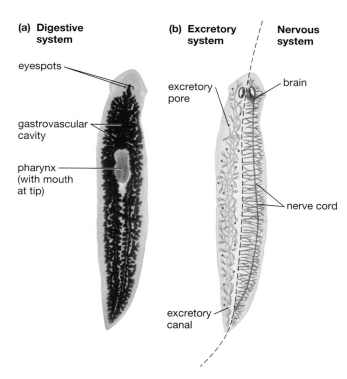

Figure 22-9 Flatworm organ systems

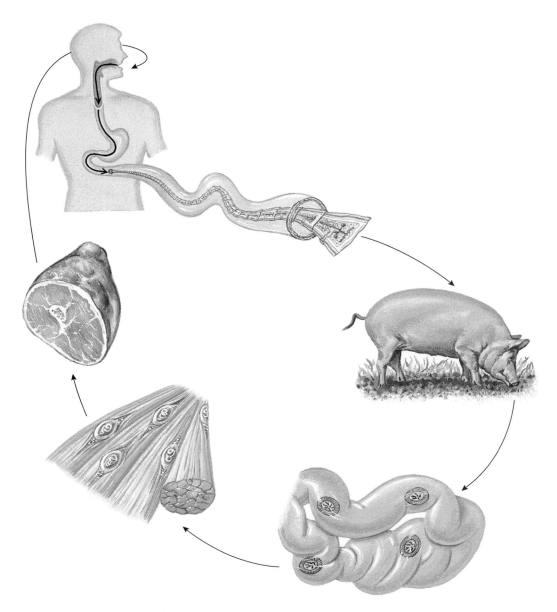

Figure 22-10 The life cycle of the human pork tapeworm

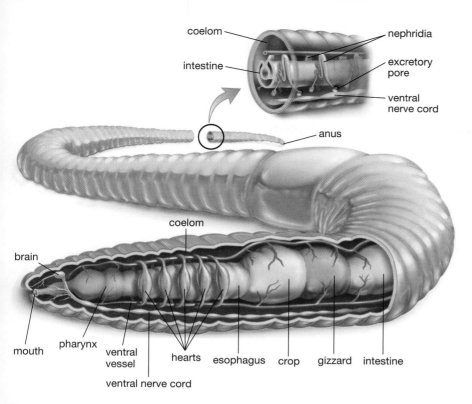

Figure 22-11   An annelid, the earthworm

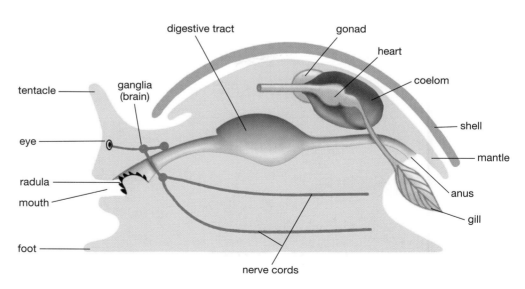

Figure 22-13   A generalized mollusk

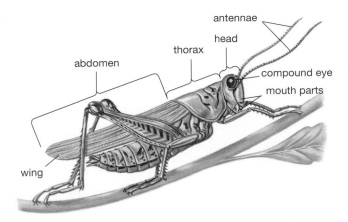

Figure 22-19 Segments are fused and specialized in insects

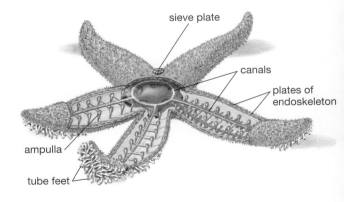

(a)

Figure 22-28a The water-vascular system of echinoderms

(a) Lancelet

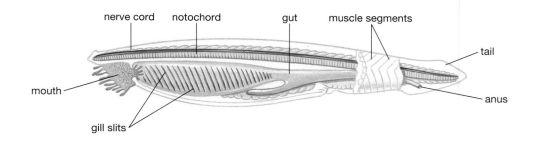

nerve cord   notochord   gut   muscle segments

tail

mouth

anus

gill slits

(b) Tunicate

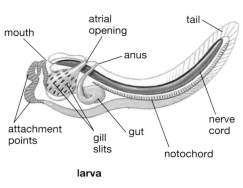

mouth

atrial opening

tail

anus

nerve cord

attachment points

gill slits

gut

notochord

larva

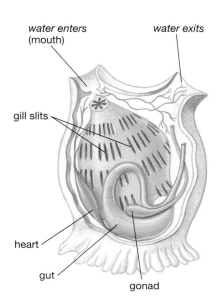

water enters (mouth)   water exits

gill slits

heart

gut

gonad

Figure 23-2   Invertebrate chordates

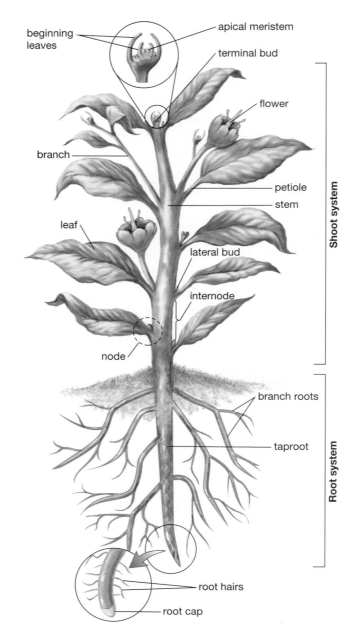

Figure 24-1 Flowering plant structure
Media Activity 24.1 Plant Anatomy

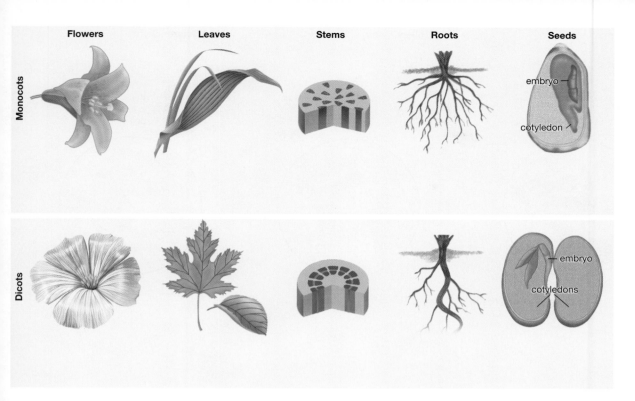

Figure 24-2 Monocots and dicots compared

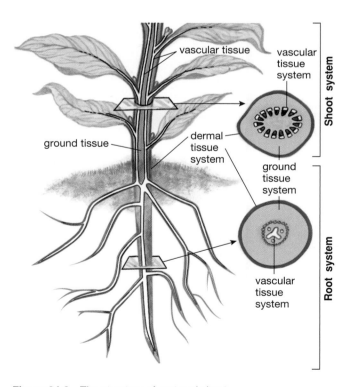

Figure 24-3 The structure of root and shoot

(a) Parenchyma

potato

stored starch

thin primary cell wall

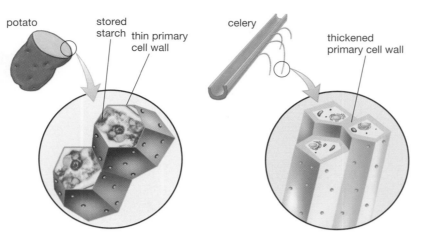

(b) Collenchyma

celery

thickened primary cell wall

(c) Sclerenchyma

pear

thin primary cell wall

thick secondary cell wall

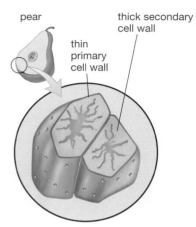

Figure 24-5 The structure of ground tissue

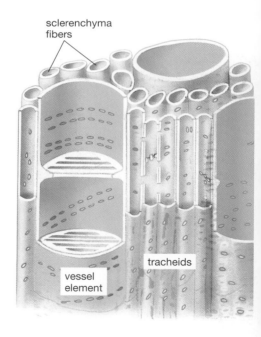

sclerenchyma fibers

tracheids

vessel element

Figure 24-6 The structure of xylem

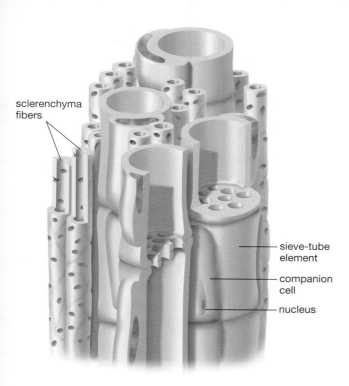

sclerenchyma
fibers

sieve-tube
element

companion
cell

nucleus

Figure 24-7 The structure of phloem

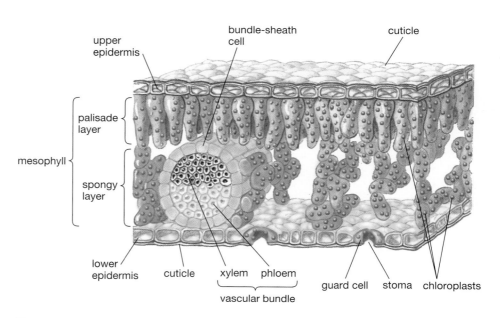

upper
epidermis

bundle-sheath
cell

cuticle

palisade
layer

mesophyll

spongy
layer

lower
epidermis

cuticle

xylem   phloem

vascular bundle

guard cell   stoma   chloroplasts

Figure 24-8 The structure of a typical dicot leaf

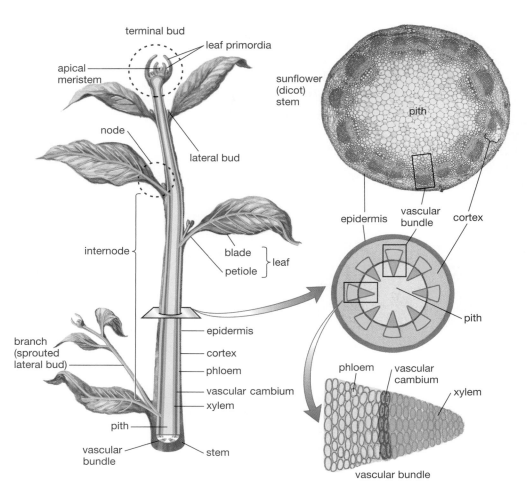

Figure 24-9 The structure of a young dicot stem
Media Activity 24.2 Primary and Secondary Growth

Labels in figure:

terminal bud
leaf primordia
apical meristem
node
lateral bud
internode
blade
petiole
leaf
branch (sprouted lateral bud)
epidermis
cortex
phloem
vascular cambium
xylem
pith
vascular bundle
stem
sunflower (dicot) stem
pith
epidermis
vascular bundle
cortex
pith
phloem
vascular cambium
xylem
vascular bundle

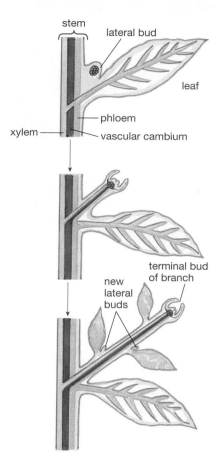

Figure 24-10   How branches form

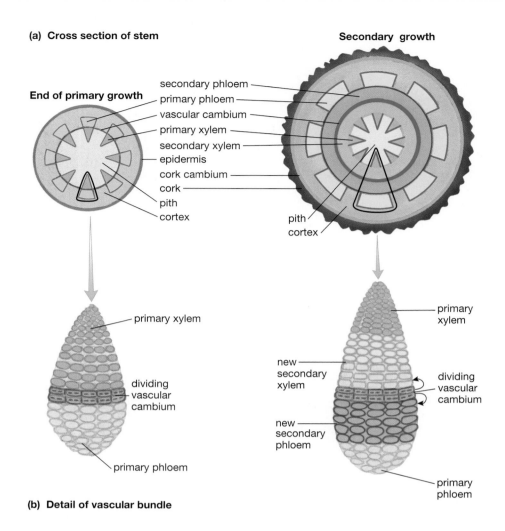

(a) Cross section of stem

Secondary growth

End of primary growth

- secondary phloem
- primary phloem
- vascular cambium
- primary xylem
- secondary xylem
- epidermis
- cork cambium
- cork
- pith
- cortex

pith
cortex

primary xylem

dividing vascular cambium

primary phloem

primary xylem

new secondary xylem

new secondary phloem

dividing vascular cambium

primary phloem

(b) Detail of vascular bundle

Figure 24-11 Secondary growth in a dicot stem

174

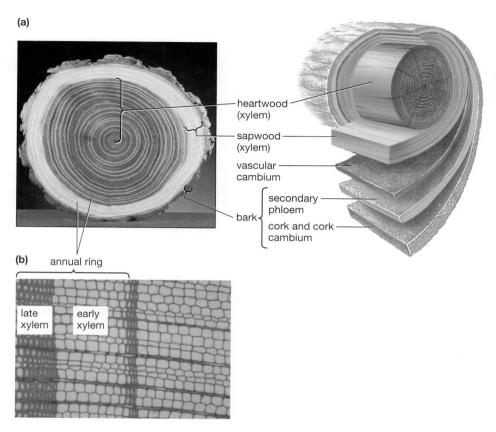

(a)

heartwood (xylem)

sapwood (xylem)

vascular cambium

bark

secondary phloem

cork and cork cambium

(b) annual ring

late xylem

early xylem

Figure 24-12 How annual tree rings are formed

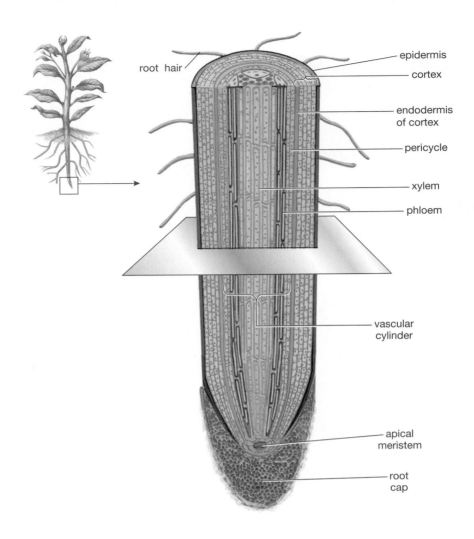

root hair

epidermis

cortex

endodermis
of cortex

pericycle

xylem

phloem

vascular
cylinder

apical
meristem

root
cap

Figure 24-15 Primary growth in roots

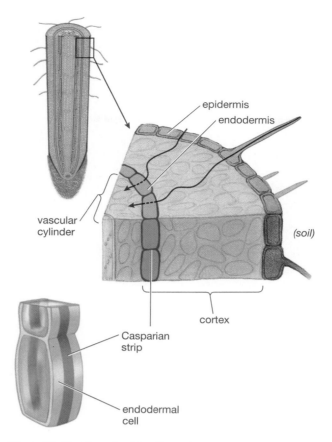

epidermis

endodermis

vascular cylinder

(soil)

cortex

Casparian strip

endodermal cell

Figure 24-18　The role of the Casparian strip

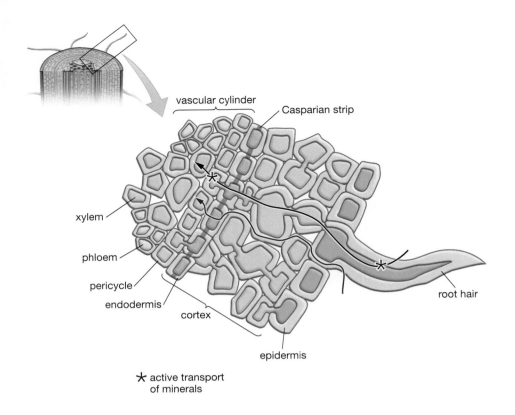

vascular cylinder

Casparian strip

xylem

phloem

pericycle

endodermis

cortex

epidermis

root hair

★ active transport
of minerals

Figure 24-19 Mineral and water uptake by roots
Media Activity 24.3 Nutrient Uptake

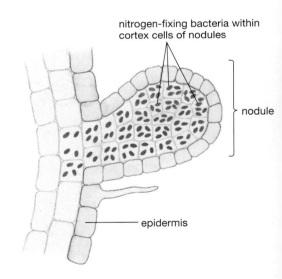

nitrogen-fixing bacteria within
cortex cells of nodules

nodule

epidermis

Figure 24-21 Nitrogen fixation in legumes

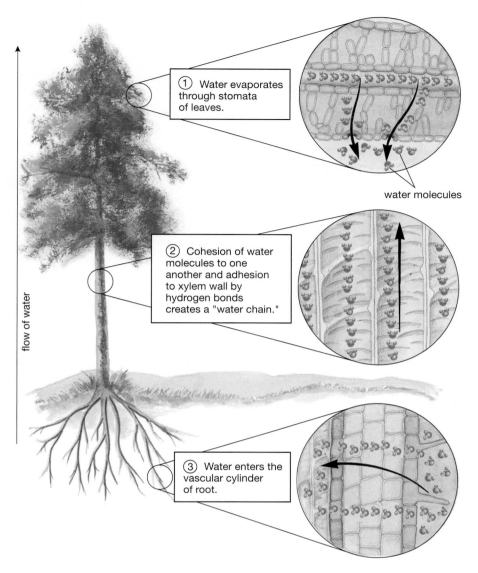

flow of water

① Water evaporates through stomata of leaves.

water molecules

② Cohesion of water molecules to one another and adhesion to xylem wall by hydrogen bonds creates a "water chain."

③ Water enters the vascular cylinder of root.

Figure 24-22 The cohesion–tension theory of water flow from root to leaf in xylem
Media Activity 24.4 Plant Transport Mechanisms

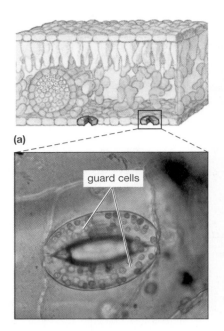

(a)

guard cells

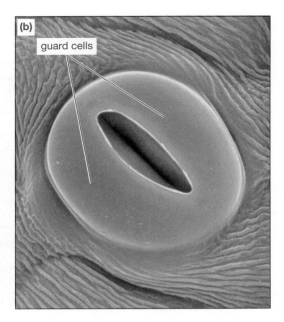

(b)

guard cells

Figure 24-23 Stomata

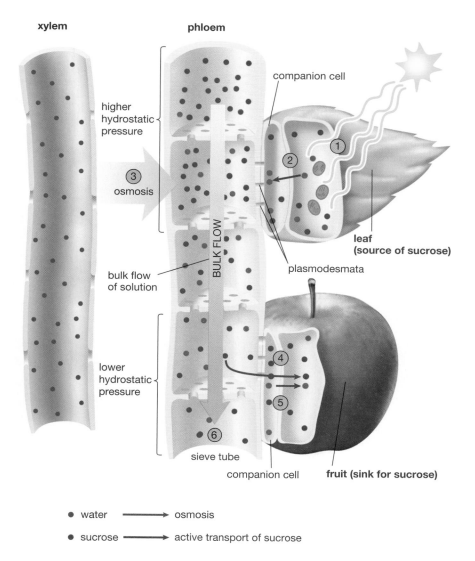

xylem

phloem

companion cell

higher
hydrostatic
pressure

③ osmosis

BULK FLOW

bulk flow
of solution

plasmodesmata

leaf
(source of sucrose)

① ②

lower
hydrostatic
pressure

④

⑤

⑥

sieve tube

companion cell

fruit (sink for sucrose)

- water ⟶ osmosis
- sucrose ⟶ active transport of sucrose

Figure 24-25   The pressure-flow theory

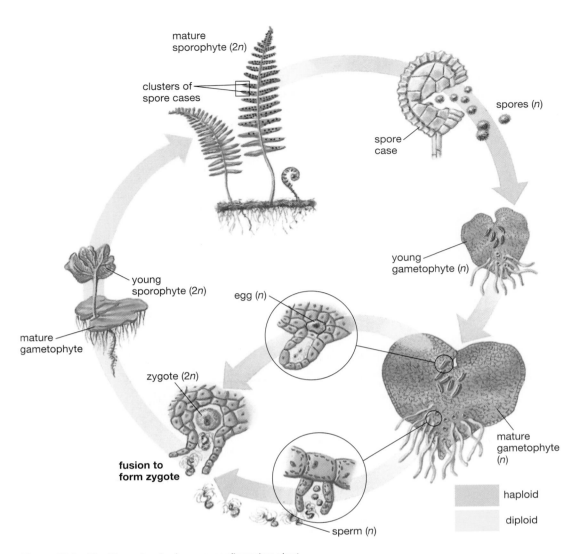

mature
sporophyte (2n)

clusters of
spore cases

spore
case

spores (n)

young
gametophyte (n)

young
sporophyte (2n)

egg (n)

mature
gametophyte

mature
gametophyte
(n)

zygote (2n)

fusion to
form zygote

sperm (n)

haploid

diploid

Figure 25-1   The life cycle of a fern—a nonflowering plant

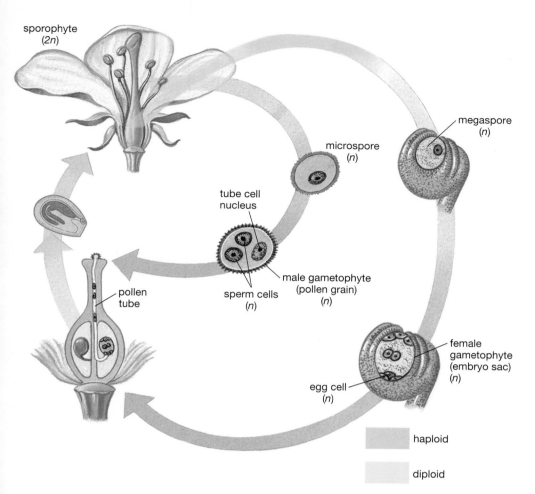

Figure 25-2 The life cycle of a flowering plant

sporophyte
(2n)

megaspore
(n)

microspore
(n)

tube cell
nucleus

male gametophyte
(pollen grain)
(n)

sperm cells
(n)

pollen
tube

female
gametophyte
(embryo sac)
(n)

egg cell
(n)

haploid

diploid

(a)

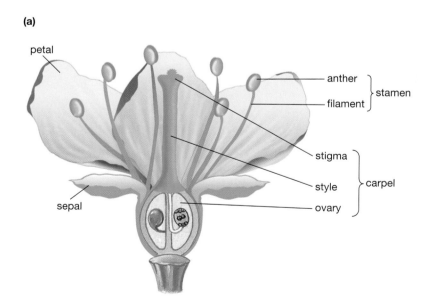

petal

anther
stamen
filament

stigma
carpel
style

sepal

ovary

Figure 25-4a A complete flower
Media Activity 25.1 Reproduction in Flowering Plants

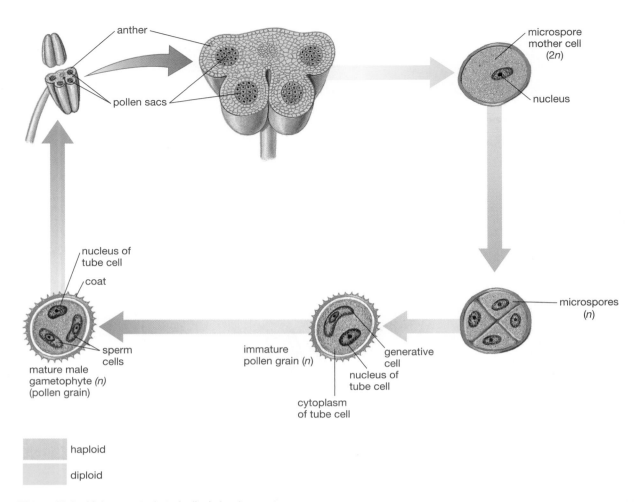

anther

pollen sacs

microspore
mother cell
(2n)

nucleus

nucleus of
tube cell

coat

sperm
cells

mature male
gametophyte (n)
(pollen grain)

immature
pollen grain (n)

generative
cell

nucleus of
tube cell

cytoplasm
of tube cell

microspores
(n)

haploid

diploid

Figure 25-6   Male gametophyte (pollen) development

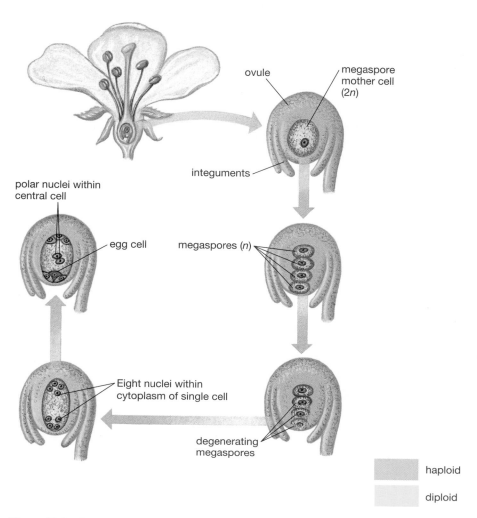

ovule

megaspore mother cell (2*n*)

integuments

polar nuclei within central cell

egg cell

megaspores (*n*)

Eight nuclei within cytoplasm of single cell

degenerating megaspores

haploid

diploid

Figure 25-9   Female gametophyte (embryo sac) development

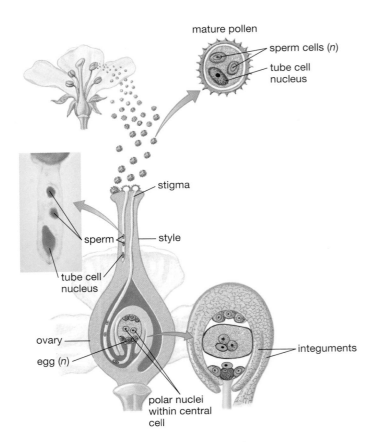

mature pollen

sperm cells (*n*)

tube cell nucleus

stigma

sperm

style

tube cell nucleus

ovary

egg (*n*)

polar nuclei within central cell

integuments

Figure 25-10 Pollination and fertilization of a flower

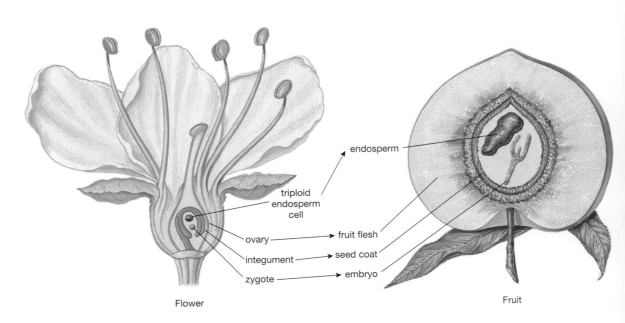

endosperm

triploid endosperm cell

ovary

integument

zygote

fruit flesh

seed coat

embryo

Flower

Fruit

Figure 25-11 Development of fruit and seeds from flower parts
Media Activity 25.2 Fruits and Seeds: Structure and Development

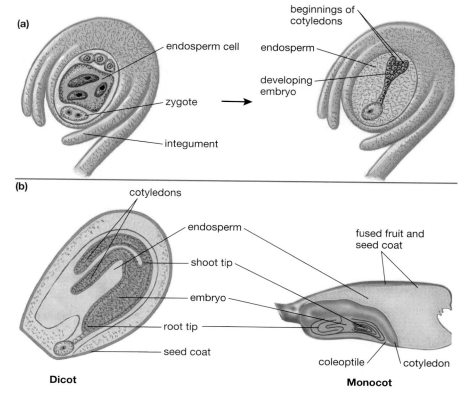

(a)

endosperm cell

zygote

integument

beginnings of
cotyledons

endosperm

developing
embryo

(b)

cotyledons

endosperm

shoot tip

embryo

root tip

seed coat

Dicot

fused fruit and
seed coat

coleoptile

cotyledon

Monocot

Figure 25-12   Seed development
Media Activity 25.2 Fruits and Seeds: Structure and Development

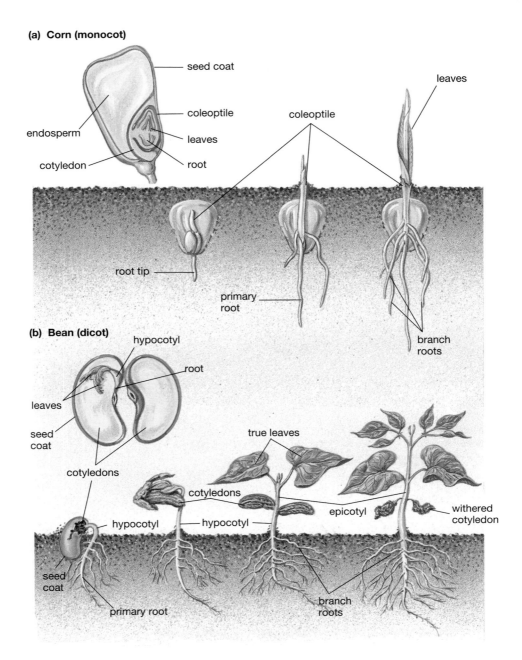

(a) Corn (monocot)

seed coat

coleoptile

coleoptile

leaves

endosperm

leaves

cotyledon

root

root tip

primary root

branch roots

(b) Bean (dicot)

hypocotyl

root

leaves

seed coat

cotyledons

true leaves

cotyledons

epicotyl

withered cotyledon

hypocotyl

hypocotyl

seed coat

primary root

branch roots

Figure 25-13 Seed germination

(a) Shoot bends upward

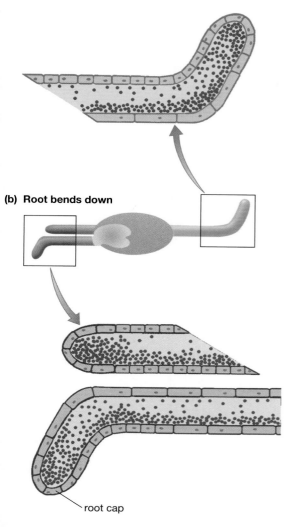

(b) Root bends down

root cap

Figure 26-1a,b The mechanism of gravitropism in shoots and roots

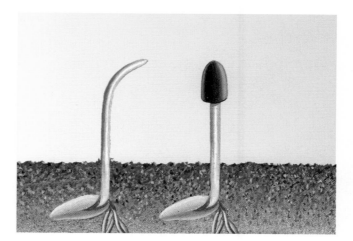

Figure 26-UN01 The Darwins' studies of phototropism

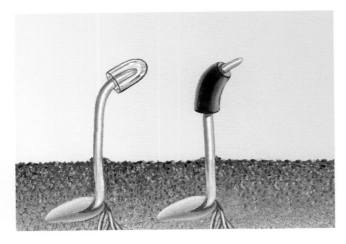

Figure 26-UN02 The Darwins' studies of phototropism

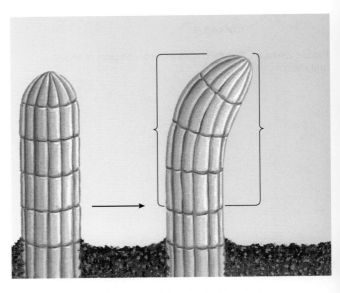

Figure 26-UN03 The Darwins' studies of phototropism

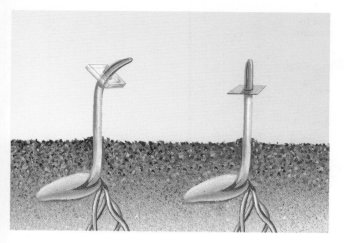

Figure 26-UN04 Peter Boyson-Jensen's and Fritz Went's experiments

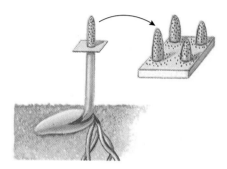

Figure 26-UN05 Peter Boyson-Jensen's and Fritz Went's experiments

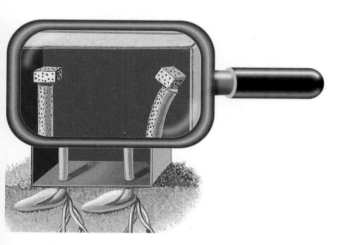

Figure 26-UN06 Peter Boyson-Jensen's and Fritz Went's experiments

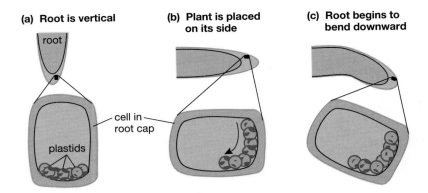

(a) Root is vertical

root

cell in
root cap

plastids

**(b) Plant is placed
on its side**

**(c) Root begins to
bend downward**

Figure 26-2 Starch-filled plastids allow plants to sense gravity

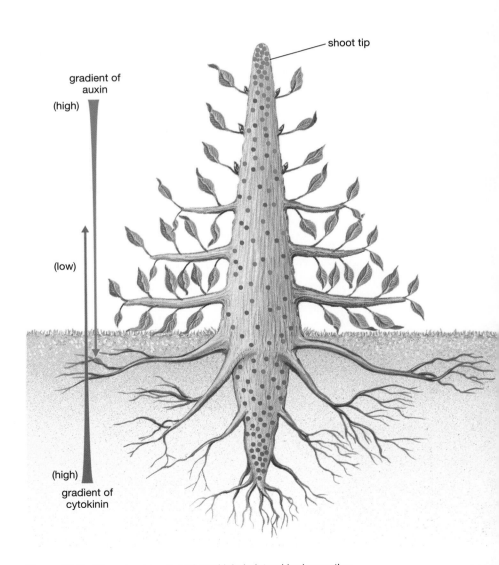

shoot tip

gradient of
auxin

(high)

(low)

(high)

gradient of
cytokinin

Figure 26-3 The role of auxin and cytokinin in lateral bud sprouting

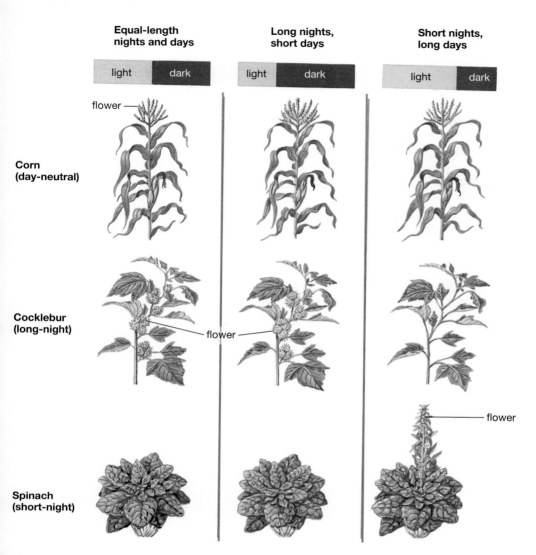

Equal-length nights and days	Long nights, short days	Short nights, long days
light dark	light dark	light dark

Corn (day-neutral)

flower

Cocklebur (long-night)

flower

Spinach (short-night)

flower

Figure 26-4 The effects of night length on flowering
Media Activity 26.2 Plant Responses to Phytochrome

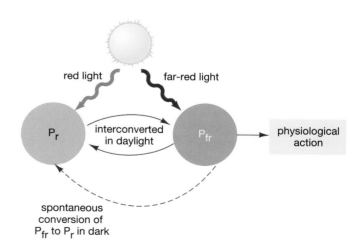

red light   far-red light

P_r interconverted in daylight P_{fr} →   physiological action

spontaneous conversion of P_{fr} to P_r in dark

Figure 26-5 The light-sensitive pigment phytochrome

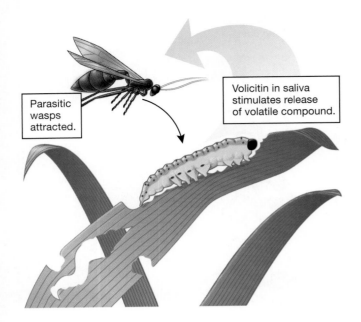

Figure 26-8 A chemical cry for help

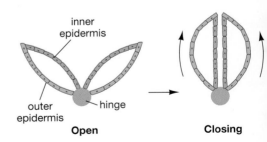

Figure 26-UN07 Venus flytrap leaves

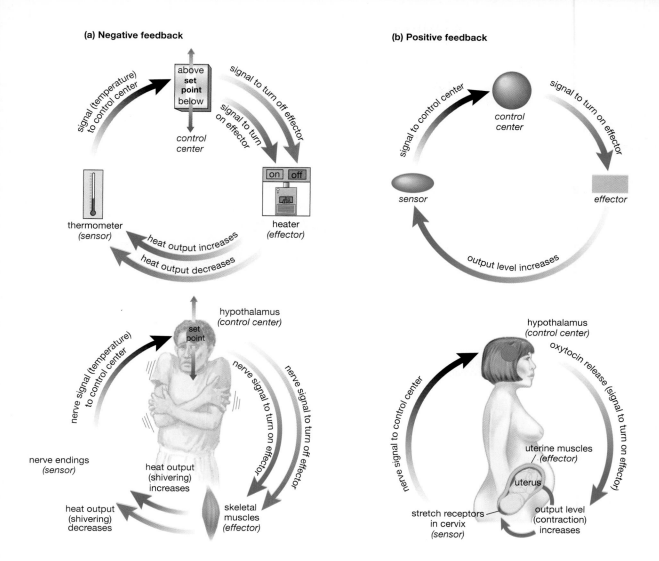

(a) Negative feedback

signal (temperature) to control center

above **set point** below

control center

signal to turn off effector

signal to turn on effector

on off

heater *(effector)*

heat output increases

heat output decreases

thermometer *(sensor)*

hypothalamus *(control center)*

set point

nerve signal (temperature) to control center

nerve signal to turn on effector

nerve signal to turn off effector

nerve endings *(sensor)*

heat output (shivering) increases

heat output (shivering) decreases

skeletal muscles *(effector)*

(b) Positive feedback

signal to control center

control center

signal to turn on effector

sensor

effector

output level increases

hypothalamus *(control center)*

oxytocin release (signal to turn on effector)

nerve signal to control center

uterine muscles / *(effector)*

uterus

stretch receptors in cervix *(sensor)*

output level (contraction) increases

Figure 27-1 Positive and negative feedback
Media Activity 27.1 Homeostasis

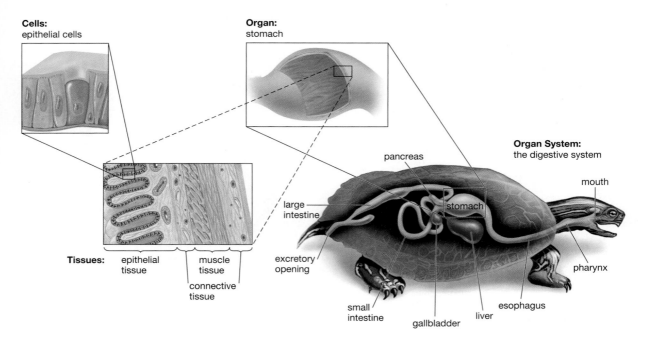

Cells:
epithelial cells

Organ:
stomach

Organ System:
the digestive system

pancreas

large intestine

stomach

mouth

Tissues: epithelial tissue

muscle tissue

connective tissue

excretory opening

small intestine

gallbladder

liver

esophagus

pharynx

Figure 27-2 Cells, tissues, organs, and organ systems

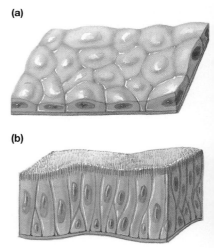

(a)

(b)

Figure 27-3 Examples of epithelial tissue

Table 27-1   Major Vertebrate Organ Systems

Organ System	Major Structures	Physiological Role
Circulatory system 	Heart, blood vessels, blood	Transports nutrients, gases, hormones, metabolic wastes; also assists in temperature control
Lymphatic/ immune system 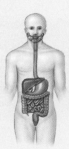	Lymph, lymph nodes and vessels, white blood cells	Carries fat and excess fluids to blood; destroys invading microbes
Digestive system 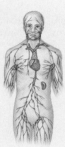	Mouth, esophagus, stomach, small and large intestines, glands producing digestive secretions	Supplies the body with nutrients that provide energy and materials for growth and maintenance
Urinary system 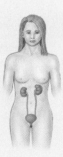	Kidneys, ureters, bladder, urethra	Maintains homeostatic conditions within bloodstream; filters out cellular wastes, certain toxins, and excess water and nutrients
Respiratory system 	Nose, pharynx, trachea, lungs (mammals, birds, reptiles, amphibians), gills (fish and some amphibians)	Provides an area for gas exchange between the blood and the environment; allows oxygen acquisition and carbon dioxide elimination

Table 27-1 Major Vertebrate Organ Systems

Organ System	Major Structures	Physiological Role
Endocrine system 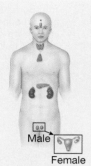 Male / Female	A variety of hormone-secreting glands and organs, including the hypothalamus, pituitary, thyroid, pancreas, adrenals, ovaries, and testes	Controls physiological processes, typically in conjunction with the nervous system
Nervous system 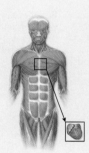	Brain, spinal cord, peripheral nerves	Controls physiological processes in conjunction with the endocrine system; senses the environment, directs behavior
Muscular system 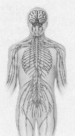	Skeletal muscle Smooth muscle Cardiac muscle	Moves the skeleton Controls movement of substances through hollow organs (digestive tract, large blood vessels) Initiates and implements heart contractions
Skeletal system 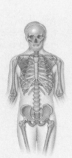	Bones, cartilage, tendons, ligaments	Provides support for the body, attachment sites for muscles, and protection for internal organs
Reproductive system 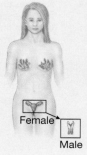 Female / Male	Males: testes, seminal vesicles, prostate gland, penis Female (mammal): ovaries, oviducts, uterus, vagina, mammary glands	Male: produces sperm, inseminates female Female (mammal): Produces egg cells, nurtures developing offspring

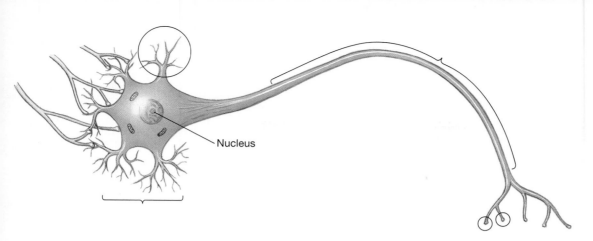

Nucleus

Figure 27-9   Nerve tissue

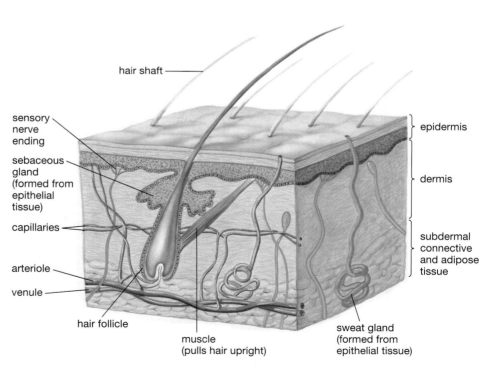

hair shaft

sensory
nerve
ending

sebaceous
gland
(formed from
epithelial
tissue)

capillaries

arteriole

venule

hair follicle

muscle
(pulls hair upright)

epidermis

dermis

subdermal
connective
and adipose
tissue

sweat gland
(formed from
epithelial tissue)

Figure 27-10   Skin

(a) Open circulatory system

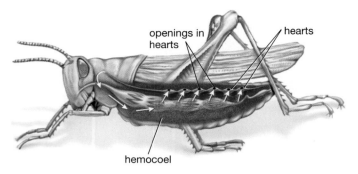

openings in hearts

hearts

hemocoel

(b) Closed circulatory system

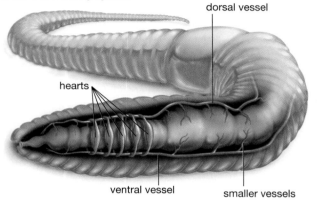

dorsal vessel

hearts

ventral vessel

smaller vessels

Figure 28-1 Open and closed circulatory systems
Media Activity 28.1 Circulatory Systems

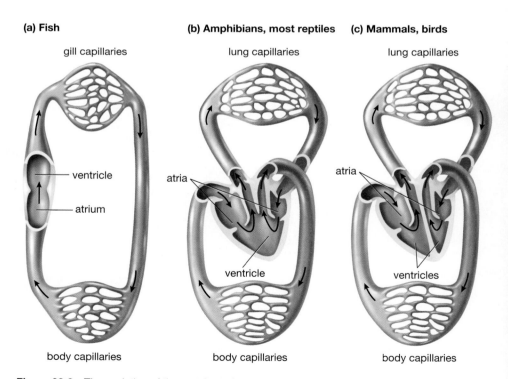

(a) Fish

gill capillaries

ventricle

atrium

body capillaries

(b) Amphibians, most reptiles

lung capillaries

atria

ventricle

body capillaries

(c) Mammals, birds

lung capillaries

atria

ventricles

body capillaries

Figure 28-2 The evolution of the vertebrate heart

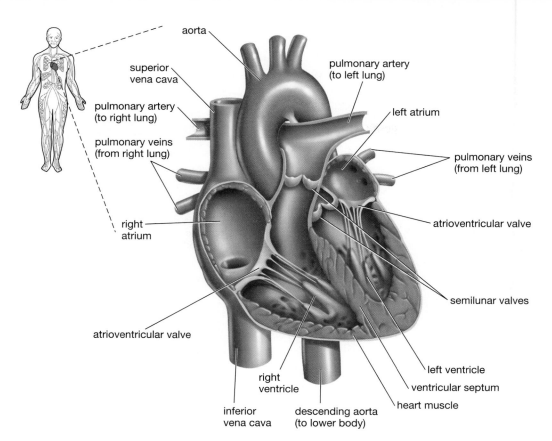

aorta

superior
vena cava

pulmonary artery
(to right lung)

pulmonary veins
(from right lung)

right
atrium

atrioventricular valve

pulmonary artery
(to left lung)

left atrium

pulmonary veins
(from left lung)

atrioventricular valve

semilunar valves

left ventricle

ventricular septum

heart muscle

inferior
vena cava

right
ventricle

descending aorta
(to lower body)

Figure 28-3 The human heart and its valves and vessels
Media Activity 28.2 Heart Structure and Function

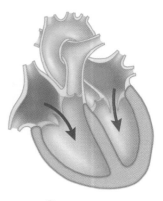 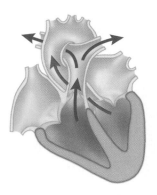 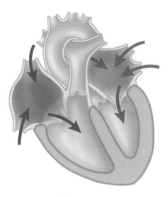

① Atria contract, forcing blood into the ventricles.

② Then the ventricles contract, forcing blood through arteries to the lungs and the rest of the body.

③ The cycle ends as the heart relaxes.

Figure 28-4 The cardiac cycle
Media Activity 28.2 Cardiac Cycle

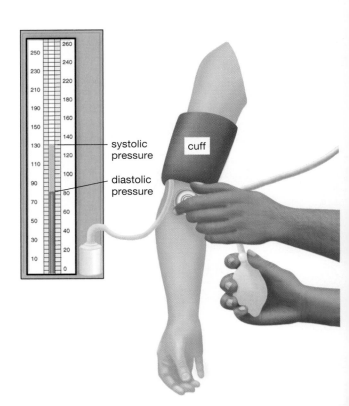

systolic pressure

diastolic pressure

cuff

Figure 28-5 Measuring blood pressure
Media Activity 28.4 Blood Pressure

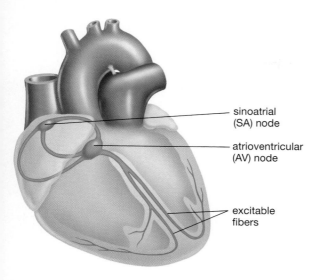

Figure 28-6 The heart's pacemaker and its connections

sinoatrial
(SA) node

atrioventricular
(AV) node

excitable
fibers

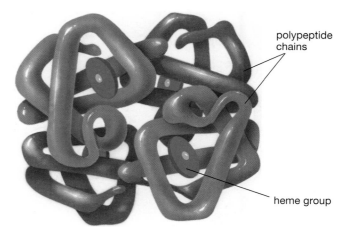

Figure 28-9 Hemoglobin

polypeptide
chains

heme group

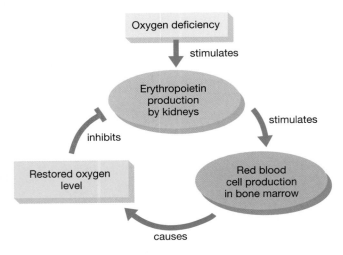

Figure 28-10 Red blood cell regulation by negative feedback

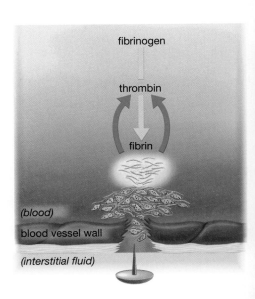

Figure 28-13a Blood clotting

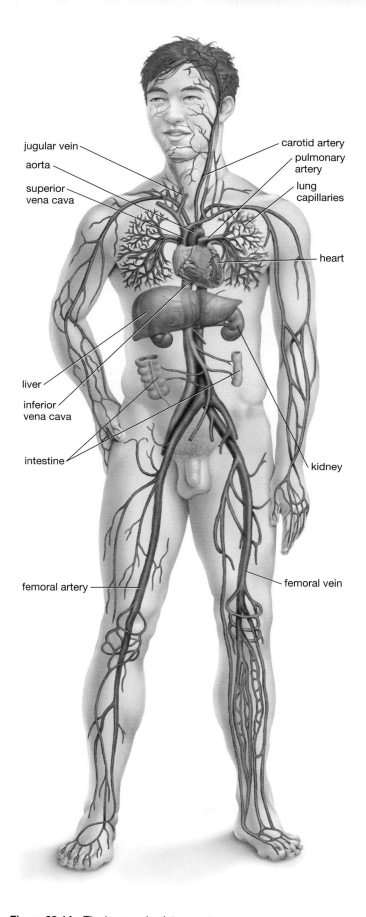

jugular vein

aorta

superior
vena cava

liver

inferior
vena cava

intestine

femoral artery

carotid artery

pulmonary
artery

lung
capillaries

heart

kidney

femoral vein

Figure 28-14   The human circulatory system

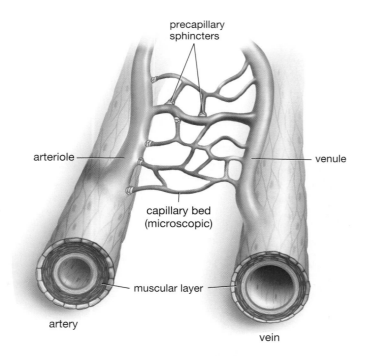

Figure 28-15   Structures and interconnections of blood vessels

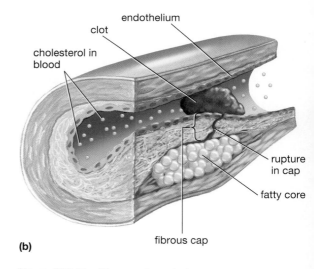

(b)

Figure E28-3b   Plaques clog arteries

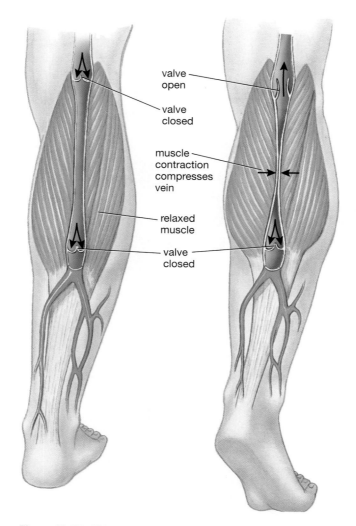

Figure 28-17   Valves direct blood flow in veins

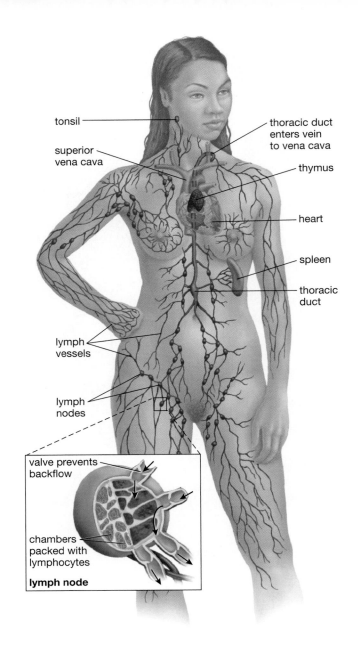

Figure 28-18 The human lymphatic system

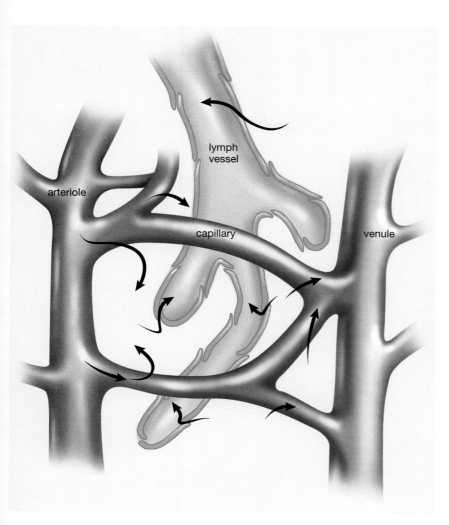

Figure 28-19 Lymph capillary structure

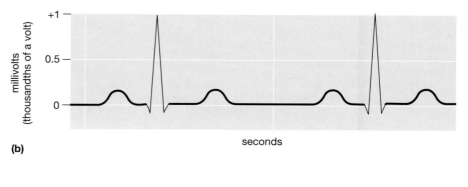

(b)

seconds

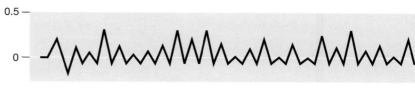

(c)

Figure E28-4b,c The electrocardiogram

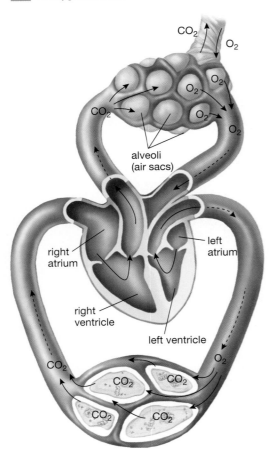

Oxygenated blood
Deoxygenated blood

CO_2 O_2

O_2

O_2

O_2

CO_2

O_2

alveoli
(air sacs)

right
atrium

left
atrium

right
ventricle

left ventricle

CO_2 O_2

CO_2 CO_2

CO_2 CO_2

Figure 29-2 An overview of gas exchange
Media Activity 29.1 Gas Exchange

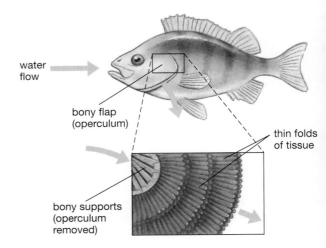

water
flow

bony flap
(operculum)

thin folds
of tissue

bony supports
(operculum
removed)

Figure 29-3 Gills exchange gases with water

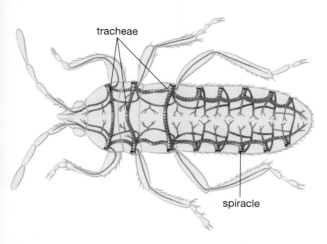

Figure 29-4   Insects breath via trachea

(a) Bird respiratory system

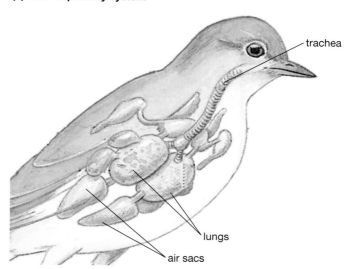

Figure 29-6a   The bird respiratory system is extremely efficient

(a)

(b)

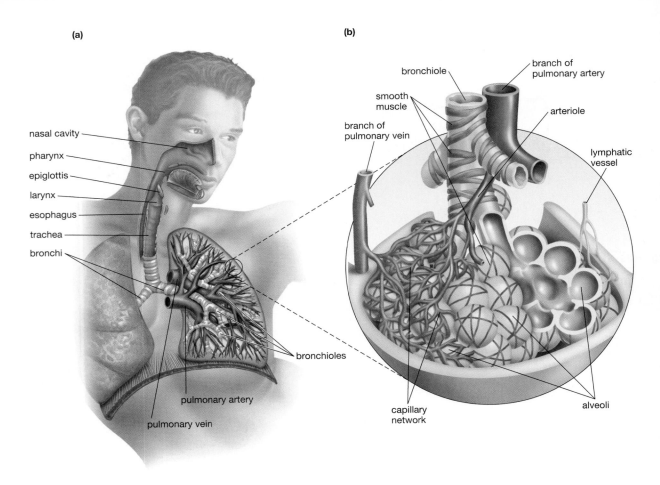

nasal cavity

pharynx

epiglottis

larynx

esophagus

trachea

bronchi

pulmonary artery

pulmonary vein

bronchioles

bronchiole

smooth muscle

branch of pulmonary vein

branch of pulmonary artery

arteriole

lymphatic vessel

capillary network

alveoli

Figure 29-7   The human respiratory system
Media Activity 29.2 Human Respiratory Anatomy

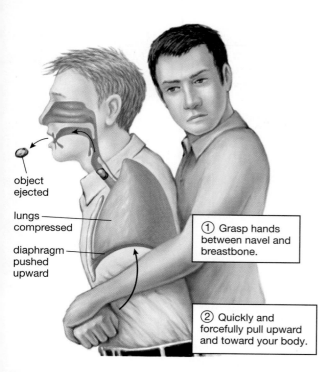

object
ejected

lungs
compressed

diaphragm
pushed
upward

① Grasp hands
between navel and
breastbone.

② Quickly and
forcefully pull upward
and toward your body.

Figure 29-8 The Heimlich maneuver can save lives

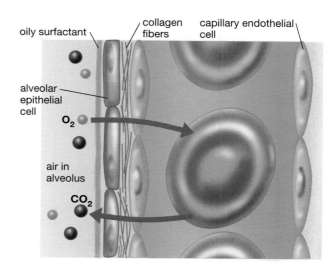

oily surfactant

collagen
fibers

capillary endothelial
cell

alveolar
epithelial
cell

O_2

air in
alveolus

CO_2

Figure 29-9 Gas exchange between alveoli and capillaries

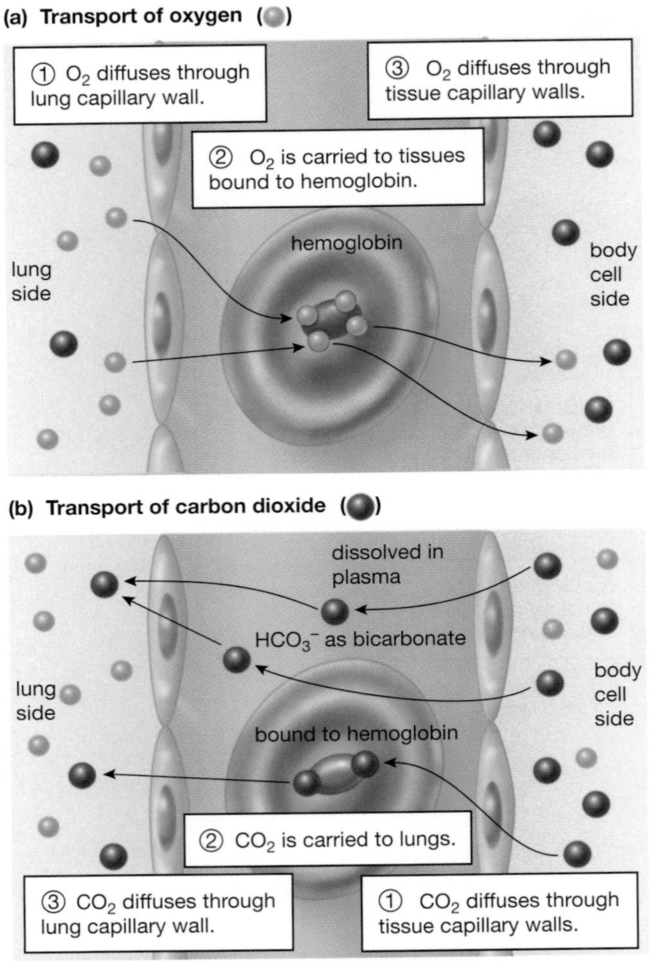

(a) Transport of oxygen (⬤)

① O_2 diffuses through lung capillary wall.

③ O_2 diffuses through tissue capillary walls.

② O_2 is carried to tissues bound to hemoglobin.

hemoglobin

lung side

body cell side

(b) Transport of carbon dioxide (⬤)

dissolved in plasma

HCO_3^- as bicarbonate

lung side

body cell side

bound to hemoglobin

② CO_2 is carried to lungs.

③ CO_2 diffuses through lung capillary wall.

① CO_2 diffuses through tissue capillary walls.

Figure 29-10   The chemistry and mechanism of gas exchange
Media Activity 29.3 Oxygen and Carbon Dioxide Transport

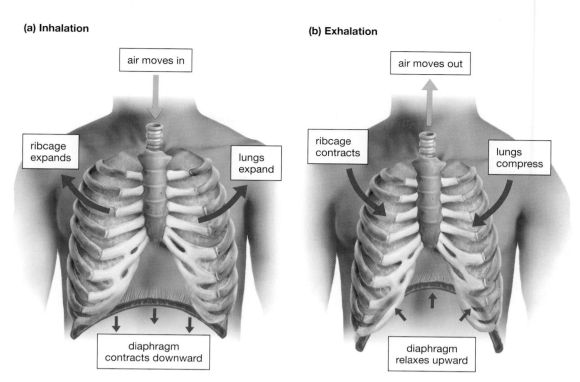

(a) Inhalation

air moves in

ribcage expands

lungs expand

diaphragm contracts downward

(b) Exhalation

air moves out

ribcage contracts

lungs compress

diaphragm relaxes upward

Figure 29-11   The mechanics of breathing

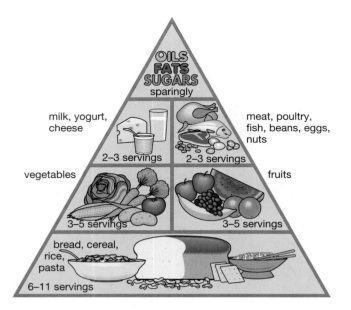

Figure 30-3 The Food Guide Pyramid

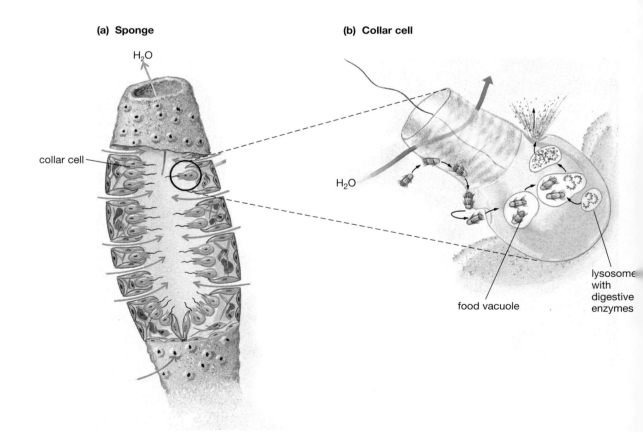

Figure 30-5 Intracellular digestion in a sponge

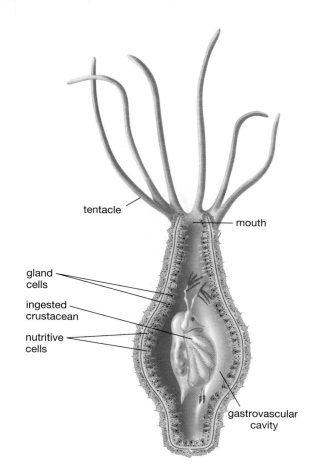

(b)

Figure 30-6b Digestion in a sac

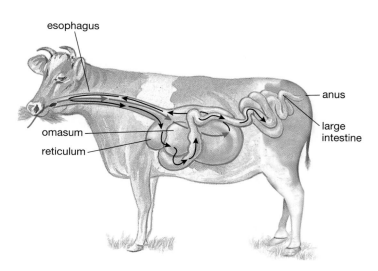

Figure 30-7 The ruminant digestive system

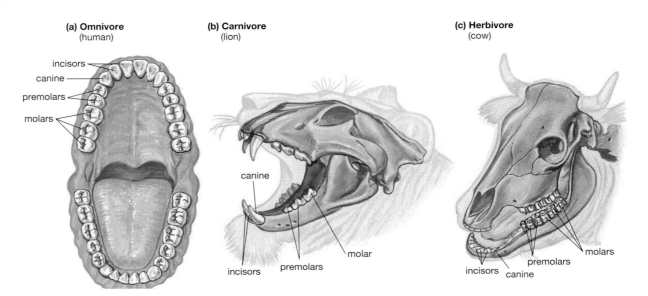

(a) Omnivore
(human)

incisors
canine
premolars
molars

(b) Carnivore
(lion)

canine

incisors premolars

molar

(c) Herbivore
(cow)

molars

incisors
canine
premolars

Figure 30-8 Teeth evolved to suit different diets

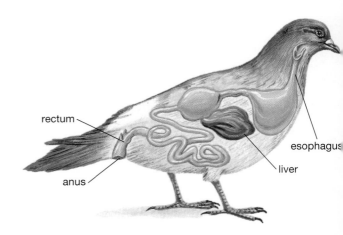

rectum

anus

esophagus

liver

Figure 30-9 Bird digestive adaptations

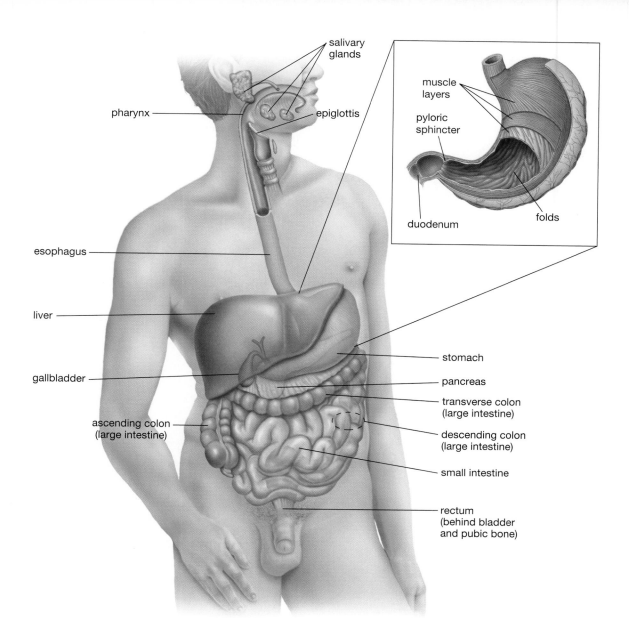

salivary glands

pharynx

epiglottis

esophagus

liver

gallbladder

ascending colon
(large intestine)

muscle layers

pyloric sphincter

duodenum

folds

stomach

pancreas

transverse colon
(large intestine)

descending colon
(large intestine)

small intestine

rectum
(behind bladder
and pubic bone)

Figure 30-10   The human digestive tract
Media Activity 30.1 The Digestive System

(a) Before swallowing

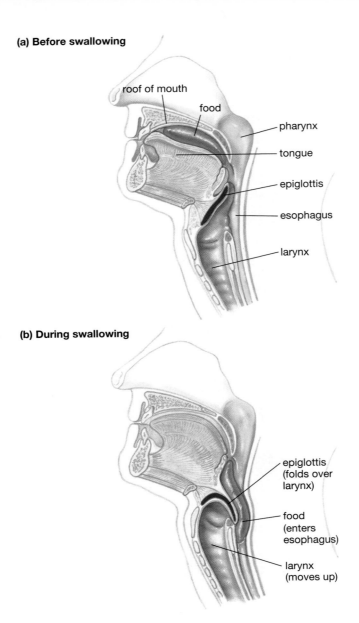

roof of mouth

food

pharynx

tongue

epiglottis

esophagus

larynx

(b) During swallowing

epiglottis
(folds over
larynx)

food
(enters
esophagus)

larynx
(moves up)

Figure 30-11   The challenge of swallowing
Media Activity 30.2 Physical and Chemical Digestion

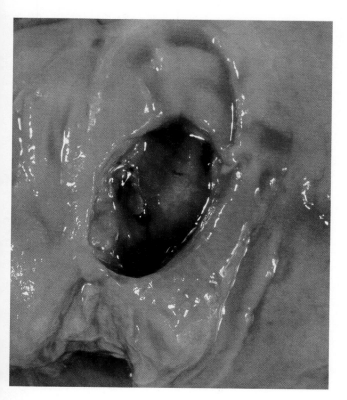

Figure E30-2   An ulcer

(a) Small intestine

fold of
intestinal
lining

**(b) Fold of intestinal
lining**

villi

(c) Villus

lacteal

capillaries

intestinal
gland

arteriole

lymph
vessel

venule

(d) Cells of villi

microvilli

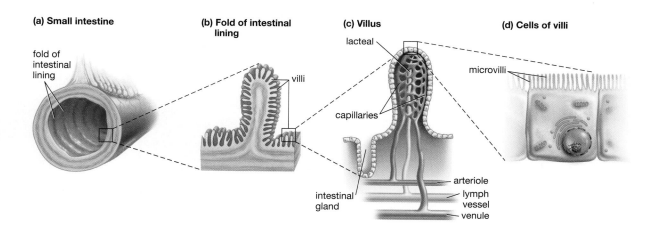

Figure 30-12   The small intestine

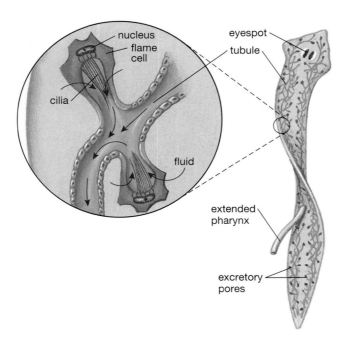

Figure 31-1 The simple excretory system of a flatworm

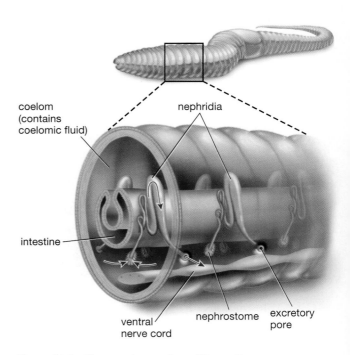

Figure 31-2 The excretory system of the earthworm

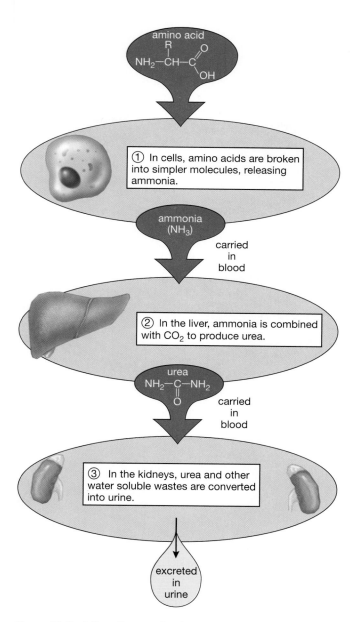

Figure 31-3 A flow diagram showing the formation and excretion of urea

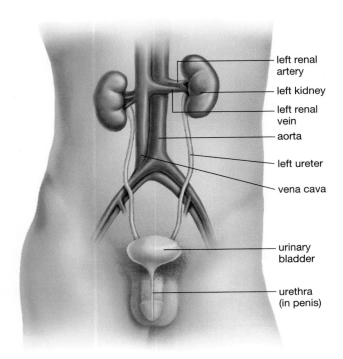

left renal
artery

left kidney

left renal
vein

aorta

left ureter

vena cava

urinary
bladder

urethra
(in penis)

Figure 31-4 The human urinary system
Media Activity 31.4 Urinary System Anatomy

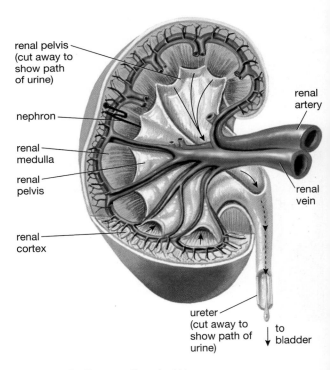

renal pelvis
(cut away to
show path
of urine)

nephron

renal
medulla

renal
pelvis

renal
cortex

renal
artery

renal
vein

ureter
(cut away to
show path of
urine)

to
bladder

Figure 31-5 Cross section of a kidney

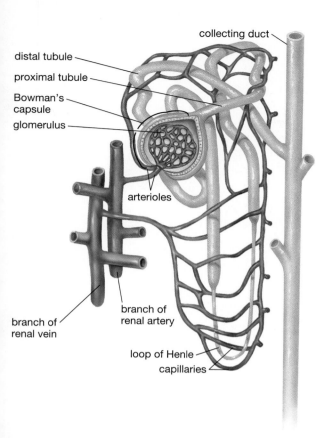

Figure 31-6   An individual nephron and its blood supply

Figure 31-7   Urine formation in the nephron

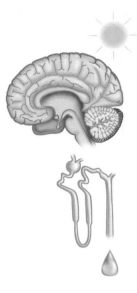

Figure 31-8 Dehydration stimulates ADH release and water retention

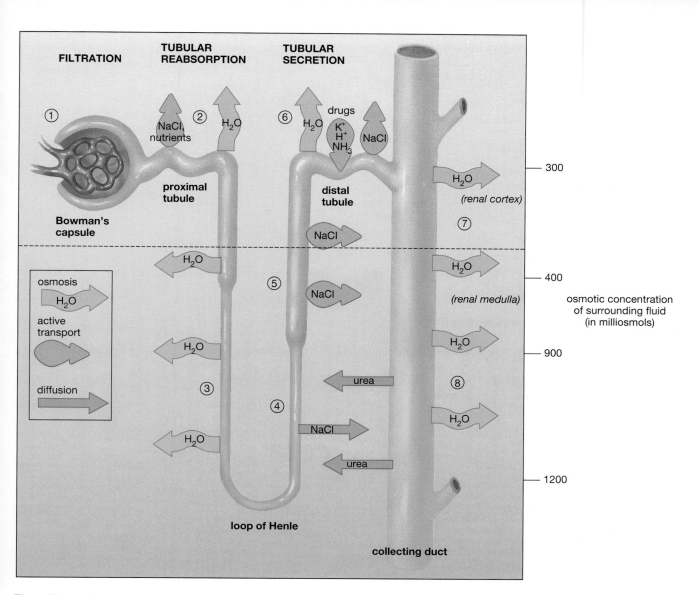

Figure E31-1 Details of urine formation
Media Activity 31.2 Urine Formation

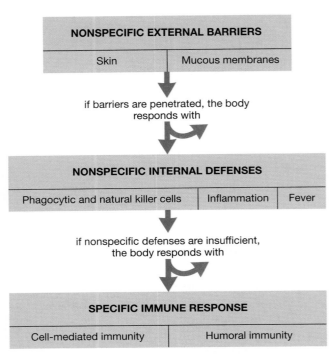

NONSPECIFIC EXTERNAL BARRIERS

Skin	Mucous membranes

if barriers are penetrated, the body
responds with

NONSPECIFIC INTERNAL DEFENSES

Phagocytic and natural killer cells	Inflammation	Fever

if nonspecific defenses are insufficient,
the body responds with

SPECIFIC IMMUNE RESPONSE

Cell-mediated immunity	Humoral immunity

Figure 32-1 Levels of defense against infection
Media Activity 32.1 Defense Against Infectious Agents

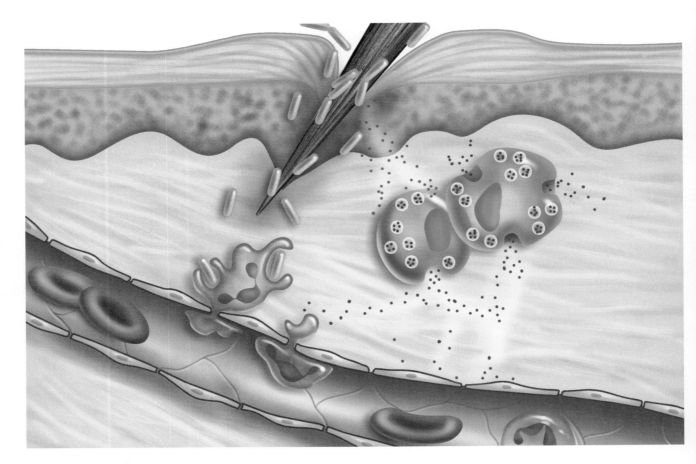

Figure 32-4 The inflammatory response
Media Activity 32.2 Inflammation

Table 32-1 The Body's Cellular Armory

Mast Cells	Connective tissue cells that release histamine; important in the inflammatory response
Neutrophils	White blood cells that engulf invading microbes
Macrophages	White blood cells that engulf invading microbes and present antigens
Natural killer cells	White blood cells that destroy infected or cancerous cells
B cells	Lymphocytes that produce antibodies
Plasma cells	Offspring of B cells that secrete antibodies into the bloodstream
Memory B cells	Offspring of B cells that provide future immunity against invasion by the same antigen
T cells	Lymphocytes that regulate the immune response or kill certain types of cells
Cytotoxic T cells	Offspring of T cells that destroy specific targeted cells, including foreign eukaryotic cells, infected body cells, or cancerous body cells
Helper T cells	Offspring of T cells that stimulate immune responses by both B cells and cytotoxic T cells
Memory T cells	Offspring of T cells that provide future immunity against invasion by the same antigen

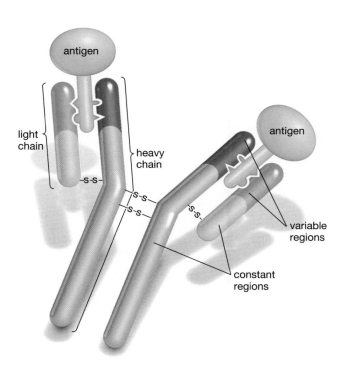

Figure 32-5   Antibody structure

229

(a) Antibody bound to the surface of a B cell recognizes microbes bearing foreign antigens.

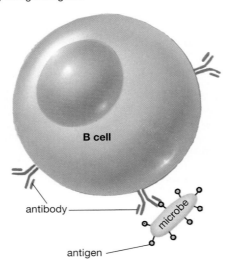

(b) Circulating antibodies bind to antigens on a microbe and promote phagocytosis by a macrophage.

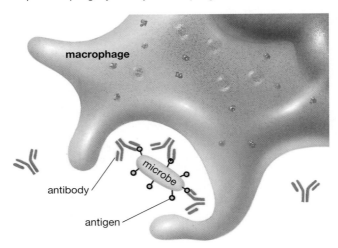

Figure 32-6 Some functions of antibodies

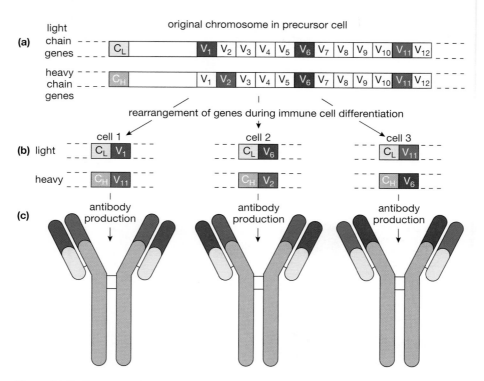

Figure 32-7 Recombination produces antibody genes

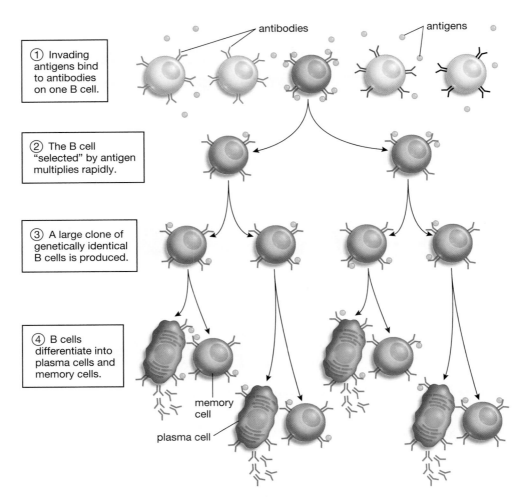

Figure 32-8 Clonal selection among B cells by invading antigens
Media Activity 32.3 Clonal Selection

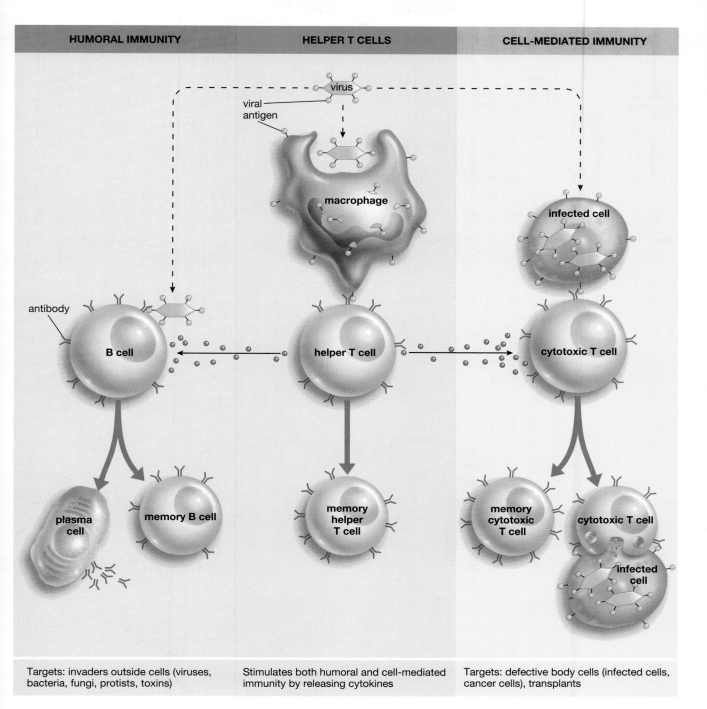

Figure 32-11 A summary of humoral and cell-mediated immune responses

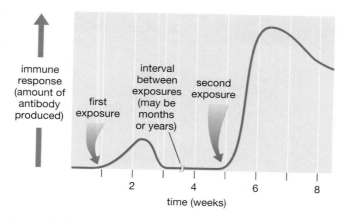

Figure 32-12 Memory cells and the immune response

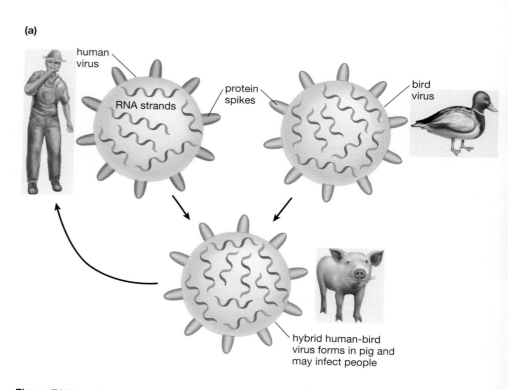

Figure E32-1a Formation of deadly new strains of influenza

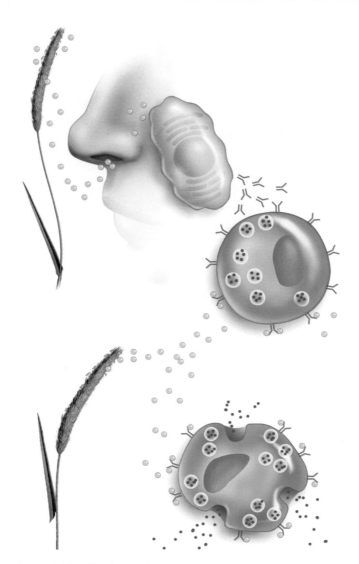

Figure 32-13   Allergic reactions

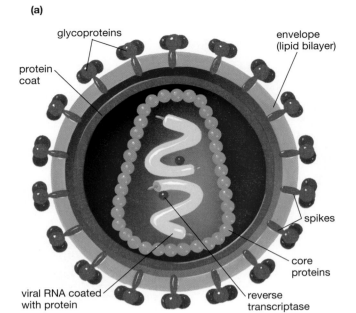

Figure 32-14a   HIV
Media Activity 32.4 Effects of HIV on the Immune System

Table 33-1 How Cells Communicate

Communication		Chemical Messengers	Mechanism of Transmission	Examples
Direct		Ions, small molecules	Direct movement through gap junctions linking cytoplasm of adjacent cells	Ions flowing between cardiac muscle cells
Paracrine		Local hormones	Diffusion through extracellular fluid to nearby cells bearing receptors	Prostaglandins
Endocrine		Hormones	Carried in the bloodstream to near or distant cells bearing receptors	Insulin
Synaptic		Neurotransmitters	Diffusion from a neuron across a narrow synaptic cleft to cell bearing receptors	Acetylcholine

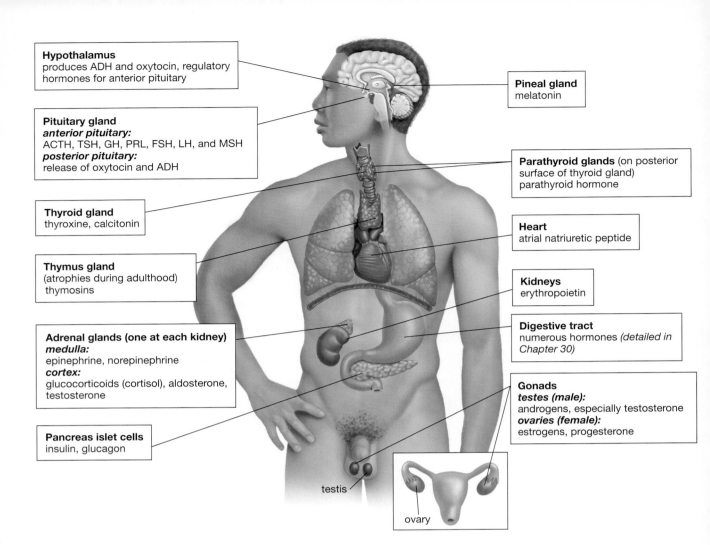

Hypothalamus
produces ADH and oxytocin, regulatory hormones for anterior pituitary

Pituitary gland
anterior pituitary:
ACTH, TSH, GH, PRL, FSH, LH, and MSH
posterior pituitary:
release of oxytocin and ADH

Thyroid gland
thyroxine, calcitonin

Thymus gland
(atrophies during adulthood)
thymosins

Adrenal glands (one at each kidney)
medulla:
epinephrine, norepinephrine
cortex:
glucocorticoids (cortisol), aldosterone, testosterone

Pancreas islet cells
insulin, glucagon

Pineal gland
melatonin

Parathyroid glands (on posterior surface of thyroid gland)
parathyroid hormone

Heart
atrial natriuretic peptide

Kidneys
erythropoietin

Digestive tract
numerous hormones *(detailed in Chapter 30)*

Gonads
testes (male):
androgens, especially testosterone
ovaries (female):
estrogens, progesterone

testis

ovary

Figure 33-1   Major mammalian endocrine glands and their secretions

238

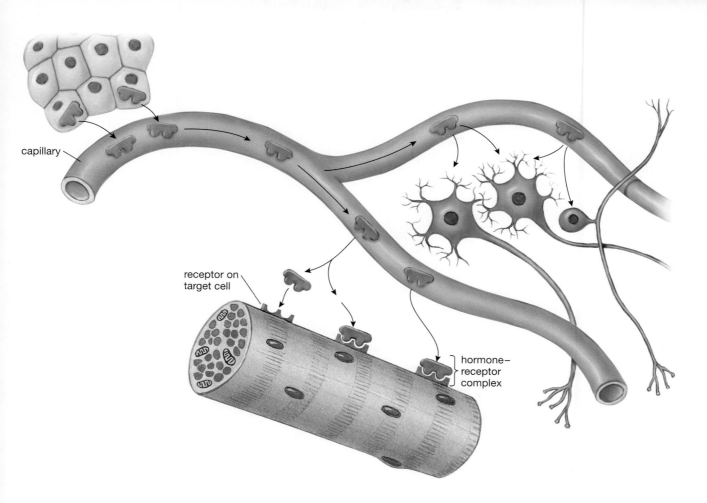

Figure 33-2 Endocrine glands, hormones, and target cells

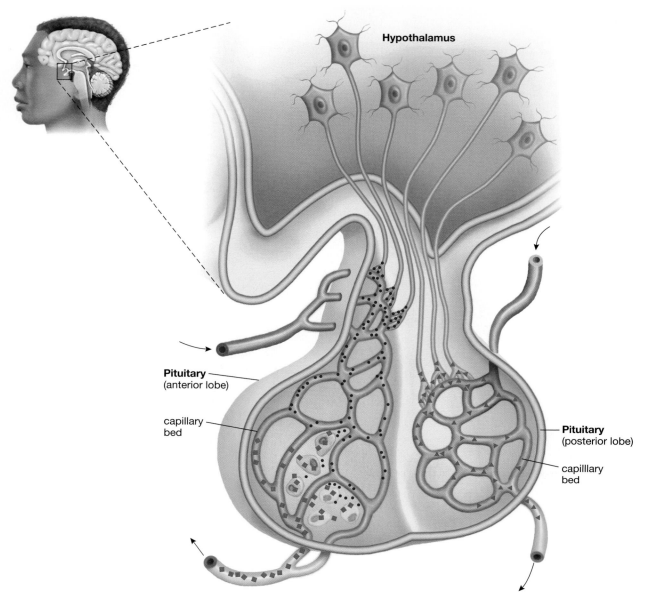

Hypothalamus

Pituitary
(anterior lobe)

capillary
bed

Pituitary
(posterior lobe)

capilllary
bed

Figure 33-3 The hypothalamus controls the pituitary
Media Activity 33.1 Hypothalamic Control of the Pituitary

(a) Amino acid and peptide hormones

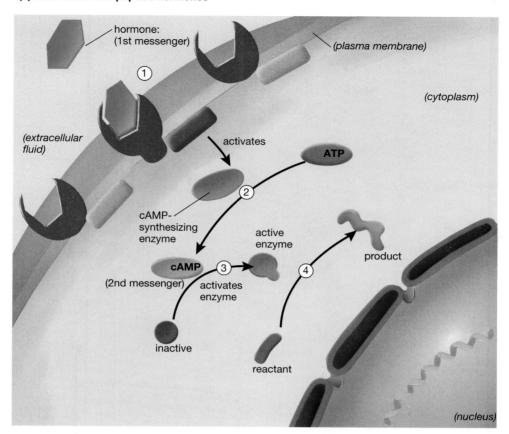

Figure E33-1a Mechanisms of hormone action
Media Activity 33.2 Modes of Actions of Hormones

(b) Steroid hormones

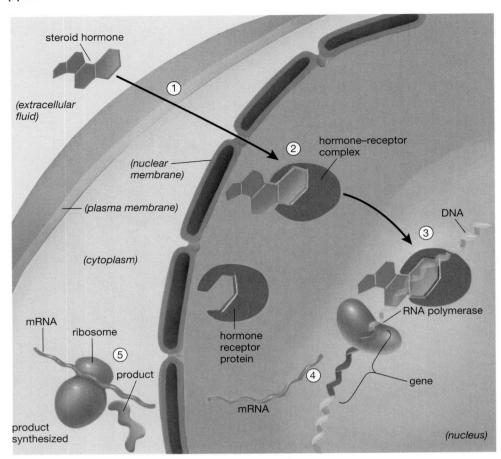

Figure E33-1b Mechanisms of hormone action
Media Activity 33.2 Modes of Action of Hormones

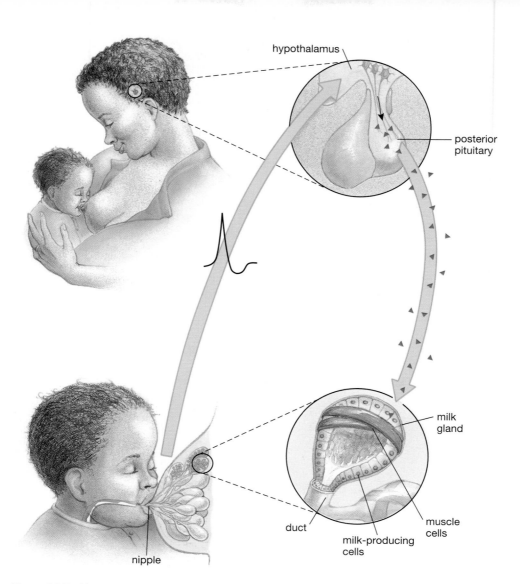

Figure 33-5 Hormones and breast-feeding

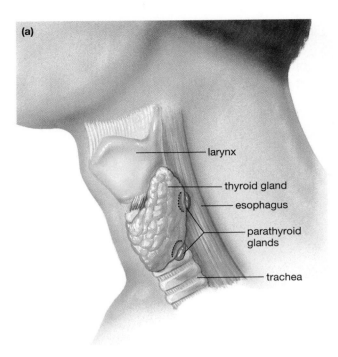

(a)

larynx

thyroid gland

esophagus

parathyroid glands

trachea

Figure 33-6a The thyroid and parathyroid glands

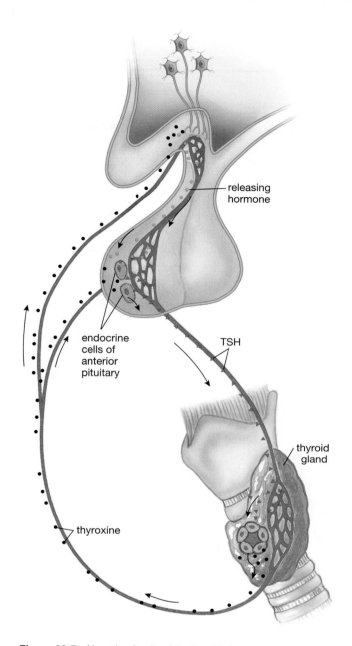

releasing
hormone

endocrine
cells of
anterior
pituitary

TSH

thyroid
gland

thyroxine

Figure 33-7 Negative feedback in thyroid gland function

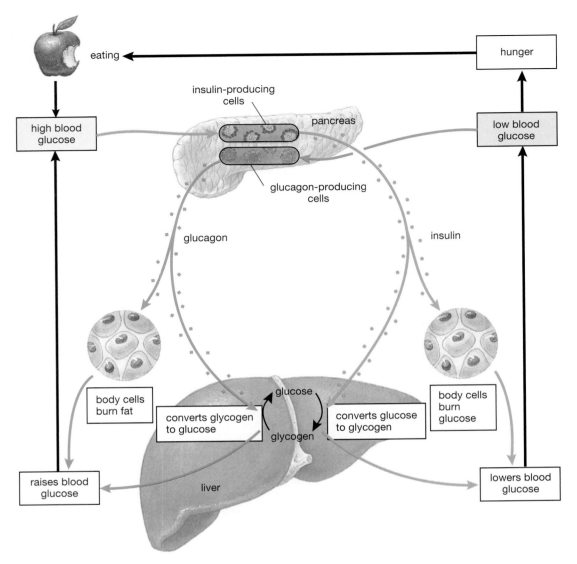

Figure 33-8 The pancreas controls blood glucose levels

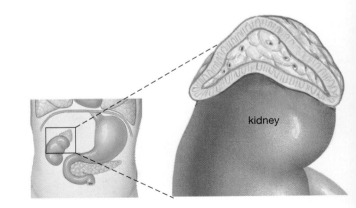

Figure 33-9 The adrenal glands

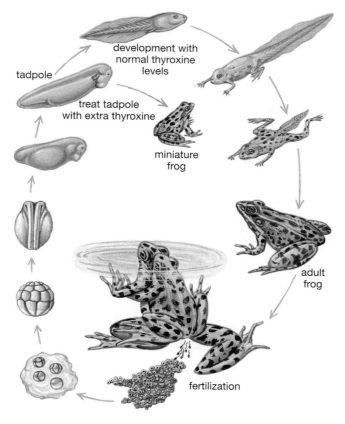

tadpole

development with
normal thyroxine
levels

treat tadpole
with extra thyroxine

miniature
frog

adult
frog

fertilization

Figure 33-11 Thyroxine controls metamorphosis in amphibians

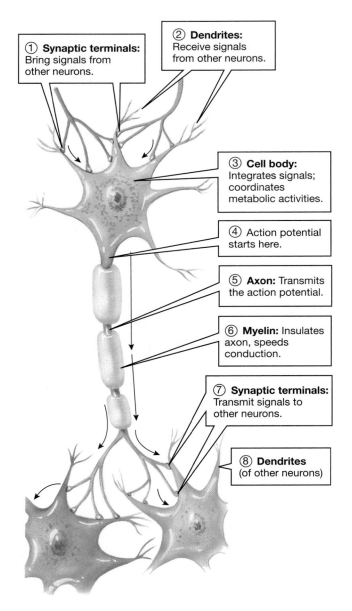

① **Synaptic terminals:** Bring signals from other neurons.

② **Dendrites:** Receive signals from other neurons.

③ **Cell body:** Integrates signals; coordinates metabolic activities.

④ Action potential starts here.

⑤ **Axon:** Transmits the action potential.

⑥ **Myelin:** Insulates axon, speeds conduction.

⑦ **Synaptic terminals:** Transmit signals to other neurons.

⑧ **Dendrites** (of other neurons)

Figure 34-1 A nerve cell, showing its specialized parts and their functions

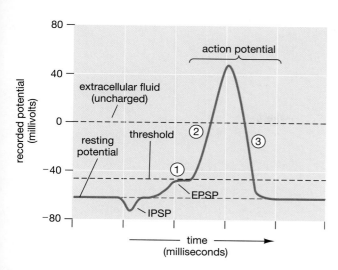

Figure 34-2 The electrical events during an action potential

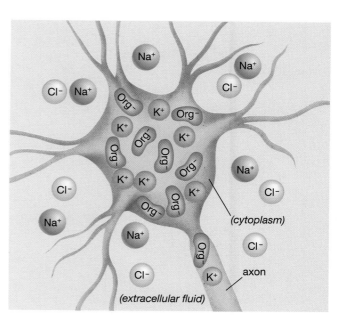

Figure E34-1 The neuron maintains ionic gradients
Media Activity 34.1 The Nervous System: Electrical Signals

resting potential

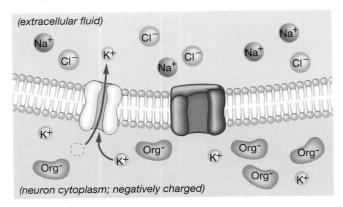

Figure 34-UN02 Resting potential
Media Activity 34.1 The Nervous System: Electrical Signals

action potential **resting potential restored**

Figure 34-UN03 Action potential, resting potential restored
Media Activity 34.1 The Nervous System: Electrical Signals

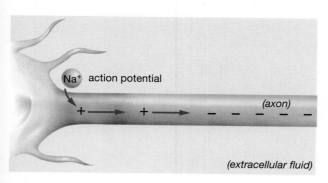

Figure 34-UN04   Action potential
Media Activity 34.1 The Nervous System: Electrical Signals

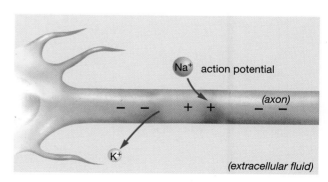

Figure 34-UN05   Action potential
Media Activity 34.1 The Nervous System: Electrical Signals

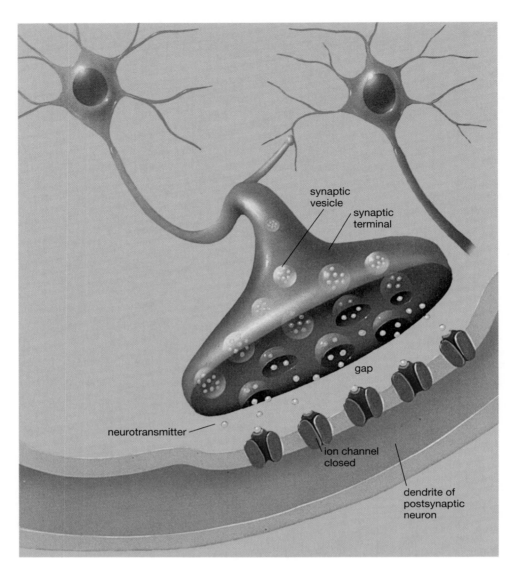

Figure 34-3 The structure and operation of the synapse
Media Activity 34.2 The Nervous System: Synapse

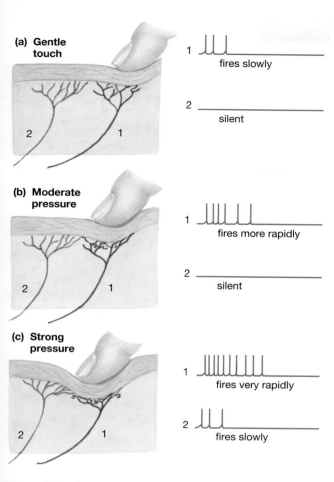

(a) Gentle touch

1 — fires slowly

2 — silent

(b) Moderate pressure

1 — fires more rapidly

2 — silent

(c) Strong pressure

1 — fires very rapidly

2 — fires slowly

Figure 34-4   Signaling stimulus intensity

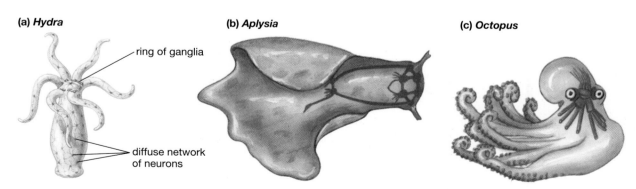

(a) Hydra

ring of ganglia

diffuse network of neurons

(b) Aplysia

(c) Octopus

Figure 34-5   Nerve net and cephalization

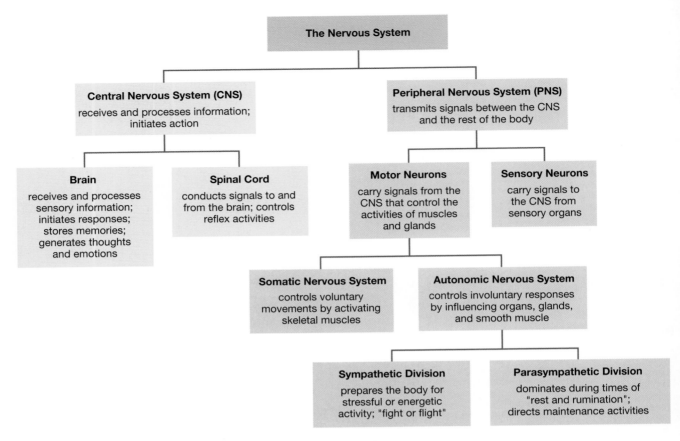

Figure 34-6 The organization and functions of the vertebrate nervous system

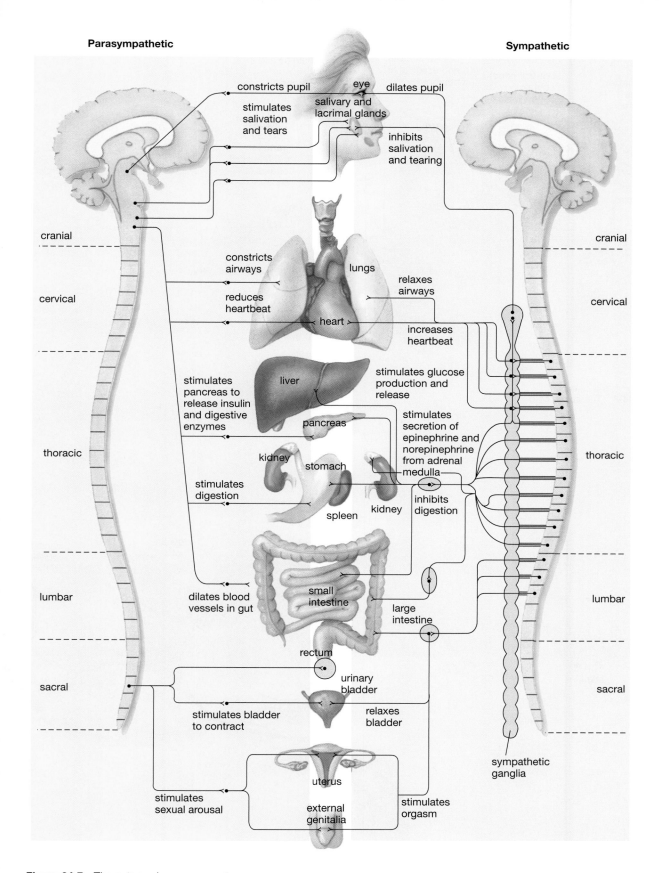

Parasympathetic

Sympathetic

constricts pupil
eye
dilates pupil

stimulates salivation and tears

salivary and lacrimal glands

inhibits salivation and tearing

cranial

cranial

constricts airways

lungs

relaxes airways

cervical

cervical

reduces heartbeat

heart

increases heartbeat

stimulates pancreas to release insulin and digestive enzymes

liver

stimulates glucose production and release

pancreas

stimulates secretion of epinephrine and norepinephrine from adrenal medulla

thoracic

kidney

stomach

thoracic

stimulates digestion

spleen

kidney

inhibits digestion

small intestine

dilates blood vessels in gut

large intestine

lumbar

lumbar

rectum

urinary bladder

sacral

sacral

stimulates bladder to contract

relaxes bladder

sympathetic ganglia

uterus

stimulates sexual arousal

external genitalia

stimulates orgasm

Figure 34-7 The autonomic nervous system

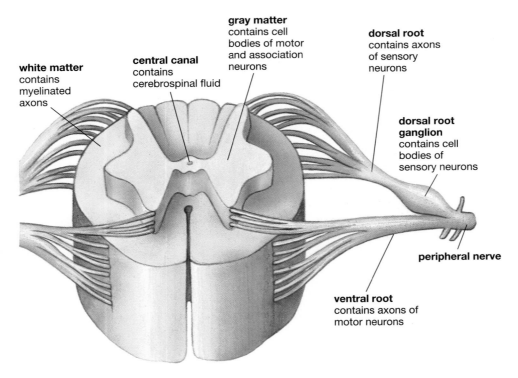

white matter
contains
myelinated
axons

central canal
contains
cerebrospinal fluid

gray matter
contains cell
bodies of motor
and association
neurons

dorsal root
contains axons
of sensory
neurons

**dorsal root
ganglion**
contains cell
bodies of
sensory neurons

peripheral nerve

ventral root
contains axons of
motor neurons

Figure 34-8 The spinal cord

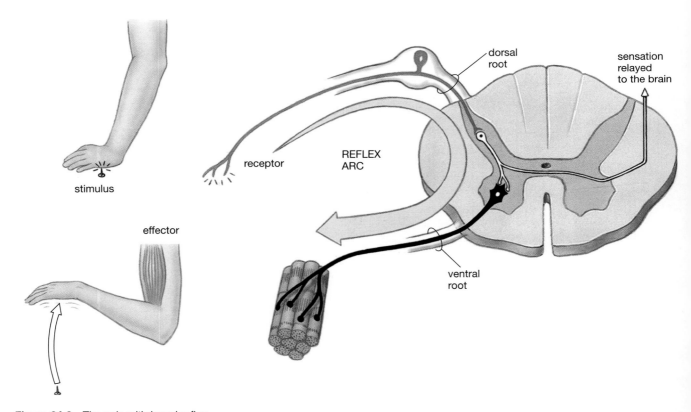

stimulus

receptor

REFLEX
ARC

dorsal
root

sensation
relayed
to the brain

effector

ventral
root

Figure 34-9 The pain-withdrawal reflex
Media Activity 34.3 Reflex Arc

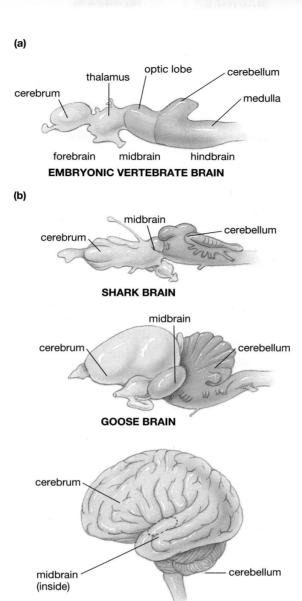

(a)

cerebrum
thalamus
optic lobe
cerebellum
medulla

forebrain   midbrain   hindbrain

EMBRYONIC VERTEBRATE BRAIN

(b)

midbrain
cerebrum
cerebellum

SHARK BRAIN

midbrain
cerebrum
cerebellum

GOOSE BRAIN

cerebrum

midbrain
(inside)
cerebellum

HUMAN BRAIN

Figure 34-10   A comparison of vertebrate brains

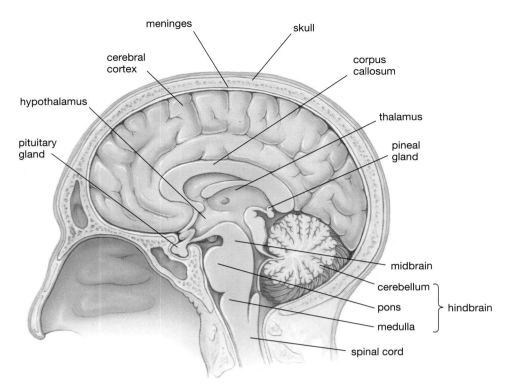

Figure 34-11 The human brain
Media Activity 34.4 Brain Structure

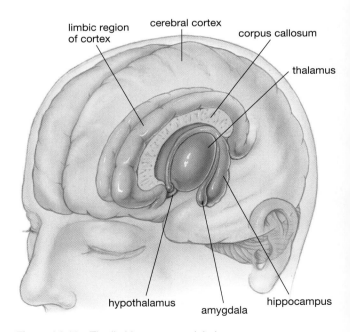

Figure 34-12 The limbic system and thalamus

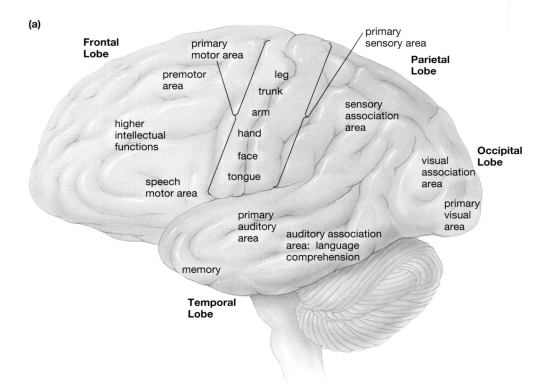

(a)

Frontal Lobe

primary motor area

premotor area

higher intellectual functions

speech motor area

leg
trunk
arm
hand
face
tongue

primary sensory area

Parietal Lobe

sensory association area

Occipital Lobe

visual association area

primary visual area

primary auditory area

auditory association area: language comprehension

memory

Temporal Lobe

(b)

Left hemisphere

1. Controls right side of body
2. Input from right visual field, right ear, left nostril
3. Centers for language, mathematics

Right hemisphere

1. Controls left side of body
2. Input from left visual field, left ear, right nostril
3. Centers for spatial perception, music, creativity

Figure 34-13 The cerebral cortex

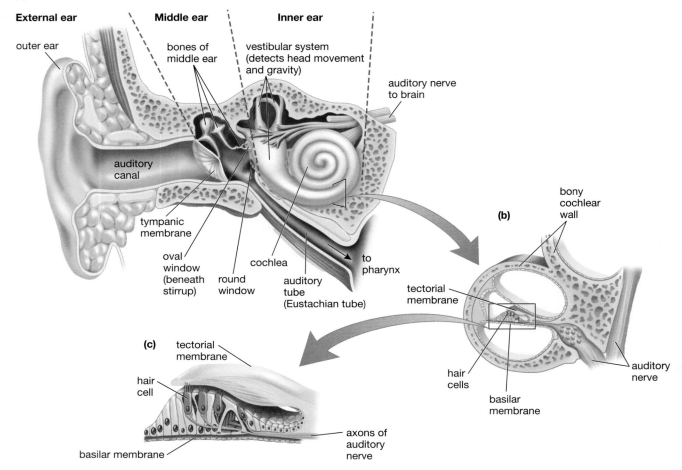

External ear

outer ear

auditory
canal

Middle ear

bones of
middle ear

tympanic
membrane

oval
window
(beneath
stirrup)

round
window

Inner ear

vestibular system
(detects head movement
and gravity)

auditory nerve
to brain

cochlea

auditory
tube
(Eustachian tube)

to
pharynx

(b)

bony
cochlear
wall

tectorial
membrane

hair
cells

basilar
membrane

auditory
nerve

(c)

tectorial
membrane

hair
cell

basilar membrane

axons of
auditory
nerve

Figure 34-15 The human ear

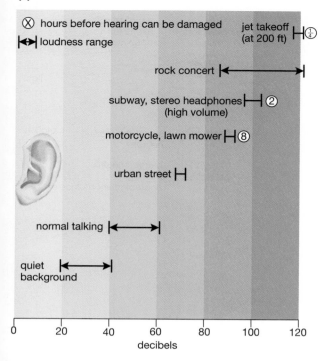

(b)

(X) hours before hearing can be damaged

|◄►| loudness range

jet takeoff
(at 200 ft) |--| (¼)

rock concert |◄--------►|

subway, stereo headphones |--| (2)
(high volume)

motorcycle, lawn mower |--| (8)

urban street |--|

normal talking |◄----►|

quiet
background |◄--►|

0   20   40   60   80   100   120
decibels

Figure 34-16b Loud sounds can damage hair cells

(a) Compound eyes

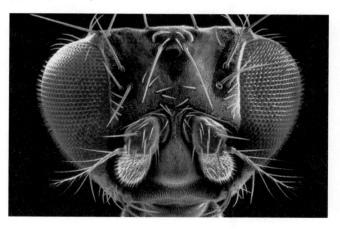

(b) Ommatidia   **Single ommatidium**

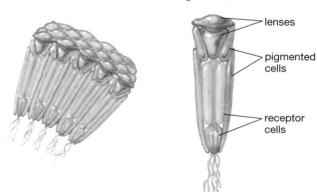

lenses

pigmented
cells

receptor
cells

Figure 34-17 Compound eyes

261

(a) Anatomy of the human eye

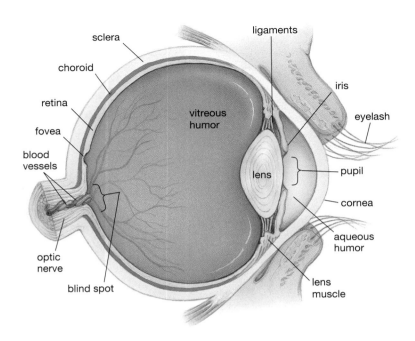

sclera
choroid
retina
fovea
blood vessels
optic nerve
blind spot
vitreous humor
ligaments
iris
eyelash
lens
pupil
cornea
aqueous humor
lens muscle

Figure 34-18 The human eye
Media Activity 34.5 Vertebrate Eye

(b) Layers of the retina

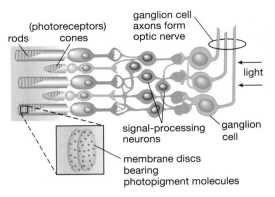

ganglion cell axons form optic nerve
(photoreceptors)
rods   cones
light
signal-processing neurons
ganglion cell
membrane discs bearing photopigment molecules

(a) Normal eye

retina

(b) Nearsighted eye (long eyeball)

(c) Farsighted eye (short eyeball)

Figure 34-19 Focusing in the human eye

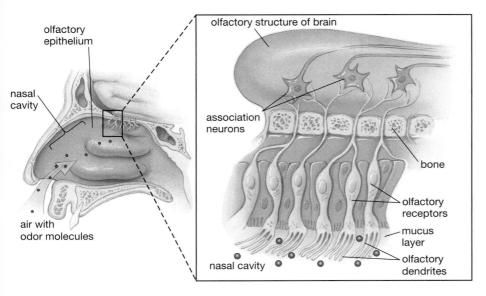

Figure 34-22 Human olfactory receptors

(a) The human tongue

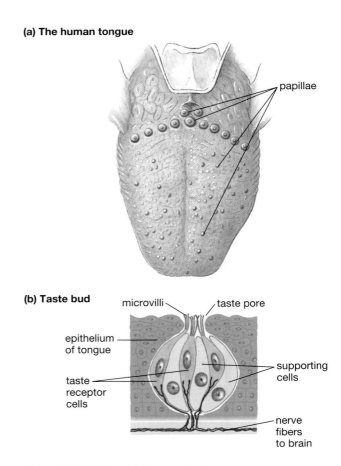

papillae

(b) Taste bud

microvilli

taste pore

epithelium of tongue

taste receptor cells

supporting cells

nerve fibers to brain

Figure 34-23 Human taste receptors

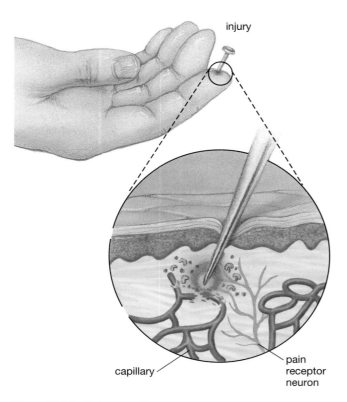

Figure 34-24   Pain perception

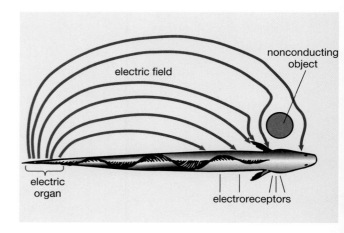

Figure 34-26   Electrolocation

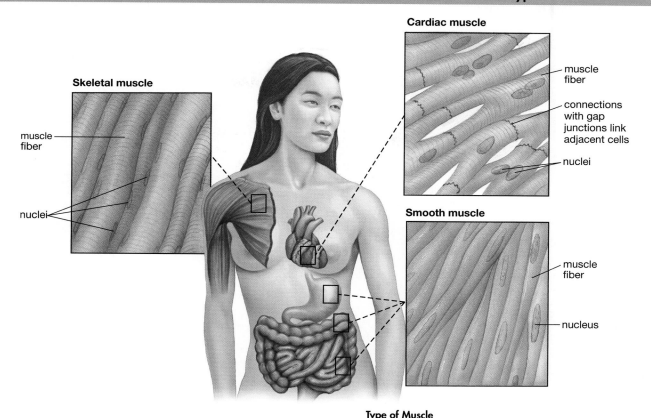

Skeletal muscle

muscle fiber

nuclei

Cardiac muscle

muscle fiber

connections with gap junctions link adjacent cells

nuclei

Smooth muscle

muscle fiber

nucleus

| | Type of Muscle | | |
Property	Smooth	Cardiac	Skeletal
Muscle appearance	Nonstriated	Irregular striations	Regular striations
Cell shape	Spindle	Branched	Spindle
Number of nuclei	One per cell	One or more per cell	Many per cell
Speed of contraction	Slow	Intermediate	Slow to rapid
Contraction caused by	Spontaneous, stretch, nervous system, hormones	Spontaneous	Nervous system
Function	Controls movement of substances through hollow organs and tubes	Pumps blood	Moves the skeleton
Voluntary control	Usually no*	Usually no*	Yes

*Smooth and cardiac muscles usually contract without conscious control. In some cases, however, their contractions may be initiated or modified voluntarily. For example, heart rate can be voluntarily slowed after biofeedback training, and bladder contractions are initiated consciously.

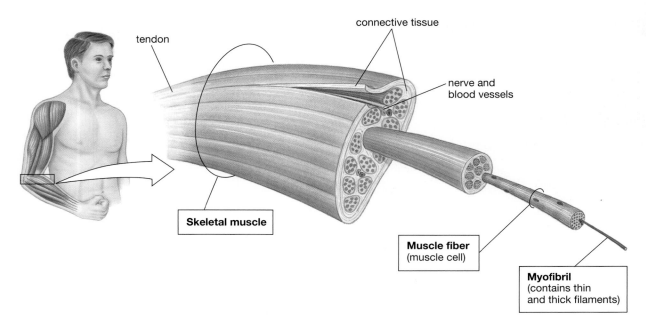

tendon

connective tissue

nerve and
blood vessels

Skeletal muscle

Muscle fiber
(muscle cell)

Myofibril
(contains thin
and thick filaments)

Figure 35-1   Skeletal muscle structure
Media Activity 35.1 Muscle Structure

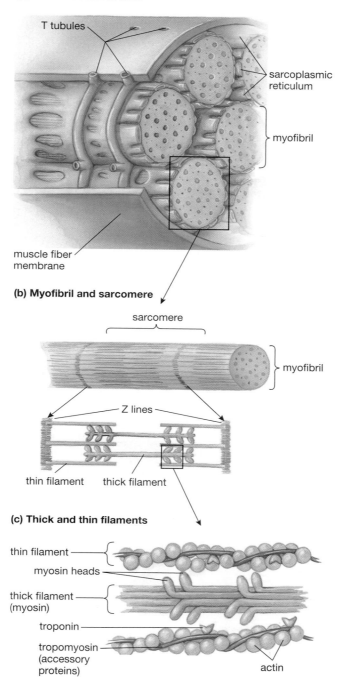

(a) Cross section of fiber

T tubules

sarcoplasmic reticulum

myofibril

muscle fiber membrane

(b) Myofibril and sarcomere

sarcomere

myofibril

Z lines

thin filament   thick filament

(c) Thick and thin filaments

thin filament

myosin heads

thick filament (myosin)

troponin

tropomyosin (accessory proteins)

actin

Figure 35-2 A skeletal muscle fiber
Media Activity 35.1 Muscle Structure

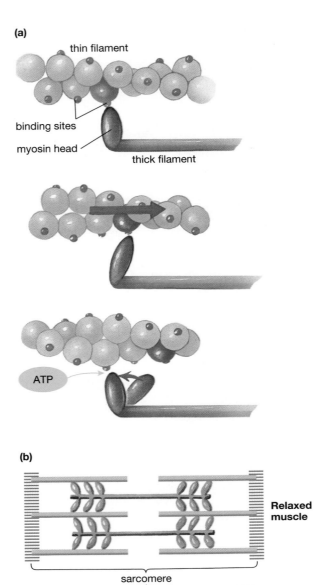

(a)

thin filament

binding sites

myosin head

thick filament

ATP

(b)

Relaxed muscle

sarcomere

Contracted muscle

Figure 35-3 Muscle contraction
Media Activity 35.2 Muscle Contraction

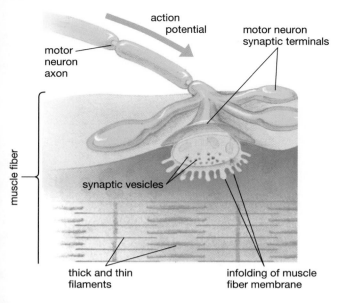

action
potential

motor neuron
synaptic terminals

motor
neuron
axon

muscle fiber

synaptic vesicles

thick and thin
filaments

infolding of muscle
fiber membrane

Figure 35-4a The neuromuscular junction

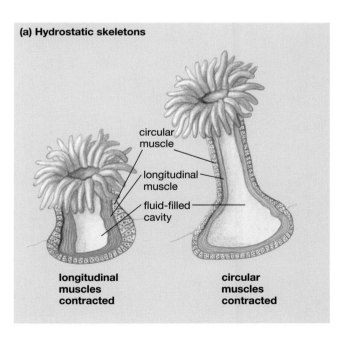

(a) Hydrostatic skeletons

circular
muscle

longitudinal
muscle

fluid-filled
cavity

**longitudinal
muscles
contracted**

**circular
muscles
contracted**

Figure 35-5a Not all skeletons are made of bone; hydrostatic skeletons

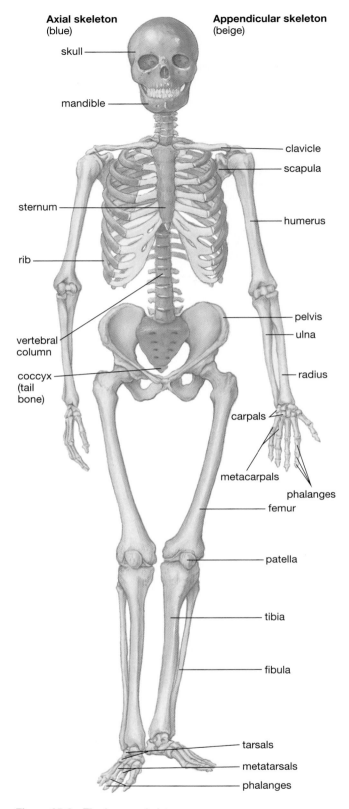

Axial skeleton (blue)

Appendicular skeleton (beige)

skull

mandible

clavicle

scapula

sternum

humerus

rib

vertebral column

pelvis

ulna

radius

coccyx (tail bone)

carpals

metacarpals

phalanges

femur

patella

tibia

fibula

tarsals

metatarsals

phalanges

Figure 35-6   The human skeleton

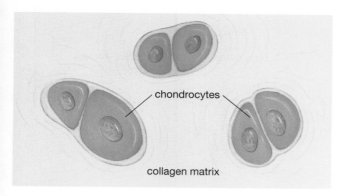

Figure 35-8 Cartilage

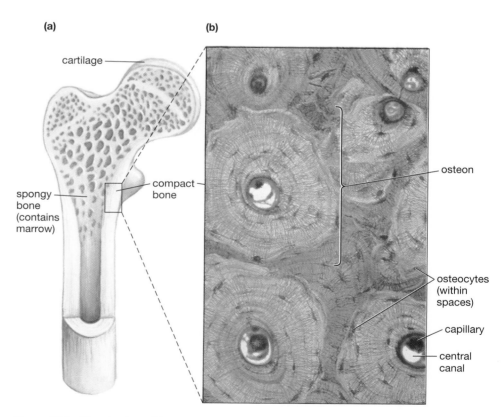

Figure 35-9 The structure of bone

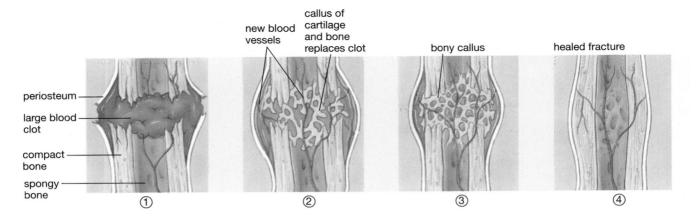

Figure E35-1 The steps in bone repair

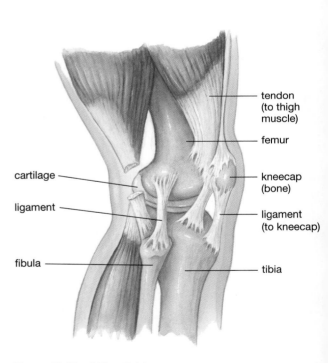

Figure 35-10 A hinge joint

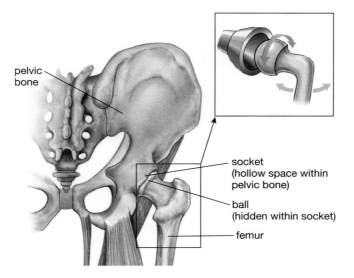

pelvic
bone

socket
(hollow space within
pelvic bone)

ball
(hidden within socket)

femur

Figure 35-11   Ball and socket joint

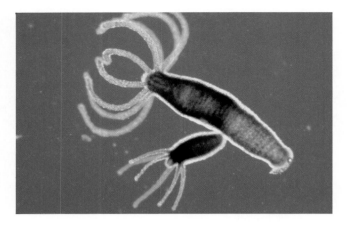

Figure 36-1 Budding

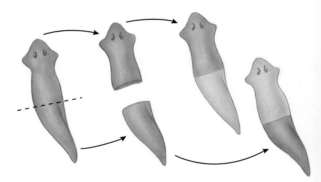

Figure 36-2 Fission followed by regeneration

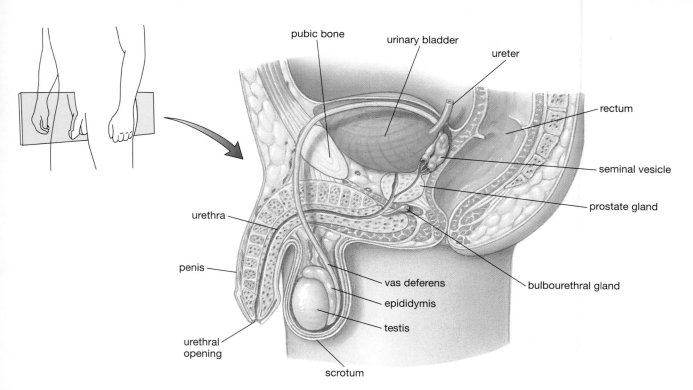

Figure 36-8 The human male reproductive tract
Media Activity 36.1 Human Reproductive System

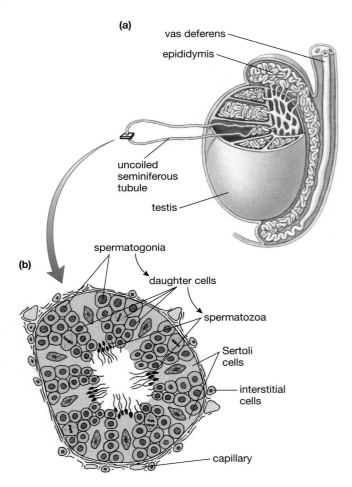

(a)

vas deferens

epididymis

uncoiled
seminiferous
tubule

testis

(b)

spermatogonia

daughter cells

spermatozoa

Sertoli
cells

interstitial
cells

capillary

Figure 36-9   The structures involved in spermatogenesis

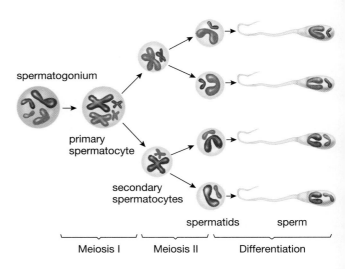

spermatogonium

primary
spermatocyte

secondary
spermatocytes

spermatids   sperm

Meiosis I   Meiosis II   Differentiation

Figure 36-10   Sperm are produced by meiosis

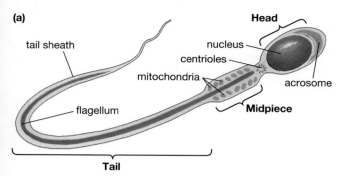

(a)

tail sheath

flagellum

Tail

mitochondria

centrioles

nucleus

Head

acrosome

Midpiece

Figure 36-11a   A human sperm cell

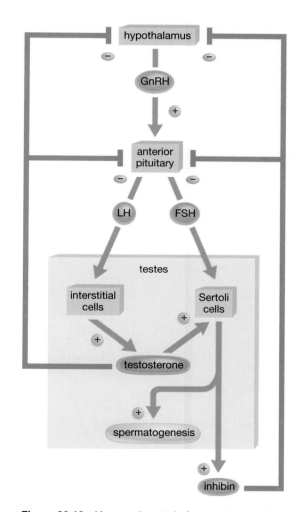

Figure 36-12   Hormonal control of spermatogenesis

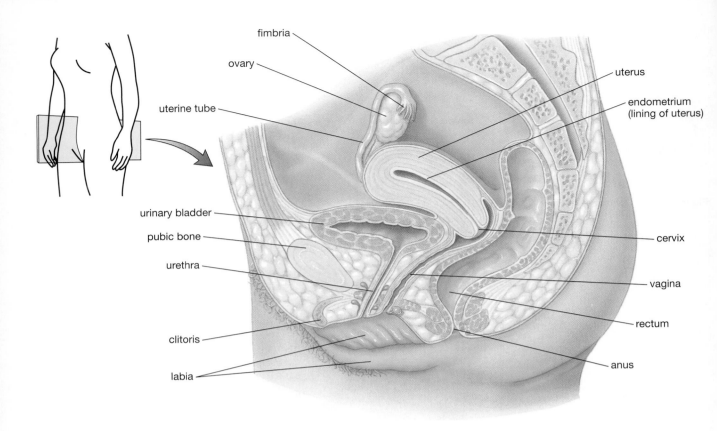

Figure 36-13 The human female reproductive tract
Media Activity 36.1 Human Reproductive System

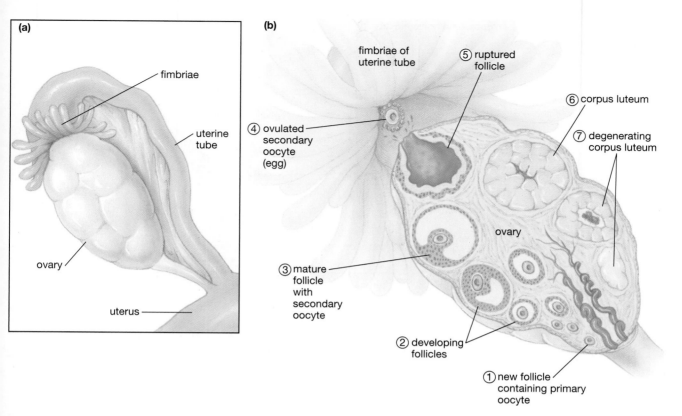

(a)

fimbriae

uterine tube

ovary

uterus

(b)

fimbriae of uterine tube

④ ovulated secondary oocyte (egg)

⑤ ruptured follicle

⑥ corpus luteum

⑦ degenerating corpus luteum

ovary

③ mature follicle with secondary oocyte

② developing follicles

① new follicle containing primary oocyte

Figure 36-14   The structures involved in oogenesis

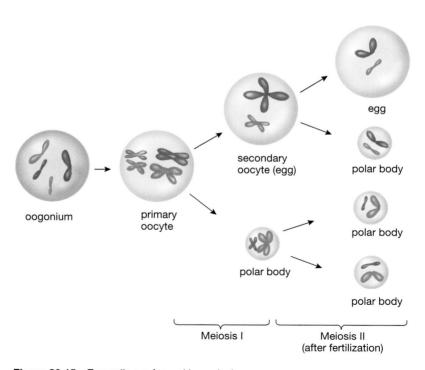

oogonium

primary oocyte

secondary oocyte (egg)

egg

polar body

polar body

polar body

polar body

Meiosis I

Meiosis II (after fertilization)

Figure 36-15   Egg cells are formed by meiosis

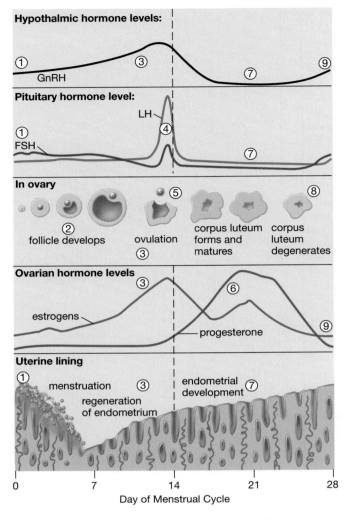

Figure E36-1 Hormonal control of the menstrual cycle
Media Activity 36.2 Hormonal Control of the Menstrual Cycle

(a) Relaxed

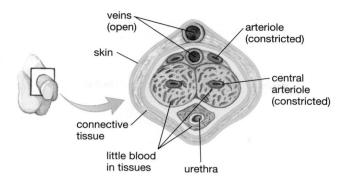

(b) Erect

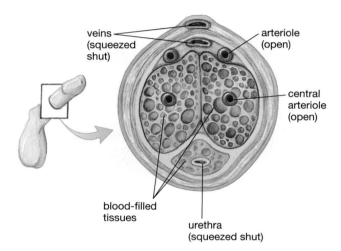

Figure 36-17 Changes in blood flow within the penis cause erection

(a)

secondary oocyte (egg)

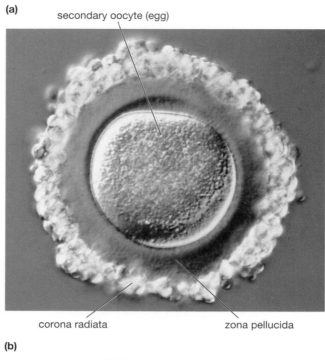

corona radiata   zona pellucida

(b)

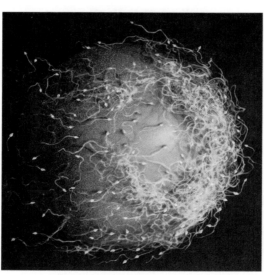

Figure 36-18 The secondary oocyte and fertilization

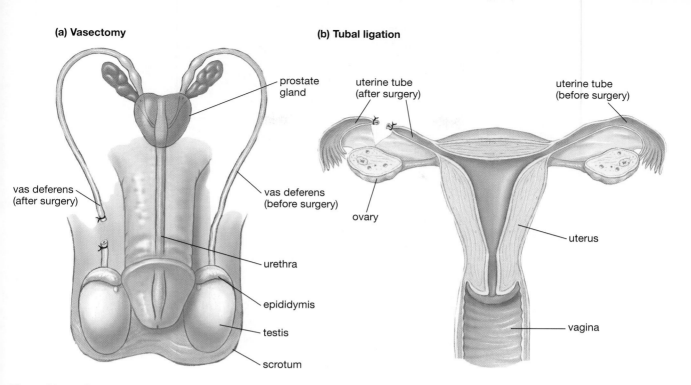

(a) Vasectomy

(b) Tubal ligation

prostate gland

uterine tube (after surgery)

uterine tube (before surgery)

vas deferens (after surgery)

vas deferens (before surgery)

ovary

uterus

urethra

epididymis

vagina

testis

scrotum

Figure 36-19 Sterilization

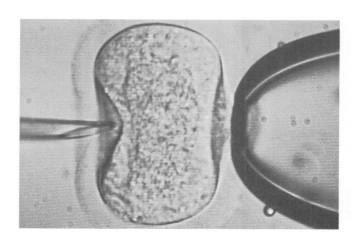

Figure E36-2 Piercing an egg to inject a sperm cell

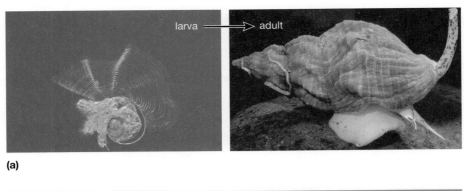

larva ⟶ adult

(a)

larva ⟶ adult

(b)

Figure 37-1 Indirect development

Figure 37-2   Direct development

Table 37-1 Vertebrate Embryonic Membranes

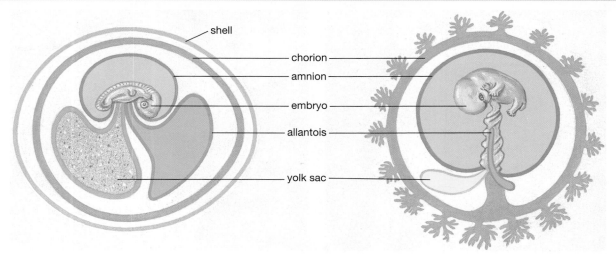

Reptile   Mammal

| Membrane | Reptilian Embryo | | Mammalian Embryo | |
	Structure	Function	Structure	Function
Chorion	Membrane lining inside shell	Acts as respiratory surface; regulates exchange of gases and water between embryo and air	Fetal contribution to placenta	Provides surface for exchange of gases, nutrients, and wastes between embryo and mother
Amnion	Sac surrounding embryo	Encloses embryo in fluid	Sac surrounding embryo	Encloses embryo in fluid
Allantois	Sac connected to embryonic urinary tract; capillary-rich membrane lining inside of chorion	Stores wastes (especially urine); acts as respiratory surface	Provides blood vessels of umbilical cord	Carries blood between embryo and placenta
Yolk sac	Membrane surrounding yolk	Contains yolk as food; digests yolk and transfers nutrients to embryo	"Empty" membranous sac	Forms blood cells

ectoderm   mesoderm   endoderm

(a) The blastula just before gastrulation.

(b) Cells migrate at the start of gastrulation.
Cells migrating in will form the endoderm and
mesoderm layers of the gastrula; the cells
remaining on the surface will form ectoderm.

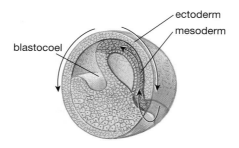

ectoderm
mesoderm
blastocoel

(c) Mesoderm differentiates.

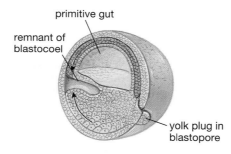

primitive gut
remnant of
blastocoel
yolk plug in
blastopore

Figure 37-3   A blastula becomes a gastrula
Media Activity 37.1 Stages of Animal
Development

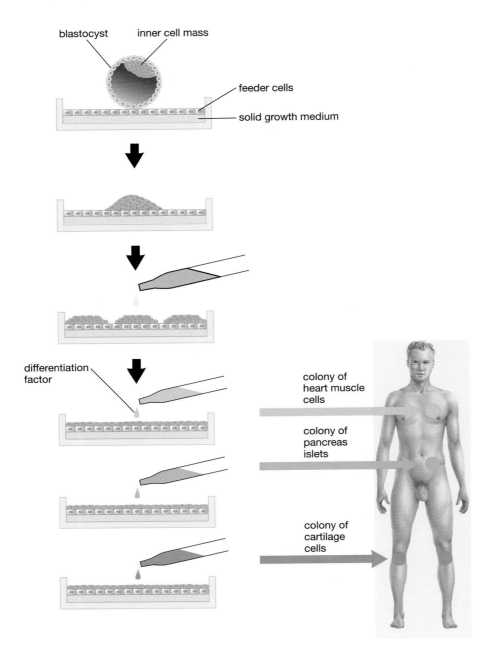

Figure E37-1 Culturing stem cells from a blastocyst

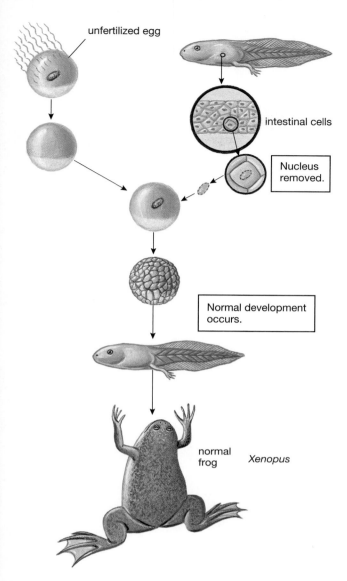

unfertilized egg

intestinal cells

Nucleus removed.

Normal development occurs.

normal frog   *Xenopus*

Figure 37-4   Cells retain all of their genes during differentiation
Media Activity 37.2 Control of Development

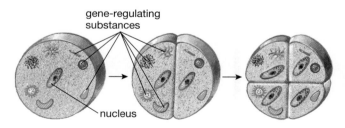

gene-regulating substances

nucleus

Figure 37-5   Distribution of gene-regulating substances

(a) Transplanted dorsal lip of blastopore induces formation of a second tadpole.

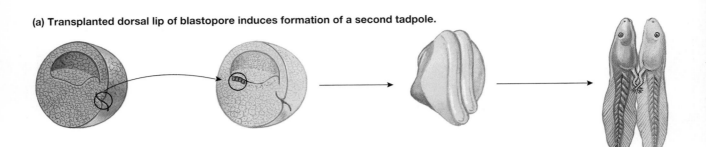

(b) Transplanted future skin cells are induced to form neural tissue.

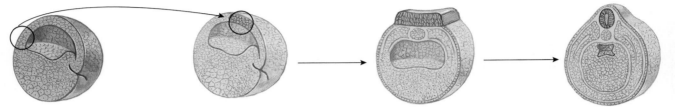

Figure 37-6 Induction and its role in differentiation

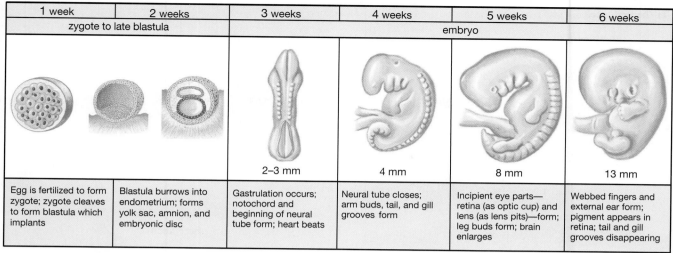

1 week	2 weeks	3 weeks	4 weeks	5 weeks	6 weeks
zygote to late blastula		embryo			
		2–3 mm	4 mm	8 mm	13 mm
Egg is fertilized to form zygote; zygote cleaves to form blastula which implants	Blastula burrows into endometrium; forms yolk sac, amnion, and embryonic disc	Gastrulation occurs; notochord and beginning of neural tube form; heart beats	Neural tube closes; arm buds, tail, and gill grooves form	Incipient eye parts— retina (as optic cup) and lens (as lens pits)—form; leg buds form; brain enlarges	Webbed fingers and external ear form; pigment appears in retina; tail and gill grooves disappearing

7 weeks	8 weeks	9 weeks	10 weeks	11 weeks	12 weeks
embryo		fetus			
18 mm	30 mm	50 mm	61 mm	73 mm	87 mm
Webbed toes form; bones begin to harden; back straightens; eyelids form	Upper limbs bend at elbows; genitalia begin to differentiate; fingers are distinct	Toes separate; eyelids develop; major parts of brain are present	Chin grows; nostrils separate; face appears human; genitals appear male or female	Well-defined neck appears; genitalia are complete; sucking reflex appears	

4 months	5 months	6 months	7 months	8 months	9 months
fetus					
140 mm	190 mm	230 mm	270 mm	300 mm	350 mm
Blood cells form; all major organs form; head and body hair appear; movements are felt by mother		Fetus may be viable if born; eyelids open; lungs and lung circulation develop; may suck thumb; fat deposited under skin		Fat deposits increase; body hair is lost; head hair is well developed; most senses are well developed; fetus turns head down in uterus	

for reference: 10 mm

Figure 37-7   Human embryonic development
Media Activity 37.3 Human Development

(a) The first week

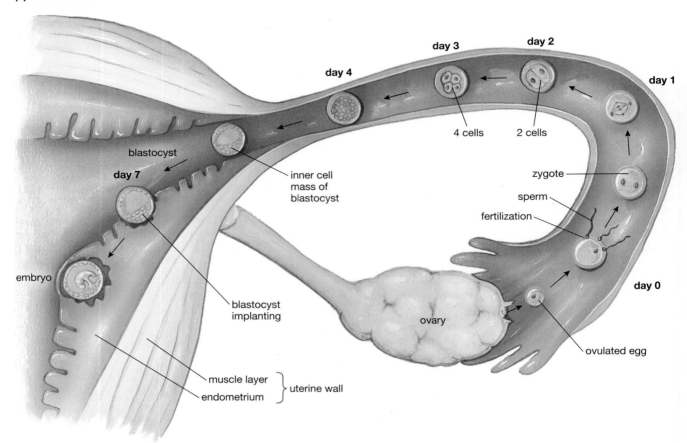

Figure 37-8a   The journey of the egg

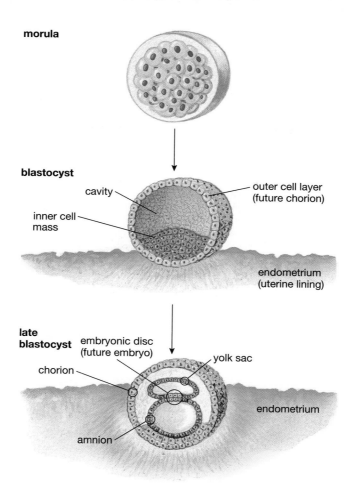

morula

blastocyst

cavity

inner cell mass

outer cell layer (future chorion)

endometrium (uterine lining)

late blastocyst

embryonic disc (future embryo)

chorion

yolk sac

amnion

endometrium

Figure 37-9 Human development during the first and second weeks

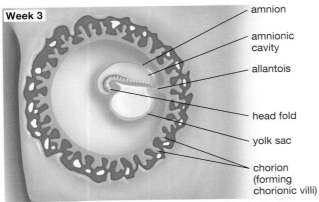

Week 3

- amnion
- amnionic cavity
- allantois
- head fold
- yolk sac
- chorion (forming chorionic villi)

(a) The embryo is suspended in amniotic fluid. Chorionic villi carry embryonic blood vessels into the endometrium, beginning the formation of the placenta.

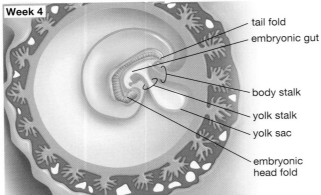

Week 4

- tail fold
- embryonic gut
- body stalk
- yolk stalk
- yolk sac
- embryonic head fold

(b) Endoderm forms the embryonic gut (future digestive tract), which is connected to the yolk sac by the yolk stalk. The body stalk carries embryonic blood into the chorionic villi.

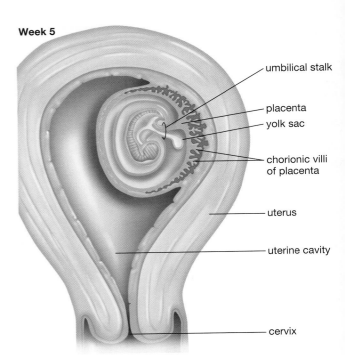

Week 5

- umbilical stalk
- placenta
- yolk sac
- chorionic villi of placenta
- uterus
- uterine cavity
- cervix

(c) The embryo bulges into the uterus, and the placenta is restricted to one side. The umbilical stalk (future umbilical cord) exchanges wastes and nutrients.

Figure 37-10 Human development during the third, fourth, and fifth weeks

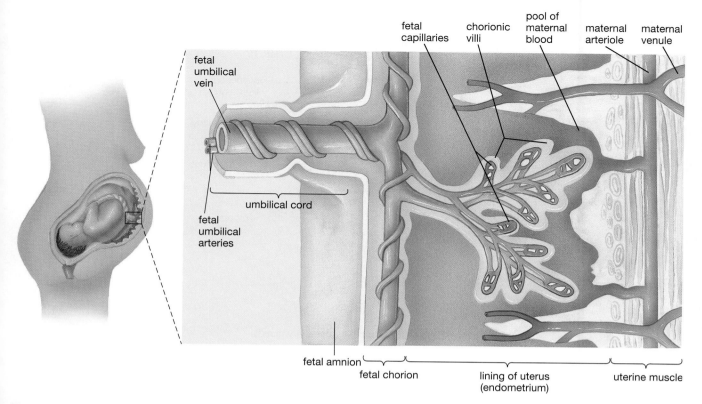

fetal
umbilical
vein

fetal
capillaries

chorionic
villi

pool of
maternal
blood

maternal
arteriole

maternal
venule

fetal
umbilical
arteries

umbilical cord

fetal amnion

fetal chorion

lining of uterus
(endometrium)

uterine muscle

Figure 37-12 The placenta

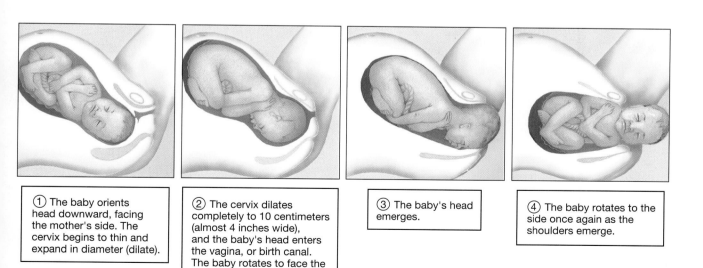

① The baby orients head downward, facing the mother's side. The cervix begins to thin and expand in diameter (dilate).

② The cervix dilates completely to 10 centimeters (almost 4 inches wide), and the baby's head enters the vagina, or birth canal. The baby rotates to face the mother's back.

③ The baby's head emerges.

④ The baby rotates to the side once again as the shoulders emerge.

Figure 37-13 Delivery

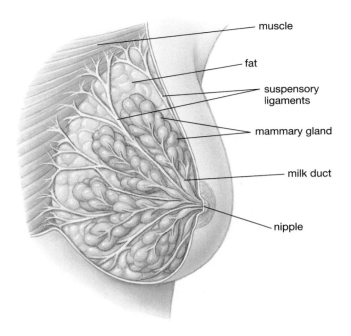

muscle

fat

suspensory ligaments

mammary gland

milk duct

nipple

Figure 37-14 The structure of the mammary glands

Figure 38-2 Habituation in a sea anemone

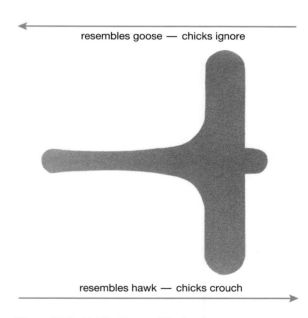

Figure 38-5 Habituation modifies innate responses

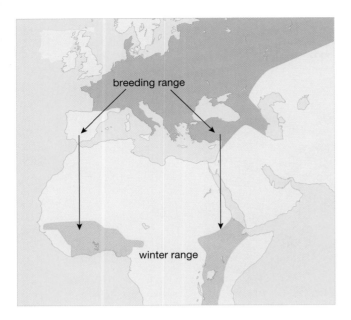

Figure 38-7 Genes influence migratory behavior

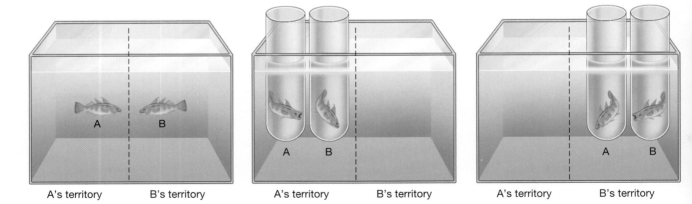

Figure 38-19 Territory ownership and aggression

(a) A male, inconspicuously colored, leaves the school of males and females to establish a breeding territory.

(b) As his belly takes on the red color of the breeding male, he displays aggressively at other red-bellied males, exposing his red underside.

(c) Having established a territory, the male begins nest construction by digging a shallow pit that he will fill with bits of algae cemented together by a sticky secretion from his kidneys.

(d) After he tunnels through the nest to make a hole, his back begins to take on the blue courting color that makes him attractive to females.

(e) An egg-carrying female displays her enlarged belly to him by assuming a head-up posture. Her swollen belly and his courting colors are passive visual displays.

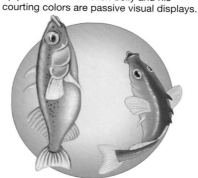

(f) Using a zigzag dance, he leads her to the nest.

(g) After she enters, he stimulates her to release eggs by prodding at the base of her tail.

(h) He enters the nest as she leaves and deposits sperm, which fertilize the eggs.

Figure 38-23 Courtship of the three-spined stickleback

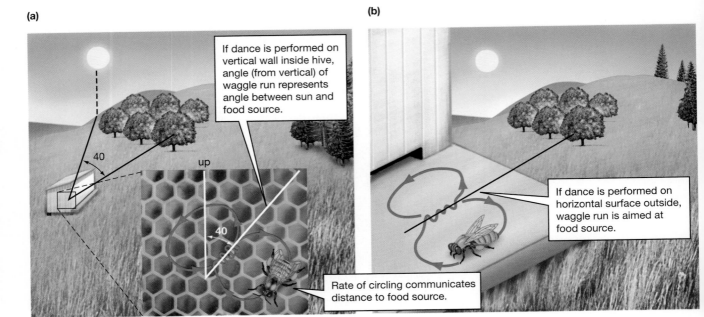

(a)

If dance is performed on vertical wall inside hive, angle (from vertical) of waggle run represents angle between sun and food source.

40

up

40

Rate of circling communicates distance to food source.

(b)

If dance is performed on horizontal surface outside, waggle run is aimed at food source.

Figure 38-26 Bee language: the waggle dance
Media Activity 38.2 Communication in Honeybees

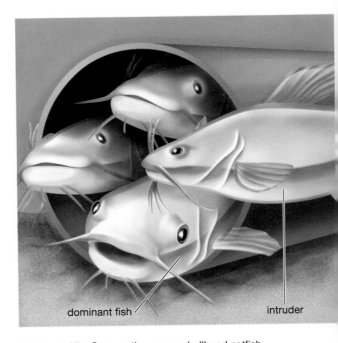

dominant fish

intruder

Figure 38-27 Cooperation among bullhead catfish

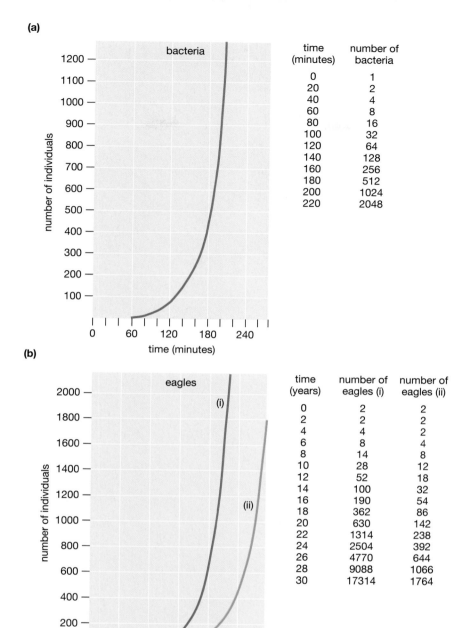

(a)

time (minutes)	number of bacteria
0	1
20	2
40	4
60	8
80	16
100	32
120	64
140	128
160	256
180	512
200	1024
220	2048

(b)

time (years)	number of eagles (i)	number of eagles (ii)
0	2	2
2	2	2
4	4	2
6	8	4
8	14	8
10	28	12
12	52	18
14	100	32
16	190	54
18	362	86
20	630	142
22	1314	238
24	2504	392
26	4770	644
28	9088	1066
30	17314	1764

Figure 39-1 Exponential growth curves are J-shaped

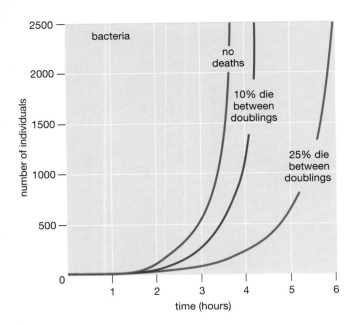

Figure 39-2 The effect of death rates on population growth

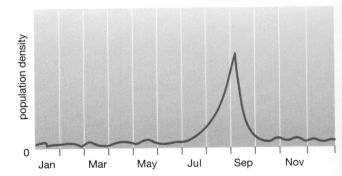

Figure 39-3 A boom-and-bust population cycle

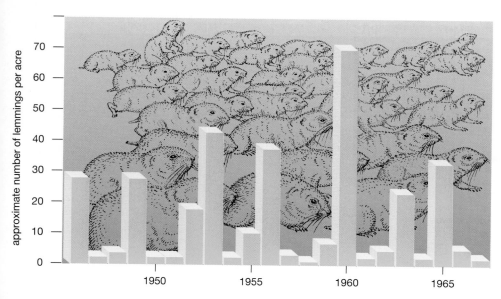

Figure 39-4 Lemming population cycles follow a boom-and-bust pattern

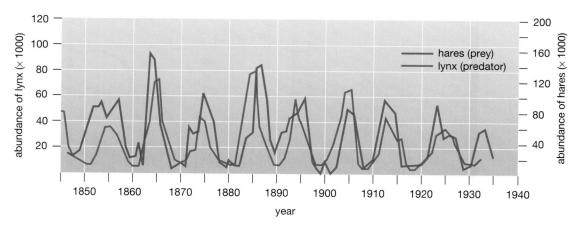

Figure E39-1 Population cycles in predators and prey

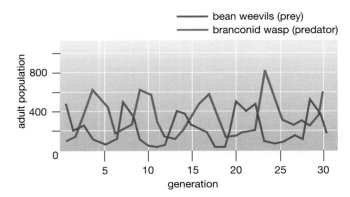

Figure E39-2 Experimental predator—prey curves

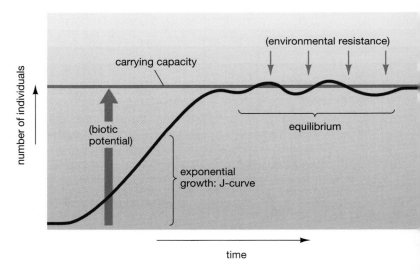

Figure 39-5 The S-curve of population growth

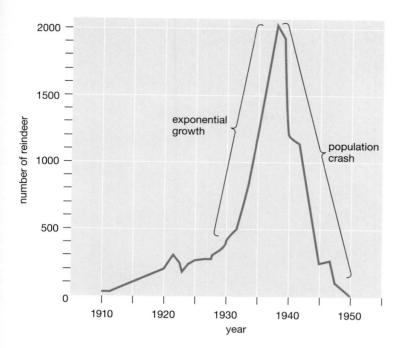

Figure 39-6 The effects of exceeding carrying capacity

Figure 39-9 Survivorship curves

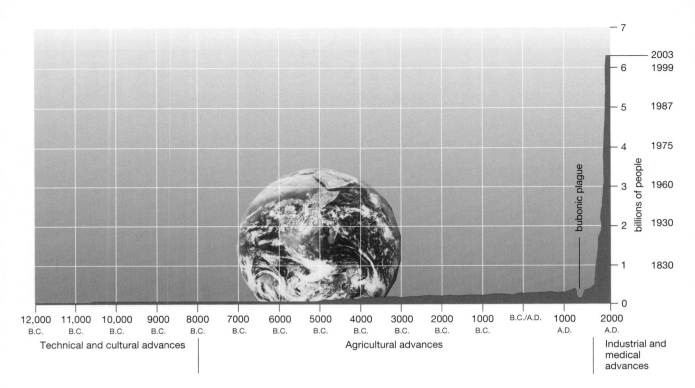

Figure 39-10 Human population growth
Media Activity 39.2 Human Population Growth and Regulation

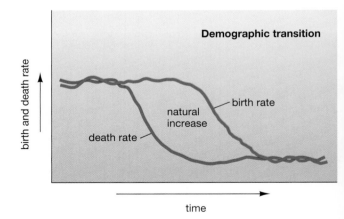

Figure 39-UN01 The demographic transition

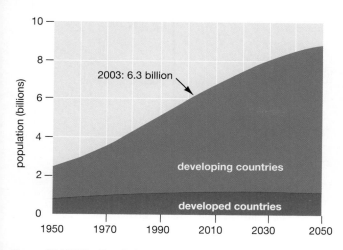

Figure 39-UN02 Populations of developed and developing countries

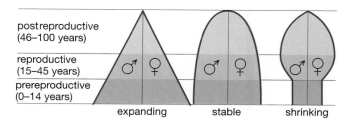

Figure 39-UN03 Age structure diagrams

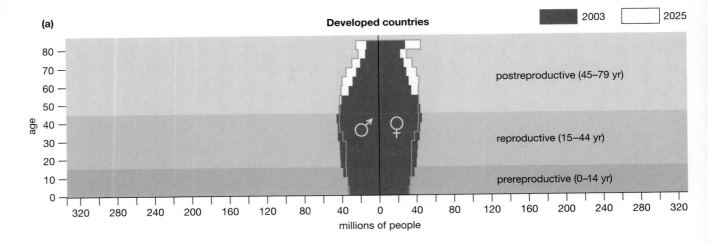

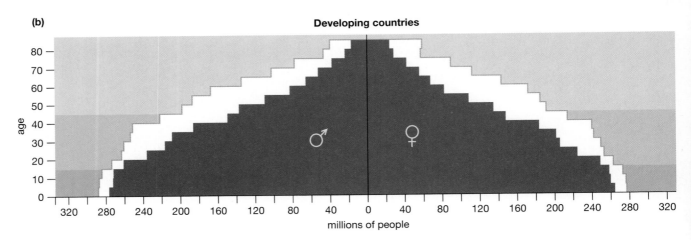

Figure 39-11 Age structures compared

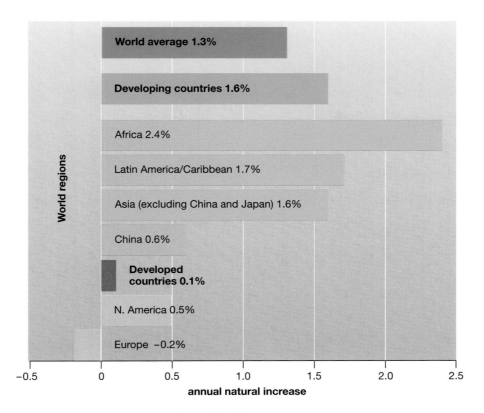

Figure 39-12 Population change by world regions

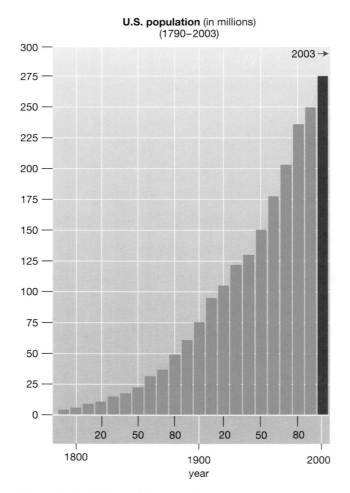

Figure 39-13 U.S. population growth

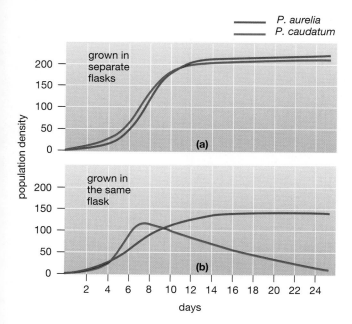

Figure 40-1 Competitive exclusion

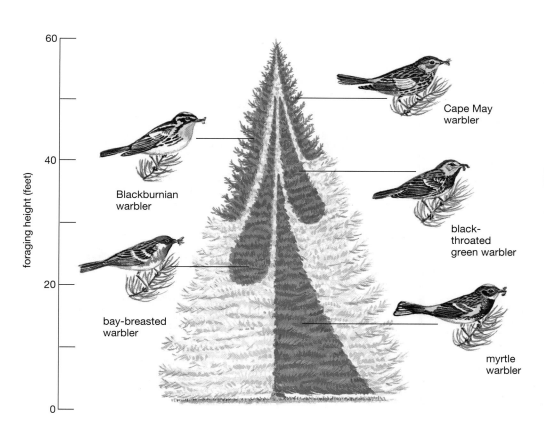

Figure 40-2 Resource partitioning

Figure 40-15　Primary succession
Media Activity 40.3 Primary Succession: Glacier Bay, Alaska

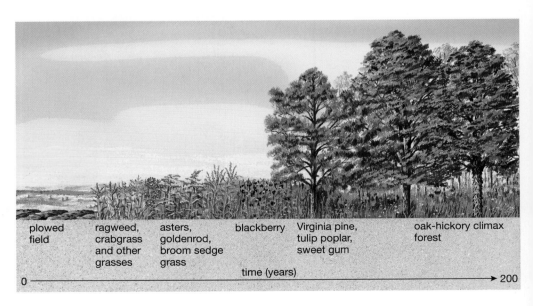

Figure 40-16　Secondary succession

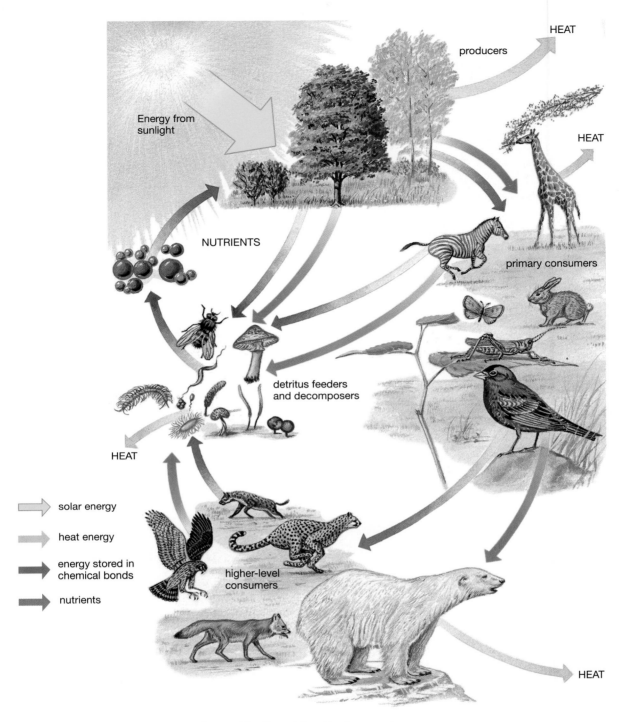

Figure 41-1 Energy flow, nutrient cycling, and feeding relationships in ecosystems
Media Activity 41.1 Ecology Models - Building a Food Web

The following labels appear in the figure:

HEAT

producers

Energy from sunlight

HEAT

NUTRIENTS

primary consumers

detritus feeders and decomposers

HEAT

solar energy

heat energy

energy stored in chemical bonds

nutrients

higher-level consumers

HEAT

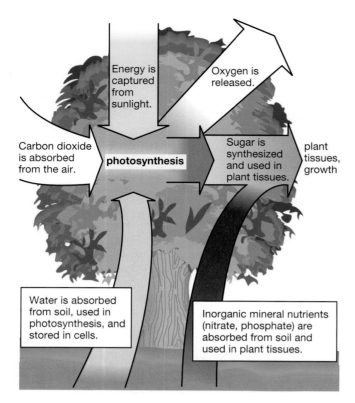

Figure 41-2   Primary productivity: photosynthesis

Figure 41-3   Ecosystem productivity compared

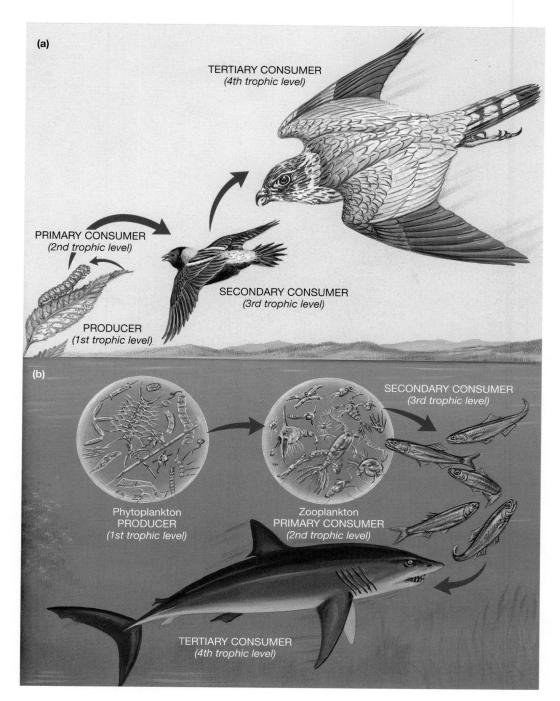

(a)

TERTIARY CONSUMER
(4th trophic level)

PRIMARY CONSUMER
(2nd trophic level)

SECONDARY CONSUMER
(3rd trophic level)

PRODUCER
(1st trophic level)

(b)

SECONDARY CONSUMER
(3rd trophic level)

Phytoplankton
PRODUCER
(1st trophic level)

Zooplankton
PRIMARY CONSUMER
(2nd trophic level)

TERTIARY CONSUMER
(4th trophic level)

Figure 41-4   Food chains

Figure 41-5 A food web

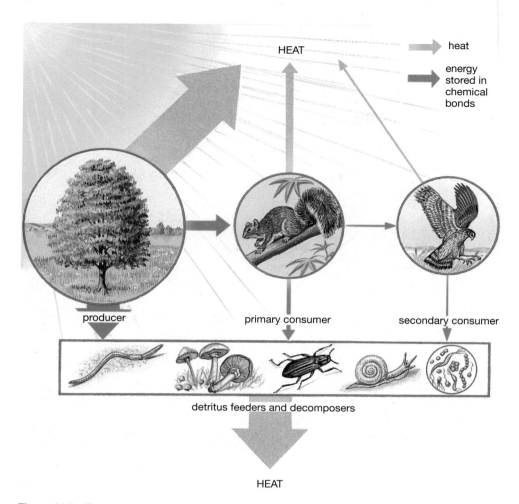

Figure 41-6 Energy transfer and loss

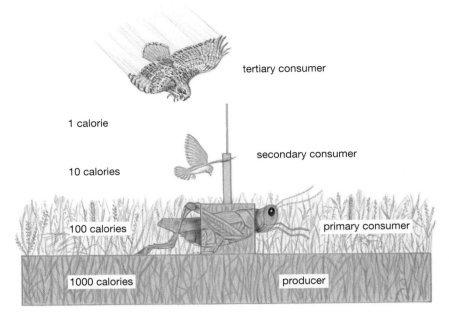

tertiary consumer

1 calorie

secondary consumer

10 calories

100 calories

primary consumer

1000 calories

producer

Figure 41-7   An energy pyramid for a prairie ecosystem

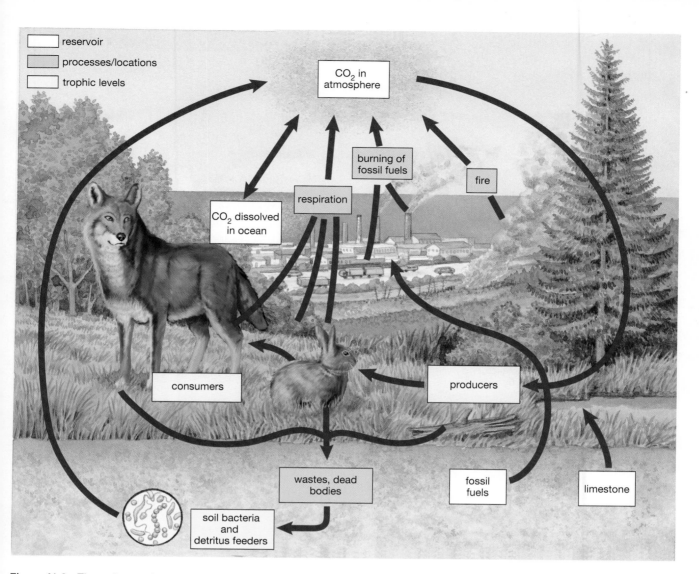

Figure 41-8 The carbon cycle
Media Activity 41.2 The Global Carbon Cycle and Greenhouse Effect

Within the figure:

- reservoir
- processes/locations
- trophic levels

CO_2 in atmosphere

burning of fossil fuels

fire

respiration

CO_2 dissolved in ocean

consumers

producers

wastes, dead bodies

fossil fuels

limestone

soil bacteria and detritus feeders

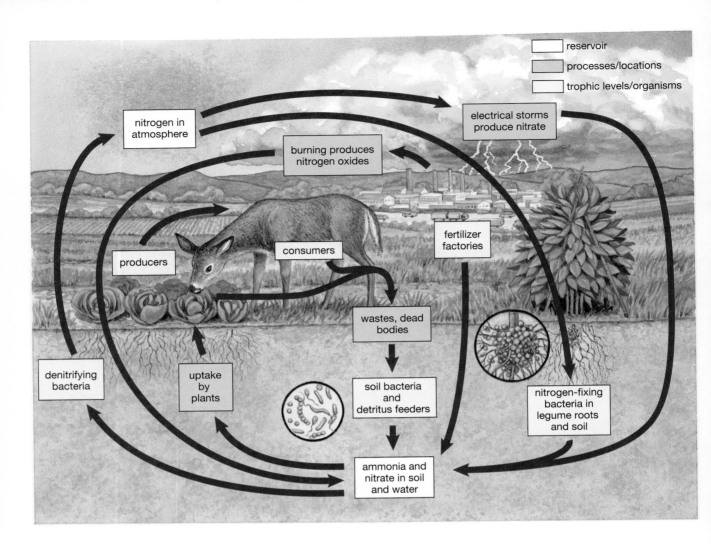

Figure 41-9 The nitrogen cycle

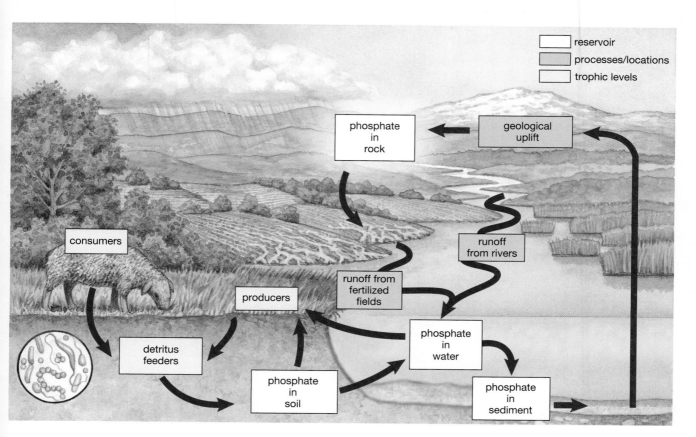

Figure 41-10   The phosphorus cycle

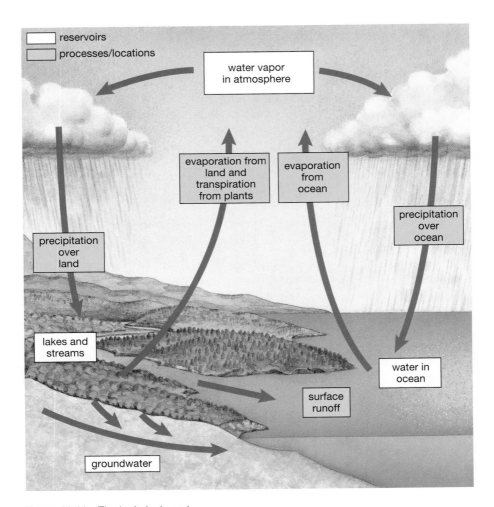

Figure 41-11 The hydrologic cycle

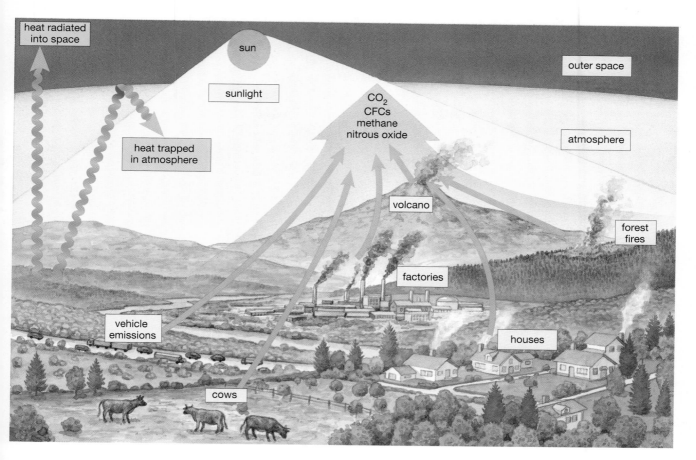

Figure 41-15 Increases in greenhouse gas emissions contribute to global warming

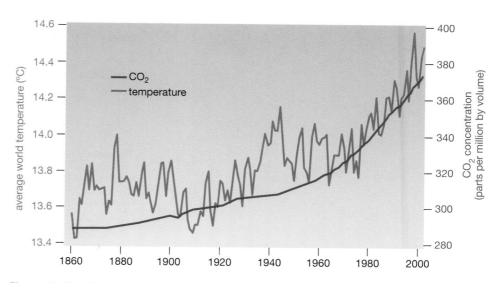

Figure 41-16 Global warming parallels CO_2 increases

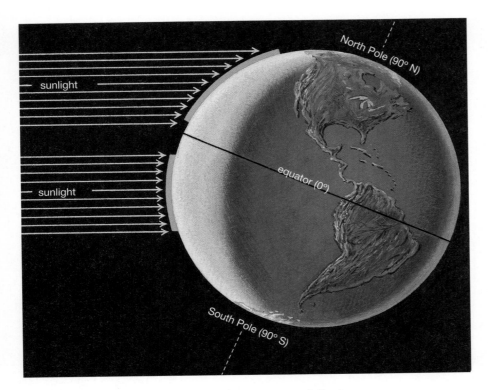

Figure 42-1   Earth's curvature and tilt produce seasons and climate

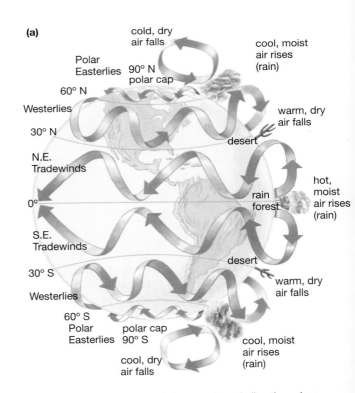

Figure 42-2a   Distribution of air currents and climatic regions

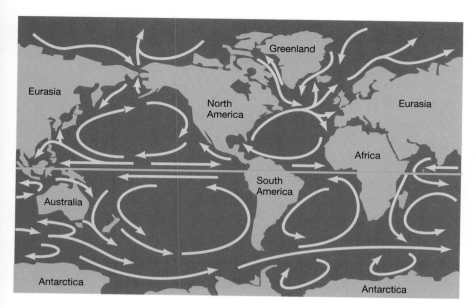

Figure 42-3   Ocean circulation patterns are called gyres

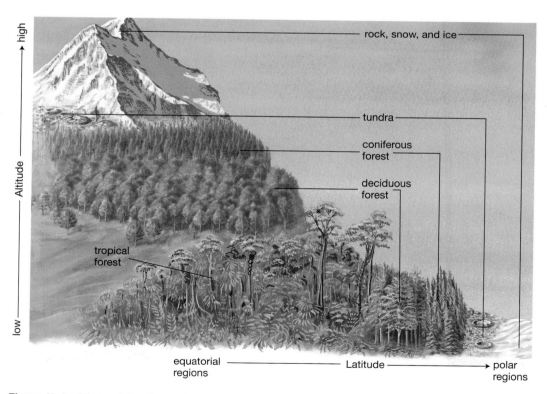

Figure 42-4   Effects of elevation on temperature

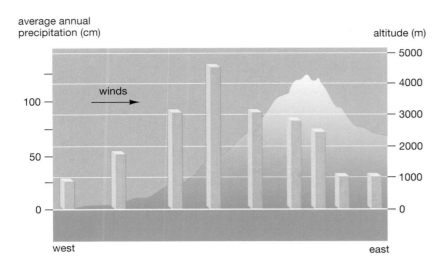

Figure 42-5 The rain shadow of the Sierra Nevada

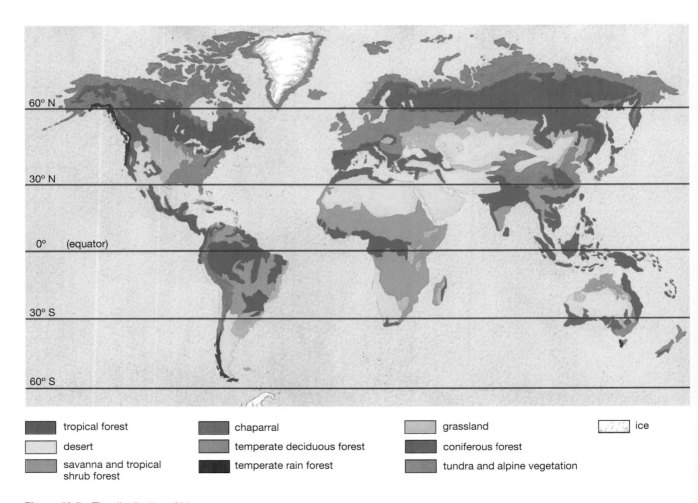

tropical forest

desert

savanna and tropical
shrub forest

chaparral

temperate deciduous forest

temperate rain forest

grassland

coniferous forest

tundra and alpine vegetation

ice

Figure 42-7 The distribution of biomes

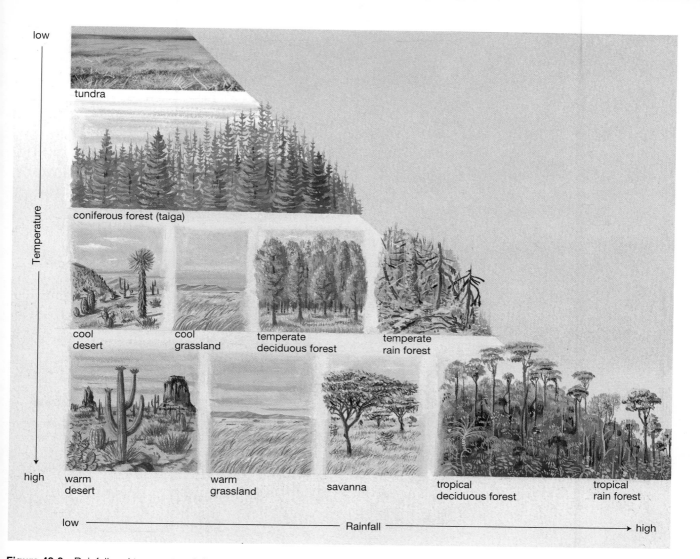

Temperature

high

tundra

coniferous forest (taiga)

cool
desert

cool
grassland

temperate
deciduous forest

temperate
rain forest

warm
desert

warm
grassland

savanna

tropical
deciduous forest

tropical
rain forest

low ——————————————————————————— Rainfall ——————————————→ high

Figure 42-8   Rainfall and temperature influence biome distribution

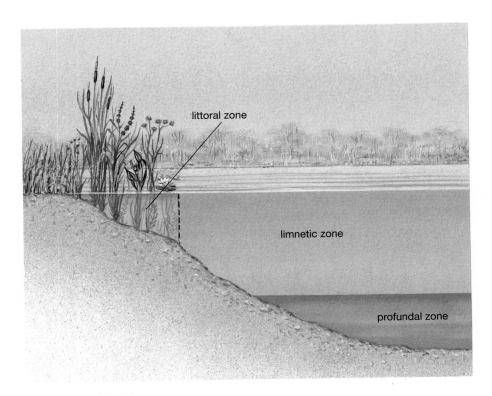

Figure 42-24 Lake life zones

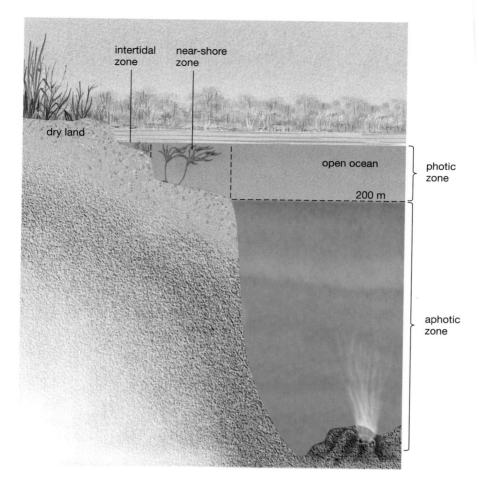

Figure 42-25 Ocean life zones

Photo Credits

Chapter 4

Page 30: Figure 4-9, Jurgen Bohmer and Linda Hufnagel/Linda Hufnagel

Chapter 5

Page 38: Figure 5-09, Don W. Fawcett/Photo Researchers, Inc.

Page 40: Figure 5-11(a), Thomas Eisner/Thomas Eisner

Page 40: Figure 5-11(b), Thomas Eisner/Thomas Eisner

Chapter 11

Page 80: Figure E11-1, Roslin Institute

Chapter 17

Page 135: Figure 17-14, Brunet Michel

Chapter 19

Page 149: Figure 19-25, Cabisco/Visuals Unlimited

Chapter 21

Page 158: Figure 21-8[L], Dr. William M. Harlow/Photo Researchers, Inc.

Page 158: Figure 21-8[R], Gilbert S. Grant/Photo Researchers, Inc.

Chapter 22

Page 163: Figure 22-9, Carolina Biological Supply Company/Phototake NYC

Chapter 24

Page 172: Figure 24-9, Ed Reschke/Peter Arnold, Inc.

Page 175: Figure 24-12(a), Runk/Schoenberger/Grant Heilman Photography, Inc.

Page 175: Figure 24-12(b), John Cunningham/Visuals Unlimited

Page 180: Figure 24-23(a), Ray Simon/Photo Researchers, Inc.

Page 180: Figure 24-23(b), Dr. Jeremy Burgess/Science Photo Library/Photo Researchers, Inc.

Chapter 25

Page 186: Figure 25-10, Carolina Biological Supply Company/Phototake NYC

Chapter 30

Page 221: Figure E30-2, Dr. E. Walker/Science Phot Library/Photo Researchers, Inc.

Chapter 34

Page 261: Figure 34-17(a), Dennis Kunkel/Dennis I Microscopy, Inc.

Chapter 35

Page 271: Figure 35-9, Manfred Kage/Peter Arnold

Chapter 36

Page 274: Figure 36-1, Biophoto Associates/Photo Researchers, Inc.

Page 282: Figure 36-18(a), Lennart Nilsson/Albert Bonniers Forlag AB

Page 282: Figure 36-18(b), Francis Leroy, Biocosmos/SPL/Custom Medical Stock Photo, Inc

Page 283: Figure E36-2, Hank Morgan/Photo Rese. Inc.

Chapter 37

Page 284: Figure 37-1(a)[L], Image Quest 3-D/NHI Limited

Page 284: Figure 37-1(a)[R], Jim Bain/NHPA Limit

Page 284: Figure 37-1(b)[L], Hans Pfletschinger/Pe Arnold, Inc.

Page 284: Figure 37-1(b)[R], Larry West/Photo Researchers, Inc.

Page 285: Figure 37-2(a), Paul A. Zahl/Photo Rese. Inc.

Page 285: Figure 37-2(b), K.H. Switak/Photo Rese. Inc.

Page 285: Figure 37-2(c), J.A.L. Cooke/Animals Animals/Earth Scenes

Page 285: Figure 37-2(d), Norbert Rosing/Oxford ! Films/Animals Animals/Earth Scenes

Chapter 39

Page 306: Figure 39-10, NASA/Johnson Space Cer